THE ENIGMA OF ROSALIE

THE ENIGMA OF ROSALIE

HARRY PRICE'S PARANORMAL MYSTERY REVISITED

by

PAUL ADAMS

WHITE CROW

www.whitecrowbooks.com

The Enigma of Rosalie

Harry Price's Paranormal Mystery Revisited.

Published and printed in the United States of America and the United Kingdom
by White Crow Books; an imprint of White Crow Productions Ltd.

For information, contact White Crow Books
at 3 Hova Villas, Hove, BN3 3DH United Kingdom,
or e-mail to info@whitecrowbooks.com.

Cover Designed by Butterflyeffect
Interior design by Velin@Perseus-Design.com

Paperback ISBN 978-1-78677-013-4
eBook   ISBN 978-1-78677-014-1

Non Fiction / Body, Mind & Spirit / Spiritualism

www.whitecrowbooks.com

For Leah, without whom this book would never have been written.

Harry Price (1881-1948),
psychical researcher extraordinaire (*Paul Adams*)

CONTENTS

INTRODUCTION

———————◆————————

Today, for many people interested in ghosts and psychic happenings, particularly modern investigators carrying out vigils in allegedly haunted locations, the environment and physical phenomena of the séance room belongs to another age, the era of the gas-lit mediums' parlour, and as such has little relevance to the contemporary paranormal scene. Unlike their distinguished Victorian predecessors, whose attempts to understand and come to terms with the claims of Modern Spiritualism created the discipline of organised psychical research in the early1880s, many modern parapsychologists are no longer preoccupied with the subject. For the vast majority, the reality of psychic phenomena does not automatically equate to the existence of a spirit world or the possibility of survival after death.

There are a number of reasons for this. In our apparently more sophisticated and increasingly technology-driven world, the claims of the early Spiritualists to be able to communicate with, and in certain cases make the dead reappear in solid form, can seem quaint and mildly absurd. The 'spirit' photographs of such pioneering figures as Billy Hope, William Mumler and Mrs Deane, have been explained away as nothing more than simple double-exposures; while the materialised figures of physical mediums such as Florence Cook, Marthe Béraud (Eva C.) and the famous Helen Duncan, whose wartime 'witchcraft' trial made her something of a Spiritualist martyr, have, according to the sceptics, been exposed as nothing but fraud and cheesecloth.

In spite of the exposures, (the volume of fraud in the early decades of the development of the Spiritualist movement should not be underestimated), *materialisation*, the rarest form of physical mediumship, has seemingly been demonstrated in every decade since the middle of the 1800s and still takes place today, although the number of mediums currently carrying out public demonstrations – in the United Kingdom at least – can be counted on the fingers of one hand. Those who believe that physical materialisation is real and valid often cite fast-paced modern life as leaving little time for potential mediums to develop the ability. In many cases this can take years to achieve within the environment of a sympathetic home circle. It has also been stated amongst commentators of a Spiritualist persuasion that only one person in ten million has the necessary physiology that spirit people can work with[1].

Despite this, the past thirty years have seen the subject of physical mediumship experiencing something of a renaissance, due in no small part to the activities of Robin Foy, a former RAF pilot and paper trade salesman, who began attending a home circle sitting for physical phenomena near Leicester in 1973. During the 1970s and 1980s, Foy took part in several Spiritualist circles and attended sittings with Leslie Flint (1911-1994), well known in the post-war years as a direct voice medium. In 1990, Foy established the Noah's Ark Society (NAS), promoting the study and safe practice of physical mediumship through organised lectures and seminars that encouraged like-minded people to set up small home circles for the development of physical phenomena. A similar project had been created in the 1930s by a prominent Spiritualist, Noah Zerdin, (1888-1972) after whom the new organisation was named. Following a move to the village of Scole in Norfolk, Foy created his own home circle with his wife, Sandra, and two trance mediums, Alan and Diana Bennett. Beginning in 1992, what has become known as the 'Scole Experiment', one of the most important developments in the history of physical mediumship took place over a period of five years[2].

Foy and his friends, known as the Scole Experimental Group (SEG), claimed to be able to contact and interact with a spirit team of discarnate souls who were keen to provide physical scientific proof of their existence and the reality of survival after death. This was to be carried out by undertaking a series of controlled experiments, the results of which were to be made known by the SEG through an educational organisation that the spirit team directed to be called the New Spiritual Science Foundation. The members of the Foundation were not Spiritualists in the formal sense of the word, but were a group of people, incarnate and discarnate, who had come together to share a spiritual message with the rest of the world. The general distrust traded between mediums and their supporters on one side, and psychical researchers representing the scientific establishment on the other, was to be overcome by allowing suitably qualified observers to take part in, and report on, certain areas of the SEG's activities, in effect experimental sittings (or physical séances to give them their traditional title) open to select members of the public.

This is, in fact, what did take place as three members of the Society for Psychical Research (SPR), Montague Keen, Arthur Ellison and David Fontana, acting in individual capacities, visited the Foy's home at Street House Farm and in total attended over thirty sittings. They and many other guests, including members of the Noah's Ark Society, reported a wealth of seemingly convincing physical phenomena. These included lights, movement of objects, the appearance of images and photographs on rolls of unexposed camera film sealed inside specially prepared containers, as well as voices and the materialisation of solid spirit hands and figures. A detailed account of their experiences running to just over 450 pages, known as *The Scole Report*[3], published under the auspices of the SPR in 1999, was subsequently considered by the late Colin Wilson to be one of the most important documents that the Society had published in its then 118-year history. Other full-length studies have included a book aimed at the popular market written by Grant and Jane Solomon, *The Scole Experiment* (1999), and *Witnessing the Impossible* (2009), a complete record of the entire Scole series of sittings compiled by Robin Foy himself from his own personal archive.

What set the work of the New Spiritual Science Foundation apart from all previous reports of physical mediums and their phenomena, was the fact that the Scole Experimental Group claimed that, in order to create the movement of objects, spirit lights, and particularly the materialisation of solid forms, the spirit team was utilising a modern 'energy-based' spirit world technology rather than the traditional séance room phenomenon of ectoplasm which had been the norm for at least the previous 100 years. The term 'ectoplasm' or 'exteriorised substance' was created in 1895 by French physician and psychical researcher, Charles Richet (1850-1935), a Nobel Laureate for medical science, to describe the materialised 'spirit' hands and other structures witnessed during his séances with the Italian physical medium, Eusapia Palladino (1854-1918), and subsequently in Algiers and Paris with a Frenchwoman, Marthe Béraud (1886-c.1943), also known as Eva Carrière or Eva C.

Ectoplasm is generally described as being a normally white amorphous substance drawn in quantities from the body of the medium, normally from the mouth, ears and nose, and also from the torso around the solar plexus. This is utilised by the communicating spirit people to create temporary physical structures (hands, faces, and at times complete human figures) in which to manifest to loved ones or other sitters within the harmonious environment of the séance room. Extremely sensitive to white light, which necessitates complete darkness as part of any materialisation séance, but visible in red light in which it can also be photographed, ectoplasm has been an essential part of physical mediumship since the first materialisations were recorded in the early years of the Spiritualist movement. One of the first mediums to demonstrate materialisation was Mrs Mary Andrews, an American physical medium from Moravia in Cayuga County, New York, who began sitting in the early 1870s. In Britain, Florence Cook, from Hackney in East London, achieved great notoriety in 1874 with her materialisation of 'Katie King'. This full-form apparition was famously investigated and photographed by the distinguished chemical scientist, Sir William Crookes. However, the idea that deceased people can return, albeit temporarily in this way, is so outside the experience of ordinary people that it is not surprising that from the very beginning, reports of this kind have been treated with derision and scepticism. Psychologist, John Beloff (1920-2006), described materialisation as 'the most bizarre phenomena of the entire paranormal repertoire[4], while Guy Lyon Playfair sums up the situation very effectively in his book, *The Flying Cow* (1975), whilst relating his own experiences of psychic and mediumistic phenomena in Brazil in the early 1970s:

> Of all psychical phenomena, materialisation must be the hardest for most of us to believe. Telepathy and clairvoyance have now become generally accepted even by much of the scientific community (about a century behind psychical researchers); reincarnation is beginning to look highly plausible...and poltergeists undoubtedly exist...But materialisation? Spirits of dead people appearing to the living, speaking to them, letting themselves be touched and examined, giving them presents as well as medical treatment and discourses on the life hereafter? For the average rational human, this is too much.[5]

According to the 'spirit team' who were working with Foy and his associates, the pioneering technology that was being used at Scole had been attempted with other Spiritualist groups in the past, but it was not until our modern times that they (i.e., the spirit workers) were able to create and sustain the phenomena on a regular basis. This new method was a mixture of *three* types of natural energy which was combined or blended together by workers in the spirit realm into a single 'creative energy' in order to produce physical effects in our world. These three sources were earth energies, which exist in various geographical locations around the planet and can be detected by dowsing; personal spiritual energy drawn from each of the participants in the circle of sitters; and spiritual energy brought from the spirit world or the spiritual dimensions by the spirit team with the express intention of creating physical phenomena. There were no physical dangers to the people taking part; the variety of physical phenomena that could be achieved was said to be limitless, and its development within a group or home circle was much faster than that which is normally obtained with a traditional developing physical medium. In fact – and this is probably the singular most important factor – *the technology did not require the presence of a traditional medium or psychic*, for, as long as there was suitable harmony between the sitters, the 'spirit team' working with them would find the most suitable person or people within the group, and work with them to achieve the results.

During the time that the New Spiritual Science Foundation was operating, it actively encouraged similar experiments to be established, producing a regular quarterly newsletter, the *Spiritual Scientist*, and a guide containing information on how best to go about setting up an experimental energy group[6]. As can be appreciated, this radical and seemingly scientifically focused approach was immensely different in attitude and concept from the "Is there anybody there?" scenario, which many people automatically think of when the subject of mediums and séances is brought up. Since the end of the Scole Experiment[7], Robin Foy has acted as an entrepreneur in the world of modern physical mediumship, as both an educator and organiser. Following the New Spiritual Science Foundation, he was one of the names behind the short-lived ISARTOP[8] research group and latterly a public website[9] dedicated to physical mediumship and its phenomena.

In March 2009, I attended a public demonstration of physical mediumship at a Spiritualist centre in Mansfield organised by Dennis and Rosalind Pearman of the Zerdin Phenomenal[10] organisation. The medium was Bill Meadows who had been sitting in a home circle comprising his wife and a small number of close family friends for the previous fifteen years. His mediumship had developed to the stage where much physical phenomena, including direct voice communication, the movement of objects and partial materialisation, was now being achieved. I had previously attended several black-out séances over the preceding two years with another physical medium who, working with traditional ectoplasm, was producing similar phenomena. What impressed me with the demonstration by the Bill Meadows Circle was that not only were the control conditions very thorough, both with regards to the securing of the medium and the sitters, but they had used the work at Scole as a blueprint and the phenomena were being produced using the relatively new 'energy' method described above. I was also able to witness the apparent materialisation of a solid spirit hand in very good red light, which a friend of mine who accompanied me to the demonstration was able to touch and hold. She said afterwards that the hand, which slid out at floor-level from underneath the curtain covering the front of the 'cabinet' where Bill had been left sitting tied into his chair, was warm and solid, had a strong grip, and appeared to be larger than the right hand of the medium which was much thinner. Bill also wore a ring (that apparently could not normally be removed) that the materialised hand did not possess.

Using the recommendations of the New Spiritual Science Foundation guide, the group, which initially had no official medium, had decided to try to sit for the development of physical phenomena and, after a period of time, Bill had been the one who was chosen by the spirit team as being suitable to work with. Following the Mansfield séance, I wrote up a report on the demonstration for my own records and began thinking about what I had experienced. Very quickly I came to realise that there might be a possible answer to what has been, for nearly eighty years, very much an enigma in the annals of psychical research and this is the singular happening which forms the subject of this book – the mystery of Harry Price and 'Rosalie'.

The 'Rosalie' case first came to public attention in 1939 following the publication of *Fifty Years of Psychical Research*, a history of organised paranormal studies written by the late Harry Price, a well known investigator and authority on the subject. Regarded today as primarily a ghost hunter, Price was extremely active on the psychic scene in the inter-war years when, like most of his contemporaries, he was heavily involved with the investigation of (primarily physical) mediums and Spiritualist phenomena in general. In his book, Price describes a séance that he said he attended in the winter of 1937 at which he encountered, in his own words, "the most remarkable case of materialization, or rather alleged materialization, I have ever witnessed."[11] Under good conditions of control, Price said he saw, touched and spoke with the solid naked form of a small child named 'Rosalie' who, he understood, had died sixteen years previously at the age of six. Seemingly, here at last was what the fifty-six year-old researcher had been searching for in over twenty years of active investigation: crushing proof that we survive the event known as 'death', that we live on in another realm which co-exists with our own physical world, and that, given the right conditions, we can return and make contact with the loved ones who have been left behind.

Despite the reservations that Price included in his account, the tone of his narrative left readers in no doubt that here was an event which was the closest he had come so far to making a shattering breakthrough. Not surprisingly, Spiritualist organisations championed Price's reporting of 'Rosalie' as entirely vindicating the tenets of the movement, while the establishment, and, in particular, organised paranormal investigation in the form of the Society for Psychical Research, with whom Price had what can best be described as an uneasy relationship during most of his career as a researcher, treated the account with the due reservation expected of scientific orthodoxy.

After Price's sudden death in 1948, former colleagues accused him of fraud and wholesale misrepresentation in his reporting of what is still his most famous case, the haunting of Borley Rectory[12], long known as 'the most haunted house in England'. Subsequently the 'Rosalie' case was looked on by the same critics as being nothing but a sensational piece of fiction inserted into what was in effect an academic textbook in order to create headline-grabbing reviews and an improvement in sales. As will be seen, the mystery of 'Rosalie' and what actually happened to Harry Price in December 1937 if, as has been suggested by some commentators, it ever happened at all, has been examined, discussed and debated at intervals over several decades.

As the whole subject of physical mediumship and its phenomena has undergone something of a revival in recent years it seemed that the 'Rosalie' case was in need of an objective re-examination in the light of the modern developments in the field of physical psychic phenomena described above. This is a subject which, if confirmed to the satisfaction of scientific orthodoxy, will bring about far reaching changes in the way we view ourselves and our position in the universe. Where 'Rosalie' is concerned, following two major examinations in the 1950s and 1960s, each reaching diametrically opposed conclusions, active investigation eventually dwindled away and effectively ceased by the mid-1970s.

Much of this book has been concerned with bringing together a considerable amount of information from many disparate sources and setting down as complete a historical record of the case as it has been possible to do. This has been achieved due to the help and support of numerous people and I would like to take a moment to thank the following: From the Society for Psychical Research, Mary Rose Barrington, Dr Tom Ruffles, Dr Melvyn Willin, Dr Alan Gauld and Karen Patel for assisting enormously with enquiries and illustrations; Frank Bowles for access to the SPR archive at Cambridge University Library; Leslie Price for allowing access to the archives of the College of Psychic Studies; Charles Harrowell and the Special Collections staff at the University of London Library for their patient co-operation and assistance; Prof Richard Wiseman, Prof Stephen Braude and Robin Foy for helping with research into physical mediumship both past and present; Margaret White for much needed technical advice; Mrs Sylvia Hill for taking the time to talk to me about the late Dr R.G. Medhurst; and Roy Stemman from *Psychic News* and Jon Beecher at White Crow Books for their interest in the project. Numerous and diverse enquiries were ably answered by Matthew Chipping of the BBC Written Archives; Lorna Jackson and Clare Cowen from the Brockley Society; Lisette Coly at the Parapsychology Foundation; Stewart Pringle at the Old Red Lion Theatre; Lisa Kenny at the British Library; Paula Best, archivist at the Wigmore Hall; Jenny Bojang and Sabrina Offord at the London Borough of Lewisham; Astrella Mullen at the London Transport Museum; Maria Paxi at the CT State Library and Allison Botelho at the New Haven Free Public Library; staff at The Magic Circle and the Royal Geographical Society; and Marlene Koenig, Robin Wall, Richard Wall and Andrew de Lotbiniere who helped with family histories and other questions. Ashley Thorpe painted the beautiful 'Rosalie' cover and Maya Humphries became 'Rosalie' for it. Other illustrations were supplied by Leighton Barrable, Andrew Clarke and Mark Davies and Laura Watson. I offer my apologies to anyone who has been omitted due to the passage of time, my failing memory and e-mails and other correspondence now being inaccessible on PC harddrives that have now, pun intended, given up the ghost. My old friend, Eddie Brazil, has followed the progress of this project from beginning to end and it would not have been possible without his support and encouragement, as well as that of my family – Leah, Aban, Idris, Isa, Sakina, Hannah and Aria. Finally, the late Peter Underwood had great personal interest in the mystery of Harry Price and 'Rosalie' and, as he assisted in so many ways with my work on this case, his absence is felt never more so than now.

In previous non-fiction books, which I have written on the paranormal, I have tried to follow the maxim that a book is about its subject not its author and I have kept my own involvement as transparent as possible. The penultimate chapter deals with my own investigation into the 'Rosalie' case and, as a result, the capital letter 'I' appears in these pages with far more frequency than I would normally like it to. In mitigation, it is possible to point out that Harry Price apologised for exactly the same situation at the beginning of his own *Search for Truth* in 1942, and, by doing the same, I find myself in good company. I hope you enjoy this book as much as I have enjoyed researching and writing it.

Paul Adams
Luton, Bedfordshire
2016

ONE

TALES FROM THE
SÉANCE ROOM

H arry Price has famously been described as 'one of the most fascinating and storm-provoking figures in psychical research'[13.] He occupies not only a unique position in the history of paranormal investigation in the first half of the twentieth century but also a major role in the case under discussion so it is important to put down, at the outset, some essential facts about him and his work, with a particular emphasis on his extensive experience with regard to the physical phenomena of the séance room. To date he has been the main subject of four full-length books while several others have included lengthy chapters covering aspects of his life and notable cases[14]. The principal biographies fall neatly into two opposing camps – one acknowledging and supportive of his achievements, the other critical and dismissive.

Price published his own autobiography as *Search for Truth – My Life for Psychical Research* in 1942. This was a readable account of his paranormal adventures which began in earnest soon after the end of World War I and continued practically without respite up until his death thirty years later. During his lifetime, Price amassed a unique archive of approximately 20,000 letters together with photographs and a collection of 13,000 books, all connected in some way with psychical research, that he bequeathed to the University of London. In 1950, Dr Paul Tabori (1908-1974), a Hungarian-born writer, broadcaster and film critic, newly appointed Literary Executor of the Harry Price estate, used this definitive source to write a lengthy biography, *Harry Price – The Biography of a Ghost-Hunter*. Tabori was a prolific writer of novels, film scripts and non-fiction works, including volumes on psychical research and the occult, and will be encountered several times during the course of the present work.

Nearly three decades were to pass before the next biography appeared, eventful years where the posthumous reputation of Harry Price as a dedicated and sincere investigator are concerned. With its title, a pun on that of Price's own memoirs, Trevor H. Hall's 1978 offering, *Search for Harry Price*, was as diametrically opposed to Paul Tabori's earlier study as it was possible to get. Hall, a chartered surveyor and estate agent from Yorkshire with a penchant for the debunking of claims for the paranormal, felt that his 'series of essays on the many and varied aspects of Price's life and activities',[15] was something of a long-awaited and definitive biography. The seeds of what remains a scathing personal attack on Price were sown only a few months after Price's death and, as will be seen, Trevor Hall is inextricably linked with much of the later criticisms of the 'Rosalie' case. In fact, parapsychologist, John L. Randall, felt it 'should be recommended to the compilers of the *Guinness Book of Records* as The Most Spiteful Book Ever Written!'[16] Hall considered Price to be a fraud and that his (i.e. Hall's) book "demonstrates that nothing that gentleman said or wrote can be trusted"[17]. After much original research among Price's own papers, former Fleet Street journalist, Richard Morris, added a fourth biography to the list with his *Harry Price – The Psychic Detective* (2006). In many ways Morris' book is a continuation of Hall's earlier work, as the author concludes his study by describing the subject as a "supreme bluffer" and a "hedonistic con man"[18].

Where Harry Price is concerned, it is very easy when writing about him to be drawn into a polemical argument. Although I am supportive of him as a genuine psychical researcher, here I am more interested in describing aspects of his paranormal career that are relevant to the field of physical materialisation mediumship, about which this book is centred, rather than fighting his corner wholesale. Psychical research is a discipline with a long history of internal friction between the many people who, over the years, have deemed – bravely it would seem – to call themselves psychical researchers. As several notable and seemingly unassailable pioneer figures such as Sir William Crookes and Edmund Gurney have had their work and reputations attacked at some point over the years, it was almost inevitable that such a flamboyant and maverick figure as Harry Price would suffer the same fate. Price himself summed up the attitude of the times as long ago as 1929 when, in an article in his own *British Journal of Psychical Research*, he made the following statement:

> I wonder how many of my readers are aware of the number of squabbles, petty jealousies and open feuds that are taking place among those investigating psychic phenomena. In nearly every country where two or more societies or investigators are working there exists a state of affairs which is little less than a scandal. Quarrels, backbiting, lawsuits, sharp practice, scandal-mongering, the gratification of personal spite, these things are rampant, to the detriment of psychical research and a paralysing drag on the wheel of progress.[19]

It was exactly this kind of personal animosity which was the cause of the main attacks on him when former colleagues – or persons within the psychical research community in the inter-war years with whom he had, sometimes out of necessity, had to associate – were quick to put the knife in after his death without fear of having to fight a libel action in court.

Harry Price was born on 17 January 1881 at 37 Red Lion Square in Holborn, London. His father was Edward Ditcher Price, a 47-year-old commercial traveller and former grocer, originally from Roddington in Shropshire. Price's mother was the much younger, Emma Randall Price (formerly Meech) who was fifteen when she married Harry's father at St. Andrew's Parish Church in Holborn on 11 January 1876. She was also pregnant at the time with Harry Price's sister who was born a few months after the marriage on 23 April 1876. Soon after his son's birth, Edward Price moved his family to an address in Chelsea and then again to New Cross in South London where they lived for a time at 6 Amersham Road. Harry's first schooling was at the London Board School in Waller Road and, at the age of eleven in January 1892, he began attending Haberdashers' Aske's Hatcham Boys' School in the nearer Pepys Road. During his school days, the Prices moved house once more to another address in New Cross, 32 St. Donatts Road, at around 1893.

Price left school some time in 1897 or 1898 and, in the ten years before he married, had several varied occupations but, in the main, followed his father's later career as a commercial traveller and juggled this with his later ongoing career in psychical investigation for the rest of his life. The years following Price's school leaving were busy ones and, apart from earning a living, Price was involved in other various activities. Goldsmiths' College is directly adjacent to St. Donatts Road and here Price attended evening classes in such subjects as photography, engineering and chemistry. He also developed what became a life-long interest in conjuring and book-collecting, particularly those devoted to legerdemain and the history of magic tricks which developed over time to volumes on the occult and Spiritualism.

Harry Price's mother, Emma, was only forty-two when she died of cancer on 18 August 1902 in St. Thomas's Home in Lambeth and he lost his father four years later from heart failure on 7 July 1906. Price's sister, Anne, was by this time married and living in a house in Waller Road. Following his father's death, Harry may have lived with her for a time, but there is evidence that he lodged with a lady called Mrs Hills at 22 Harefield Road in Brockley, a district just to the south of his old stomping ground of New Cross. This address in Brockley is about half a mile north of 10 Adelaide Road, which was the family home of Harry Price's future wife, Constance Mary Knight, whom he married on 1 August 1908 at the parish church of St. Mary's at Pulborough, West Sussex; a country village where the couple lived for the rest of their married lives.

The Brockley of Harry Price's youth was a well-to-do Victorian suburb and it plays a major role in the history of the 'Rosalie' case. It was here from around 1896 onwards that, according to his reminiscences in *Search for Truth,* Price began attending Spiritualist meetings. For a period of around ten years he was a regular visitor to a house in Manor Road (since renamed Manor Avenue) where many visiting physical mediums gave public séances. These demonstrations were normally held on a Wednesday evening and, depending on the notoriety of the guest medium present, an entrance fee of between one to five shillings a head was levied. The Manor Road circle enabled the fledgling investigator to meet many of the Victorian mediums of the day who were doing the rounds of the Spiritualist churches and meeting places. Among them were several figures of note from the early decades of English Spiritualism. They included Mrs Thomas Everitt (1825-1915), the wife of a tailor from Pentonville, who is credited as being the first medium to demonstrate the phenomenon of direct voice in England, whereby a spirit communicator speaks through the medium's own mouth and addresses the sitters. There was also the Glaswegian, David Duguid (1832-1907), mostly remembered for his automatic drawings and paintings. Both were elderly when Price saw them. Mrs Everitt limited her demonstration to a psychometry exercise, but Duguid produced some small paintings, on specially marked blank cards, which Price found initially impressive as the oil paint was still wet to the touch. However, the Scotsman was exposed a few years later in Manchester when he was found with prepared paintings hidden in his trousers.

One of the first materialisation mediums that Price met was Charles Eldred of Nottingham who was highly regarded. Full-form figures were a speciality of his mediumship and Eldred most often brought his own upholstered chair to his meetings which, soaked with his own mediumistic vibrations or power, allegedly enabled the spirits to manifest more easily. On the singular occasion that Price attended one of his séances, in the winter of 1905, several solid persons seemingly materialised and stepped out of the medium's 'cabinet', a makeshift enclosure normally created by curtaining off a corner of the séance room, inside which Eldred was ostensibly in a deep trance. The spirits included a tall man with a black beard, a Spaniard wearing a sombrero and a young girl in white, all made visible by the weak glow emanating from two pieces of paper, coated with luminous paint, which were pinned to the cabinet curtains. "It was all most interesting, but not convincing" was how Price described the sitting several years later[20]. It must have been something of a let-down as, by this time, he had been investigating Spiritualistic phenomena for a number of years and this was his first exposure to what was is considered to be the most highly developed form of physical mediumship. The year after Eldred visited Manor Road, at another sitting in London, Dr Abraham Wallace, President of the Society for the Study of Supernormal Pictures (see Chapter 12), and a man of considerable experience in psychic matters, made a point of examining Eldred's special chair and found, as he suspected, that it contained a secret compartment inside the seat in which was hidden a wealth of props that were used to create the visiting 'spirits' – they included a collapsible dummy, a mask, false wigs and beards, a tiny musical box (for ghostly music) and reaching-rods to create 'psychic touches'.

The year of Eldred's exposure, Price sat with another physical medium, Cecil Husk (1847-1920), a former professional opera singer who was noted as being able to carry out matter-through-matter experiments using steel and iron rings. However, it was materialisation that was on the bill when the fifty-nine year-old medium demonstrated for

Harry Price in Brockley. Husk had seemingly survived a séance room scandal fifteen years earlier when he had been found impersonating a 'spirit' by illuminating his face with a phosphorescent slate, and had evidently been rehabilitated enough to be invited to demonstrate at Manor Road. Despite this, Price was unimpressed with the medium's 'cheese cloth spirits'[21].

In the period that saw Harry Price's first exposure to Spiritualistic phenomena, the scientific investigation of physical mediumship began to step up a pace. The year before Price first visited Manor Road, the Society for Psychical Research had tested Italian born Eusapia Palladino (1854-1918) at Leckhampton House in Cambridge and by then, beginning in the early 1890s, she had already held dozens of séances for various teams and commissions of international observers from Italy, England, France, Germany, Russia, Poland and America. Despite the unsatisfactory result of the SPR enquiry (Eusapia was detected in fraud throughout the series of experiments by the ultra-critical sitters which included the highly sceptical researcher Richard Hodgson [1855-1905]), respected figures such as the Italian criminal anthropologist, Cesare Lombroso (1835-1909), and Dr Julien Ochorowicz (1850-1917), a Polish philosopher and psychologist, had become convinced that many aspects of her phenomena were genuine. Just over ten years later the Italian medium was effectively rehabilitated by the publication of the 'Feilding Report' whose findings have become recognised as a milestone in the history of psychical research[22].

By the time Price had seen the phoney materialisations of Eldred and Husk, Charles Richet had already photographed the long deceased Brahman Hindu, 'Bien Boa', at the eerily-sounding Villa Carmen in Algiers, courtesy of the mediumship of Marthe Béraud, and was refining aspects of paranormal phenomena under the general title of 'metapsychics'. He and other researchers would soon be championing this as a new and bone fide scientific discipline. They included Hereward Carrington (1880-1958), British-born but based for most of his life in America, the Frenchman, Gustav Geley (1868-1924) of the *Institut Métapsychique* in Paris, and, Baron Albert von Schrenck-Notzing (1862-1929) of Munich, whose controversial *Phenomena of Materialisation* dealing with Marthe Béraud's mediumship appeared in 1913. The German giant, the 'imperious tone' of whose writings 'almost commanded belief'[23] in the reality of mediumistic phenomena and the existence of ectoplasm, was one of the major figures on the psychical research scene in the opening decades of the twentieth century that the

6

amateur investigator from Holborn would later consider a colleague. In the atmosphere of the aftermath of World War I, with Spiritualist churches overflowing with people desperate to contact their lost loved ones, the nearly forty year-old Harry Price decided to try to 'reorganise' (his own expression) the psychic scene on his own terms. In June 1920, he joined the English premier league of paranormal investigation when he was elected a Member of the Society for Psychical Research. This transfer from amateur to semi-professional (Price never became a full-time salaried psychical researcher of the likes of the aforementioned Australian Richard Hodgson) had the advantage of his being able to meet and associate with some of the leading researchers, both in this country and abroad, and through them have access to séances with the leading physical mediums of the day.

One person who later claimed much of the credit for this was Dr Eric Dingwall, a Pembroke College graduate (the doctorate was obtained later from London University) who joined the Society in the same year as Price and quickly rose through the ranks to become Foreign Research Officer. He was also (for a year in 1921) the Director of the Department of Physical Phenomena for the American Society for Psychical Research. Ultimately Dingwall, whose interests included collecting clocks and studying erotic literature, would become one of the most noted and experienced psychical researchers of his day, although his forthright manner and, at times outrageous, way of expressing himself took some getting used to. The late Tony Cornell recalled[24] that when in 1954 he invited 'Ding' (as he was often known) to investigate a house (Cornell's parents') at Histon near Cambridge which was plagued by a mysterious and seemingly paranormal smell, the internationally-known researcher quickly bombarded Cornell's ghost hunting team with a mixture of questions, some practical, others off-putting, which included whether anyone had been breaking wind or had trod in dogs' mess, and (true to form) whether the men present had erections when the phenomenon occurred! Despite this, it would be true to say that his knowledge of the literature of physical séance room phenomena has probably never been bettered although I feel that, where practical investigation of physical mediumship was concerned, Price was easily his equal if not superior in experience, despite the fact that Dingwall wrote his own guide to séance room phenomena[25] and outlived him by nearly forty years.

Dingwall was nearly ten years younger than Price but the two men had much in common, including an abiding interest in book-collecting and conjuring (they were both members of the Magic Circle), and were determined to make their marks on the psychical scene. On Dingwall's return from America what initially promised to be a rewarding association began to take shape, starting with a literary collaboration that produced (in 1922) a facsimile edition of a long out of print handbook entitled *Revelations of a Spirit Medium,* an exposure of fraudulent séance room practices, originally published in America in 1891. Both men were aware that the slaughter of the trenches had driven many people towards Spiritualism and were keen to equip new investigators with the necessary skills to weed out the frauds. The reprint was achieved by sacrificing one of two copies of the scarce original, from Price's now world-class occult library, for photographic reproduction and both men added an extensive annotated bibliography from their own collections, spending several hours a day in each other's company for several weeks working on the project.

The same year that the *Revelations* reprint appeared, a call came through to the SPR from Baron von Schrenck-Notzing with a request for competent researchers to assist in his on-going investigation of a young physical medium in Munich. As Research Officer for the Society, Dingwall was the one to make the trip, and he extended an invitation to his recent collaborator to join him. Several years later he described the preparations for the visit in the following terms:

> Although Mr Price claimed to have been actively engaged in psychical research for twenty years he did not then seem to me to know very much about the scientific side of the subject ... and I soon came to the conclusion that, were he to have opportunities of observing genuine physical phenomena (if such exist) he might develop into a psychical researcher of great ability. Accordingly, at the end of May 1922 I invited Mr Price to accompany me to the series of sittings with the medium, Willi Schneider which Dr Schrenck-Notzing had asked me ... to attend in Munich. The results that were observed were so striking a nature that they impelled Mr Price to continue his studies ... [26]

As we have seen, Price had had much experience of séance room practices, albeit at a grass roots level, but most if not all he had seen was suspect if not complete and outright fraud, and Dingwall's invitation was to be the break he had been waiting for.

In later years, when recalling his first Willi Schneider sittings, Price tended to downplay Dingwall's involvement as their promising relationship gradually deteriorated over time to the point where, shortly after Price's death, the younger man willingly collaborated in the scathing attack on the Borley case and Price's entire role in it. The break up was in truth the sum of several factors. John Randall (in his SPR paper on Price) has commented that Dingwall's persistent habit of hectoring his colleagues may have caused resentment, especially as Price was that much older, while comments of the type reported by Tony Cornell, if taken the wrong way, could have caused offence. Nandor Fodor (1895-1964), a practising New York psychoanalyst and, according to Colin Wilson, one of the great unsung heroes of twentieth century psychical research, felt (and I tend to agree with him) that Price's own character was the cause of many of the problems that he had where relationships with fellow investigators was concerned. "He was a very difficult man to like, and easy to resent ... far too selfish, intent on his own glory and immensely jealous" was how Fodor summed up Price after his death, but, despite that, he respected him for his devotion to psychic matters and in 1939, the year that the 'Rosalie' case first came to public attention, considered him to be "the outstanding psychical researcher in England of that day"[27], an opinion he still held when writing in 1956. As will be seen shortly, when given the opportunity, Price tended to take the bull by the horns and go things alone with little regard to either what he may or may not have agreed with others beforehand, or what effect his actions might have on his relationships with colleagues.

Schrenck-Notzing's séance room at his apartment in the Max Josefstrasse in Munich where Dingwall and Price held their experiments with the young Austrian medium, Willi Schneider (1903-1971), was a far cry from Manor Road, Brockley, and the clumsy cheese-cloth ghosts of fakers like Charles Eldred. The following extract from one of Price's articles, written following a later series of sittings in the autumn of 1925, gives a clear indication of the type of astonishing phenomena that both men witnessed, which included direct-voice, the movement of objects, as well as partial materialisation:

> H.P. [i.e. Price] reports seeing a luminous mass on floor, between table and curtains, (roughly 2 feet square, like a semi-luminous deflated balloon). Curtains swing out and are twisted. A "hand" darts out from luminous mass (which is now smaller), snatches handkerchief off slate; throws it down; picks it up again; and replaces it on table, carefully covering the slate again. Lamp again flickers. Handkerchief

again snatched off table, and thrown on to top of lamp shade. Light flickers and handkerchief is removed from lamp by a pseudopod, in the shape of a half-formed "fist".[28]

Price and Dingwall both signed a statement to the effect that they had witnessed genuine phenomena and Dingwall, who gave a lantern slide lecture on Willi's mediumship to the SPR on their return to London (with Price operating the lantern), later boldly referred to Willi as the 'King of the Mediums'. They also agreed that should a similar subject come to light in England, a joint investigation under the auspices of the Society for Psychical Research would be undertaken.

As Dingwall suggested, the séances with Willi Schneider, who was regarded as a powerful physical medium throughout most of the 1920s, were a watershed for Price who began to capitalise on the experience and the growing notoriety that the sittings had provided. Price later went on to have over a dozen sittings with the Austrian youth who never, like his brother Rudi, became a professional medium, and went on to qualify in dentistry. However, the following year, when the opportunity arose to carry out exactly the kind of joint investigation the two men had talked about, it was Price who seized the initiative and began the kind of trail blazing that would not only make him a well known public figure in the psychic world, but create the alienation of the contemporaries with whom he continued to associate.

Early in 1923, Price made the acquaintance of a young twenty-two year-old hospital assistant named Stella Cranshaw who, it seemed, had the potential to develop as both a trance and physical medium. Accounts differ as to how their initial meeting came about – Price later said he had met her on a train journey but, as Richard Morris has since suggested[29], it seems more likely that they were introduced by a Spiritualist correspondent. Instead of contacting Eric Dingwall and the SPR, Price booked the séance room of the London Spiritualist Alliance, a move he later described as being the inaugural investigation of what was, in effect, his own rival psychical organisation to the SPR, the National Laboratory of Psychical Research. It eventually officially opened for business at the beginning of 1926 at premises in Queensberry Place, South Kensington, and Price was quick to describe it, in the opening number of his own *British Journal of Psychical Research*[30], as a 'model psychic laboratory'.

With his Stella C. sittings, he achieved total control over the proceedings which was for him of prime importance. Thirteen sittings were held between March and October 1923 (with another series of ten more much later in 1928) and Price's report, first published in the *Journal* of the American SPR in May 1924, and later (1925) in book form by the London publishers Hurst and Blackett, proved that Stella, the "electric girl" as Price later called her, was a powerful physical medium in her own right. As well as the movement of objects, a clairvoyant prediction which came true, flashes and sparks which shot about the room and the destruction of a balsa-wood table by an unseen force, eerie psychic structures similar to the ectoplasmic 'pseudopods' which had been observed in Munich made impressions on pieces of clay and a smoked glass screen.

By far the most impressive occurrence was what appeared to be a partial materialisation which was witnessed by Eric Dingwall (relegated now to the rank of guest rather than collaborator) who observed a bizarre egg-shaped body which crawled out from near the medium's foot towards the centre of the floor under the séance table. "It was white, and where the light was reflected it appeared to be opal. To the end nearest the medium was attached a thin white neck like a piece of macaroni. It advanced towards the centre and then rapidly withdrew to the shadow",[31] was how he later described it in a signed statement.

Where the furtherance of Price's career in organised psychical research was concerned, the Stella C. experiments were a resounding success. Price was able to keep the anonymity of his medium and, at the same time, compare her importance with Richet's and Schrenck-Notzing's famous subject. His report was instrumental and, in the spring of 1925, he was offered the honorary position of Foreign Research Officer of the American SPR, a post he held for six years after which it was effectively abolished due to internal changes within the Society. However, Price's rather antagonistic relationship with Walter Franklin Prince (1863-1934), the ASPR Research Officer and founder of the Boston SPR, was a factor with him finally breaking his ties with the organisation. In *Search for Truth*, Price easily summed up the advantages of going solo:

> It was exactly the sort of post I wanted. The job would take me all over Europe: to the various foreign centres of psychic activity; to those universities interested in psychics and the paranormal; and would put me in contact with fellow-investigators and scientists who were working on the same lines as myself. I should also meet the principal Continental mediums.[32]

And meet the mediums he did. For Harry Price, the 1920s and early 1930s were a catalogue of encounters with some of the most remarkable and controversial psychics of the day. They included Jean Guzik (1875-1928), a Polish weaver's son who convinced the likes of Geley, Richet and Sir Oliver Lodge of the apparent genuineness of his phenomena which famously included the materialisation of a furry ape-like animal; Price was unimpressed and called him "one of the cleverest fakers I have ever met".[33] Another Pole was a female cashier, Stanislawa P(opielska), whose ectoplasm was photographed and filmed by Schrenck-Notzing. In Warsaw, Price considered her mediumship nothing but childish tricks and, despite the Baron's forthright championing, she was caught faking phenomena in Paris in 1930.

One physical medium that Price courted in the hope of carrying out his own investigation was the notorious Mina Stinson (1888-1941), or 'Margery', wife of the noted Boston surgeon, Le Roi Goddard Crandon, a former Harvard Medical School instructor, who caused havoc amongst the American researchers and wrangled with Houdini. The Crandons refused to give a sitting at the National Laboratory and Price had to make do as a guest at a private séance in London where he was presented with one of the famous thumbprints (in heated dental wax) from the apparently materialised hand of 'Margery's' spirit guide, Walter, her late brother killed in a railroad accident in 1911. Nonplussed with much of what he witnessed, Price's suspicions were confirmed just over three years later when the ghostly thumbprints were exposed as clever fakes.

Another American psychic, who promised much but failed to deliver, was New York materialisation medium, Frank Decker, who gave Price a single séance in June 1933 that included direct voice and trumpet phenomena (the levitation of a cone-shaped device commonly used to produce spirit voices), all held in complete darkness. There was also a display of ectoplasm in red light. The sitting was in the way of a 'friendly' experiment and no proper control conditions were imposed. Price felt certain that Decker's ectoplasm, which at one point was seen frothing from the medium's mouth, was a cheap trick. Subsequently he was able to replicate the effect by holding a small amount of Kolynos toothpaste (then a popular brand) in his mouth and surmised that the New Yorker had done the same with a small tube concealed on his person. Despite agreeing to more controlled experiments, Decker and his spirit guide, 'Patsy', a newspaper seller from Chicago who had apparently been kicked to death by a horse, failed to keep a later appointment at the National Laboratory and headed back across the Atlantic. Three years later, an American spiritualist, Dr Edwin Bowers, the author of such books as *Bathing for Health* and *Nudism Exposed*, published a summation of his thirty-five year experience of séance room phenomena in which he championed Decker's mediumship unreservedly[34]. According to Bowers, regular visitors to the Decker séance room included Abdul Baha, the founder of the Bahá'í Faith, Omar Khayyám and Pythagoras.

What was probably Harry Price's most famous 'exposure' took place two years before his solitary sitting with Frank Decker when in July 1931 he accused the Scotswoman Helen Victoria Duncan (1898-1956) of being a 'regurgitator' rather than a genuine physical medium. After much wrangling behind the scenes, due to the fact that Mrs Duncan had an exclusive contract to sit only for the London Spiritualist Alliance, five séances were finally given over the course of a month, during which Price was able to take several flashlight photographs of apparent ectoplasmic forms including a hand and a materialised baby. Although the rigorous control conditions, including a full strip and cavity search and the medium being enclosed within a specially-made one-piece séance suit, made fraud seem impossible, the cold light of Price's magnesium flash told a different story. Mrs Duncan's ectoplasm appeared to be created by nothing more supernormal than lengths of muslin, a rubber surgical glove and a face made from cardboard. When the Scottish medium went into hysterics and refused to be x-rayed after the fourth sitting on 28 May, Price felt sure she had swallowed the items prior to the séance and had regurgitated the props at suitable moments inside the cabinet.

Other séance room photographs, taken by Mrs Duncan's supporters rather than psychical investigators, seem to support Price's findings and the crude materialised figures (obviously supported on wires or household items) became known as the 'coat hanger ghosts'. Instead of providing dramatic evidence of survival, these photographs, together with the fact that many Spiritualists rallied in support of the medium rather than condemning her outright, more than anything strengthened Price's statement of Modern Spiritualism being "the laughing-stock of the thinking man"[35]. However, where Helen Duncan is concerned, it is not easy to dismiss her outright. Although many mediums have been defended using the convenient get-out clause of 'mixed' mediumship (i.e. genuine phenomena reinforced with fraud due to waning powers or over-working etc.), other accounts of occurrences at her materialisation séances seem to suggest that she did have genuine abilities. This includes the Edinburgh sitting where the sinking of the British battleship *HMS Hood* by the *Bismarck* on 24 May 1941 was seemingly announced by a communicator before it had been confirmed or reported by the Admiralty[36].

An oft-repeated quote from Price's pen was that Spiritualism was 'at its best, a religion; at its worst, a "racket"'[37], but not all of his séance room investigations were disappointments. Although he was unsympathetic and at times downright hostile towards the Spiritualist movement, he was quick to champion and make public positive results. In Copenhagen, Anna Rasmussen, the 'Daylight Medium', named after her ability to perform without blackout conditions, made metal pendulums enclosed within glass cases swing by themselves under excellent control conditions in the same way that Moscow housewife, Nina Kulagina, performed for Soviet scientists in the 1970s. Price also brought the Romanian 'poltergeist girl', Eleonora Zügun, to London, and later published an extensive report on her phenomena[38]. In her presence, objects, including coins and a paper knife, moved and were projected across the room, sinister bite marks appeared on the girl's arms and hands and her face became scarred and disfigured. Price was impressed, but the most remarkable séance room investigations he was to undertake were yet to come.

In the latter part of the 1920s, Albert von Schrenck-Notzing had been carrying out extensive experiments with Rudi Schneider, whose brother, Willi, as we have seen, played an important role in introducing Harry Price to genuine séance room phenomena. Schrenck-Notzing's sudden death from an attack of appendicitis in February 1929 enabled Price to carry out what became his most successful, and ultimately most controversial physical mediumship investigation when, with typical opportunism, he quickly travelled to Munich and engaged Schneider for five sittings at the National Laboratory in London. These took place in April 1929 and were followed later in the year by another twenty-one séances which began on 14 November and continued until the middle of January 1930.

It was with Rudi that Price experienced impressive phenomena under what amounted to a watertight system of control. Rudi was restrained physically *outside* the curtained cabinet by one of the experimenters (often Price himself) and the sitters themselves were linked up by means of metallic 'socks' to an electrical circuit which indicated, by means of a warning light mounted on the wall of the séance room, whether anyone was intentionally leaving their place to fake phenomena. Price made much of this 'modern' system of controlling which in fact had been developed previously on the Continent by Fritz Grunewald (1885-1925) and whose use was later taken up by Baron Schrenck. In Rudi's presence the temperature of the room dropped and the cabinet curtains billowed out by themselves; Rudi's 'spirit' control, 'Olga,' spoke in direct voice through her medium; trigger objects, including a waste paper basket, were picked up and moved about by seemingly unseen hands, and the sitters were touched and had their clothes pulled. There was also materialisation:

> ... to our astonishment the basket emerged from between the curtains which parted and revealed to most of the onlookers a perfectly formed woman's arm, with hand and fingers ... I immediately likened the arm – and especially its upward movements – to a swan's neck and head, in a pose similar to that which the shadowgrapher makes when he throws the picture of a swan on the screen.[39]

Not surprisingly Price wanted more, and, two years, later Rudi returned to London and gave another series of séances, a total of twenty-seven in all, between 9 February and 5 May 1932. Objects moved, bells rang by themselves and a handkerchief danced off a table on to the floor. Despite the successes it all ended ultimately in disaster, some aspects of which, as will be seen in a later chapter, are relevant to the 'Rosalie' case.

Lord Charles Hope (1892-1962) was a keen psychical researcher and a Council Member of Price's National Laboratory. He was also a leading light and supporter of the Society for Psychical Research, which, effectively, made him one of Harry Price's rivals. Lord Charles took part in the Schneider séances as a sitter and also contributed financially to the project. As the experiments progressed, Price discovered through a chance remark by Rudi that, after he had finished sitting for the National Laboratory, he had agreed to undertake another series of experiments for the SPR under Lord Charles' direction. Price was furious and considered this an act of betrayal. At the twenty-fifth séance on 28 April 1932, he obtained a flashlight photograph which showed Rudi with one arm behind him free from the control. Despite having evidence of possible fraud on the Austrian's part, Price withheld the photograph on purpose for a year until after Rudi had carried out his sittings for the SPR. He then published it as part of an 'exposure' in the *Sunday Dispatch* on 5 March 1933 and a day later as part of a book-length report issued by his own organisation[40], the clear intention being to make the quality of the SPR enquiry appear doubtful and Lord Charles Hope personally look foolish.

Price's actions go a long way to supporting the view of Nandor Fodor mentioned above. Peter Underwood has also commented, that there were occasions 'where his personal self-esteem was involved, he was capable of the most extraordinary double-dealing, spite and intrigue'[41]. However, there is clear evidence that Price himself never doubted the genuineness of Rudi's mediumship and privately championed him right up until the day that he (Price) died. Where the incriminating photograph is concerned, opinions are divided. Anita Gregory, who carried out an extensive examination of Rudi's mediumship published posthumously as *The Strange Case of Rudi Schneider* (1985), felt that Price faked the photograph – a view which has been challenged by Vernon Harrison, a former president of the Royal Photographic Society, who could find no evidence of tampering. Whether the incident was a genuine accident that Price put to the "most nefarious use"[42], or whether he in fact staged the accident himself by releasing Rudi's hand on purpose (Price was controlling at the time), is open to debate.

Despite his stormy relationship with the SPR, Harry Price was a member of the Society for nearly thirty years right up until his sudden death. The rivalry that existed between the two was never far from the surface as shown in a letter to a correspondent, H.F. Rossetti of the Ministry of Labour, dated 17 June 1938 in connection with a poltergeist case. Price wrote:

> I hope that you are not going to hand your "case" of "haunting" over to the SPR. It is a long story, but there is considerable jealousy between that society and ourselves. They were furious when I founded the first psychical laboratory in this country in 1925, and I do not think they have forgiven me yet.[43]

Price need not have worried as the psychical disturbances ceased in mid August, unlike the friction between himself and his contemporaries which rumbled on.

The 1932 Rudi Schneider experiments were Price's last major practical physical mediumship investigation although, even as late as 1939, he proved his continuing interest and fascination with the subject by trying to encourage Eric Dingwall in accompanying him to séances at the Balham Psychic Research Society with the Welsh materialisation and trumpet medium, Jack Webber, who was then fast becoming a major figure in the movement. The Balham society was a Spiritualist organisation under the direction of healer, Harry Edwards (1893-1976), and in some ways Price's motivation was possibly one of trying to rekindle the success of their earlier *Revelations of a Spirit Medium* days and the Willi Schneider investigation in Munich. Despite the olive branch, Dingwall was uninterested. On 11 July 1939 he wrote to Price clearly showing his scepticism of the Welshman's séance room marvels which included the apparent dematerialisation of the medium's clothing under allegedly controlled conditions: "What are you doing about Webber? I understand he is pulling in about £10 per week or so. The coat effect with his hands held (?) sounds pretty, but I suppose the sitters on either side are holding each other's [*sic*] hands."[44]

Despite further prompting by Price, Dingwall remained noncommittal. Three days later he wrote:

> I can't help thinking it unwise of you to go to one of the ordinary séances with Webber. There is a good deal going on which wants rooting out! I don't think I want to go to any sittings as an ordinary sitter. If it was but the preliminary to a series for enquiry, good, but it won't be ... It is clear that W[ebber] is going to be somebody if he can get sufficient advertisement ... I think I won't come with you (thanks all the same) as I fancy the local officials of the [Balham] Society here have warned Webber about me and of course Edwards too.[45]

Ultimately it all came to nothing; Price never sat with Webber and the Welshman's sudden death at the young age of thirty-three of spinal meningitis on 9 March 1940 made things permanent. The only investigation of Webber's phenomena was carried out by newspapermen in conjunction with Harry Edwards who published the results as a series of annotated photographs in a book, *The Mediumship of Jack Webber* (1940). Despite the biography running to several editions in his lifetime, Edwards conveniently fails to include in any an incident at a sitting in Carshalton, Surrey, on 27 October 1939. Due to the accidental switching on of a light by Webber's father-in-law, who as in all séances took charge of the proceedings, the ostensibly entranced and secured medium was caught free of his bonds and creating a 'spirit' voice by holding the séance trumpet close to the sitters' faces[46].

Price's attitude to paranormal phenomena was clear and unambiguous and, in the closing pages of his *Fifty Years of Psychical Research*, he summed it up in the following way:

My experiences are based on thirty years' intensive experimentation, in many parts of Europe, and under conditions where fraud simply could not have occurred ... I am convinced that I have witnessed telekinetic phenomena ... I have heard raps, knocks, and other percussive phenomena, often at command, which were not produced normally. I have seen séance "lights", some percussive and some lambent, mostly of a bluish tint, which could not be explained by any laws with which we are at present acquainted. I have seen, felt, pinched, photographed and played tug-of-war with "pseudopods": teleplasmic masses resembling arms, hands, tubes, a triangular leg, a chocolate-coloured leg, a snow-man, childlike-form, luminous masses, etc., all showing volition and, in some cases, intelligence.[47]

For the remainder of the 1930s, Price's activities were mostly outside of the environment of the séance room and involved more sensational and publicity-inspired ventures. These included fire-walking experiments in Surrey and his investigation of Gef, the notorious 'talking mongoose' from the Isle of Man (whom we will return to briefly later on in this book). Following the outbreak of hostilities in September 1939, Price closed his London office and, although he made efforts to reopen it again following the end of the war, he had by this time effectively retired from active investigation. He devoted his final years to compiling his memoirs, penned an extended study of poltergeist phenomena in what became his longest book – *Poltergeist Over England* (1945) – and continued his researches at Borley, a case which had first come to his attention in 1929.

I hope that this chapter clearly demonstrates that where the investigation of physical psychic phenomena is concerned, Harry Price, whatever one may think of him as a person, was one of the most experienced researchers of his day and carried out his work in what was very much a 'golden age' of physical mediumship, the likes of which will never be seen again. Writing in his *Parapsychology: A Concise History*, the late John Beloff felt confident enough to say that "survival research can no longer be considered part of the cutting edge of parapsychology"[48], a contemporary viewpoint that suggests it is possible to explain practically all mediumistic phenomena in terms of the alleged ESP and PK (or psychokinetic) abilities of an individual medium without resorting to belief in the existence of immaterial spirits.

Not only are many modern parapsychologists disinclined to pursue survival as a worthwhile area of study but many Spiritualists also today no longer feel the need to prove anything to the scientific establishment. Unlike the founders and early pioneers of the movement, many mediums are wary of involving themselves with researchers, often citing the hostile way that certain historical figures, such as Helen Duncan, were treated by investigators in the past. There is little or no active co-operation in trying to obtain the conclusive evidence that mainstream orthodox science demands. The result is an impasse which, despite recent attempts to redress the situation[49], seems insurmountable. One of the results of this is that today's researchers sorely lack the kind of practical knowledge for investigating séance room phenomena that Harry Price possessed in abundance. Price may have courted the limelight, acted childishly and at times behaved like a bastard, but he was a hands-on practical investigator who knew, through bitter experience, when he was being deceived. He himself commented: "I must claim some authority for deciding whether fraud was possible [in his investigations] or not, as methods of deception have been a special study of mine – from necessity and not from choice – a vital study for anyone claiming to be a scientific investigator."[50]

In the 'Rosalie' case, as in no other, Price would need to rely on his considerable experience of both genuine and fraudulent phenomena. It was an investigation that began simply enough, like many others, with a telephone call ...

TWO

BACKGROUND TO AN
INVITATION

———————>●<———————

The year 1937 was a busy one for Harry Price. He was at that time, by choice, the Honorary Secretary of the University of London Council for Psychical Investigation, a grand-sounding but somewhat watered down version of his old National Laboratory which had been wound up three years previously. Despite the title, Price's organisation did not have any official connection with the University of London but grew out of his protracted lobbying to establish a Chair of Psychical Research and with it some form of honorary academic qualification in the subject for himself. At the time, the arrangement seemed to suit both parties, particularly the University, as they benefited from the permanent loan of Price's extensive occult library and later (in 1938) his laboratory apparatus, while Price drew around him an impressive Council of distinguished academics and corresponding members.

The activities of this, Price's second and last psychical organisation, reflected in some ways the gradual shift in emphasis away from the investigation of mediums and their phenomena which began to take place during the latter part of the 1930s. However, there was no real attempt as such to embrace fully the Rhine revolution at Duke University that was ushering in the new science of parapsychology with its emphasis on the statistical analysis of psychic phenomena. Rather than ESP, the fledgling years of the ULCPI involved several headline-grabbing ventures such as a radio broadcast from a haunted house and investigations of the Indian Rope Trick and similar curiosities. Despite this, articles in periodicals of the day such as "Science in the Séance Room" (*Prediction*, April 1937) and "Woman Medium's Cheese Cloth Spirits" (*Glasgow Evening News*, 21 May 1937) retained the connection with the investigations of previous years.

In March 1937, the lease on the basement premises at 13, Roland Gardens, South Kensington (out of which for the previous six years both the old National Laboratory of Psychical Research and later the ULCPI operated) expired and Price moved his London office, consisting of himself and his secretary, Miss Ethel Beenham, to a new address at 19, Berkeley Street, Mayfair. Following this short period of upheaval, Price brought his involvement with the enigma of fire-walking to a close with a second series of tests held at Carshalton in Surrey and also at Alexandra Palace where they were televised by the BBC. At the previous sessions at Carshalton in the autumn of 1935, the Kashmir mystic, Kuda Bux (1905-1981), also known as 'Professor K.B. Duke' and more famously, through his feats of apparent 'eye-less sight', as 'The Man with the X-Ray Eyes', braved the fire and Price published a report on the experiments under the auspices of his new organisation[51]. On this latest occasion, a professional fire-walker from Kanpur, Ahmed Hussain, did the honours, attempting to cross the twenty-foot long burning trench filled with paraffin-soaked logs, newspaper and charcoal. He was accompanied by Reggie Adcock, a Cambridge graduate who the same year took part in Price's investigations at Borley. Both were successful and Price enjoyed the publicity that the event and the solution of the fire-walking mystery (a combination of speed, the poor conductivity of wood and 'absolute confidence') gave to the ULCPI. Later in the year (11 August), an article by Price entitled "Last Words on the Fire-Walk" appeared in *The Listener* magazine.

When covering this period of Price's life in his book, *Harry Price – The Psychic Detective* (Chapter 11 – Writing to Hitler), Richard Morris makes much of the visit that Price paid in the middle of April 1937 to Nazi Germany where at Bonn he was entertained by a group of University academics that included philosopher, Professor Siegfried Behn, and Dr Hans Bender (1907-1991). Then an assistant at the Psychological Institute, Bender was later to become a famous figure in German parapsychology through cases such as the Rosenheim Poltergeist. Morris surmises that Nazi officials also took part in the meetings, which centred around the possibility of transferring Price's laboratory to Bonn University as the nucleus of a new Department of Psychical Research and, as such, paints a lurid picture of Price fawning over Adolf Hitler, effusing with the Nuremburg Rally and carrying out 'sinister discussions' with the Third Reich. While some aspects of Price's personal life may be questionable and for a biographer cannot be ignored, I do not see that they lessen in any way Price's competence as a psychical researcher. For the sceptic, this episode, coming as it does just before what was to be his most famous investigation, is an easy and flawed way of dismissing the validity of his work in the same way that, with typical illogical abuse, Trevor Hall argues (in the second chapter of his *Search for Harry Price*) that the actions of Edward Price in getting Emma Meech pregnant at the age of fourteen affected his future son's ability to investigate spontaneous phenomena several decades later. Suffice to say that, on his return from Germany, Price began in earnest the case which was to dominate, not only the rest of 1937, but also the remaining ten years of his life.

Borley Rectory was a rambling, red-brick house with a sinister reputation, situated in a lonely and remote part of rural Essex. The building itself was falling into disrepair; there was no electric light and water had to be hand-pumped from a well. Price had had an on and off relationship with the place since first visiting eight years previously in the company of newspapermen from the *Daily Mirror* when stories of its alleged ghosts had made national headlines. For a period of just over seventy years, from 1863 when the house was built by the Bull family to 1935 when the last occupier, the Revd Lionel Foyster moved out, four successive incumbents all reported strange and unusual experiences including the appearance of apparitions, disembodied footsteps, the movement of objects, mysterious lights, and the apparently unaided ringing of the servant bells. In 1929, the Revd Guy Eric Smith and his wife, Mabel, were adamant that they and their live-in maid, Mary Pearson, had all seen and heard things they could not explain. In the autumn of 1931, during the time that the Foysters were in residence, Price paid a short visit accompanied by members of his National Laboratory which included Kathleen 'Mollie' Goldney who, as will be seen, plays an important role in the later development of the 'Rosalie' case. On this occasion, Price was unimpressed with the Rectory 'phenomena' which, he felt, was produced fraudulently by the Rector's wife, the enigmatic Marianne Foyster, and dropped the case after a confrontation with her husband. Despite this, Borley Rectory clearly offered, under the right circumstances, the opportunity of carrying out a controlled and protracted investigation of a spontaneous haunting and Price kept in touch with contacts in the district in case things changed for the better.

In early May 1937, Price entered into correspondence with the Revd Alfred Henning who, the previous year, had been inducted into the Borley living. Unlike his predecessors he chose to live at Liston Rectory as, by then, Borley had been amalgamated with a neighbouring parish. With Borley Rectory standing empty, the time had come to see whether, under careful scrutiny, it would live up to its formidable reputation. Price negotiated a tenancy deal for six months (later extended to a year) and, on 19 May 1937, on behalf of the University of London Council for Psychical Investigation, took control of 'the most haunted house in England'.

At the outset, Price quickly realised that to be effective the investigation would require numerous and lengthy visits to Borley. Ghost hunting, when approached seriously, can be a drawn out and tedious business as phenomena do not occur on cue or at the drop of a hat. As he lived over one hundred and fifty miles away, daily visits were not possible and, although the investigation was being carried out under the auspices of the ULCPI, the people on its Council (although impressive on paper) were in fact academics rather than seasoned field researchers. The only practical option open was to recruit suitable members of the public with an interest in psychical matters to carry out the on-site enquiry, which was achieved through an advertisement in the Personal Column of *The Times* on 25 May 1937. Applicants were vetted by attending a personal interview at Berkeley Street and those that were felt suitable for the task were allowed to visit the rectory by appointment and given suitable directions (via a printed set of guidelines latterly known as the 'Blue Book of Instructions') on what to do and what to look out for during an observational period. These 'Official Observers', as they have become known, included engineers, doctors, civil servants and university graduates, and around eighty people visited Borley (mostly at weekends) during the twelve months that the investigation took place. Price later quoted forty-eight persons as assisting him but the number was boosted by observers who invited friends for whom they could vouch. Reports on their visits were submitted to Price in London and he used extracts from the material to compile a study of the rectory haunting which was published later as *'The Most Haunted House in England'* in the late summer of 1940.

With hindsight, the practicalities of Price's investigation were far from ideal and his methods and reasons for carrying out the enquiry became fair game in the wholesale attack on his work at Borley, which was instigated by the Society for Psychical Research within a year of his death. The whole subject of the Price tenancy of Borley Rectory has been discussed in detail elsewhere[52] and here I am only interested in including it as a background to events in the 'Rosalie' case. The Borley tenancy was in progress at the time that Price attended the 'Rosalie' séance and, as will be seen shortly, the séance itself was the result of events which took place involving the rectory investigation earlier the same year.

One of Price's most dedicated and objective observers was Mark Kerr-Pearse (1908-1961), a twenty-nine year-old civil servant from London. In the summer of 1937, Kerr-Pearse was between jobs, an outcome that was to be to Harry Price's great advantage as, once enrolled as an official observer, he was able to spend lengthy periods at Borley, a situation which made him an ideal investigator. This is proven by the meticulous reports that were submitted to Berkeley Street which show he followed Price's instructions to the letter. In spite of only taking part in the first six months of the investigation (as a job posting overseas required him to leave the country in November), Kerr-Pearse spent more time collectively at Borley than any other observer.

Early in September 1937, the BBC began planning a series of radio programmes on haunted houses and included an article on their forthcoming broadcasts in *The Listener.* On seeing this, Kerr-Pearse wrote (while at the rectory) to the Director of the Talks Department via the magazine and offered to relate to them his experiences at Borley which, up to that time, included footsteps, raps and other noises, together with the movement of control objects. These he said he found "interesting and convincing"[53].

During the 1930s, Harry Price had important contacts at Broadcasting House. This included a good relationship with Richard S. Lambert, at that time the founding Editor of *The Listener* who, as will be seen shortly, plays a highly important part in the 'Rosalie' story. Price had also collaborated with Seymour J. de Lotbiniere, a BBC Director and the pioneer of outside broadcasting. On 10 March 1936, the two men had taken part in a live relay from Dean Manor at Meopham in Kent in what was the first live radio broadcast from an allegedly haunted house; a "speck of radio history", according to Richard Morris, but Price was there first decades before modern day TV programmes like *Most Haunted Live* made it fashionable. The following year, on 21 July 1937, he had accompanied Price and Henry Douglas-Home to Borley for an overnight stay. Both Lambert and de Lotbiniere were clearly aware that Price was carrying out an investigation at the lonely Essex rectory and word soon got back to Berkeley Street about Kerr-Pearse's offer.

Unfortunately for the budding ghost hunter, one of Price's stipulations on being accepted as an investigator on the Borley case was that all observers had to sign a disclaimer, known as the 'Haunted House Declaration Form', agreeing to abide by the rules of the enquiry. One of these stipulations was an embargo on publicity of any kind unless authorised by the Council of the ULCPI. Price later admitted that, as a legal document, it probably wasn't worth the paper it was printed on, but a curt letter to Kerr-Pearse, together with an additional copy of the Haunted House form, was enough to quickly kill off any involvement in the BBC programme. In typical fashion, Price himself entered into a discussion with Seymour de Lotbiniere over the upcoming radio series and it was agreed that he would script and present one of the programmes about his current investigation, although Borley Rectory would not be mentioned by name. The broadcast went out at the beginning of November with Price receiving the handsome fee of £6.6s.0d (just over £350 today) for his trouble. A few days later, on 10 November 1937, an illustrated article based on Price's talk entitled "A Really Haunted House" was published in *The Listener* as part of a BBC series called "Can You Beat It?". It was a chain of events that was to create one of the most enigmatic cases in the whole of Harry Price's career in organised psychical research.

The Borley investigation continued through the autumn and into the winter of 1937. While his official observers were in action in rural Essex, Price was working on a solo project which, as he later described, was "the fulfilment of a mental resolution, made many years ago"[54]. This was to produce a continuation of one of the early classics of psychical research written by the ultra-critical investigator, Frank Podmore (1856-1910), one of the founders of the Society for Psychical Research, and published in 1902 as *Modern Spiritualism*. In producing "a sort of history", as he described it, in a letter to Sidney Glanville, another of his prominent Borley investigators, Price's book was also a continuation of the developments in the scientific study of psychic phenomena chronicled and published in Charles Richet's *Thirty Years of Psychical*

Research which appeared in an English translation in 1923. In bringing things up to date, Price added on another couple of decades and called his book *Fifty Years of Psychical Research* and, under this title, it was eventually published early in 1939 while he was working on his first Borley book.

On Wednesday 8 December 1937, over a month after *The Listener* article appeared, Harry Price took his usual train from Pulborough to London. At Berkeley Street he had his usual correspondence to deal with, plus a luncheon appointment. During the morning, Ethel Beenham put through a telephone call to his office. According to Price, the lady caller was "educated and cultured" and she had a story to tell. As Price listened, one can only wonder what thoughts were going through his head. Perhaps, given his known attitude a short time afterwards, it was a case of having heard it all before, as one might expect after spending the best part of the previous thirty years among the mediums and their many extraordinary claims.

In the account subsequently published in *Fifty Years of Psychical Research*, Price only ever refers to his female informant as "Mrs X" but, as will be shown later, it was established several years after his death that her surname was Mortimer. She told him that she had been encouraged to contact him personally after reading the "Haunted House" article in the previous month's *Listener* in which he stated at the outset that he had been investigating such buildings for thirty years, and, as Price described it, 'was impressed with my efforts to "ascertain the truth" in such matters'. As well as the flattery (which was grist to the mill as far as Price was concerned), there was also an interesting proposition which had been inspired by his bold assertion about the quality of the phenomena occurring at Borley: "She told me that she had noted that I could 'guarantee a ghost' in a particular haunted house which I mentioned in my broadcast; she, too, could 'guarantee a ghost', but one of a much more objective nature than any I had experienced."[55] This was in the form of a home circle, which was held regularly on a Wednesday evening at her house, located in one of the 'better-class' London suburbs. According to Mrs X, it was here that every week, a "little girl spirit" by the name of Rosalie, *always* materialised. Price himself would be able to experience this astonishing phenomenon as long as a few house rules were followed. As he later recalled, although he expected there to be conditions attached, he was "genuinely astonished" as to the simplicity of Mrs X's requirements. They were as follows:

1. The identity of the circle sitters, including Mrs X and her husband, were not to be disclosed to anyone.
2. Likewise, the address of the house where the séances took place was not to be revealed; nor was its locality.
3. As long as this anonymity was maintained, Price was free to write and publish a report about the sitting wherever and whenever he wished.
4. The sitting was in the way of a one-off chance to experience what Mrs X claimed was genuine materialisation phenomena. Even if he was "impressed with the proceedings" and thought the phenomena worthy of further study, no scientific inquiry would be permitted. This was because 'the mother of "Rosalie", who attended each sitting, was "terrified that her girl might be frightened away"' and the Wednesday sittings were treated by her as a kind of "sacred communion" between mother and spirit child.
5. No light sources such as torches or matches were to be brought to the séance and Price would not be allowed to touch the materialisation or speak to it, or carry out any kind of experimentation without prior permission.
6. The arrangement between Price and the circle members was to be a "gentlemen's agreement" and, as such, would not require a written contract or a disclaimer to be signed.

Initially this list looks unimpressive, if one were hoping that some kind of breakthrough in the investigation of physical mediumship phenomena was going to be achieved. The home circle and its location was to remain nameless, there would be no chance of further scientific study in an independent location and Price, in the role of a guest, was unable to carry out any kind of experimentation during the course of the sitting. The overall result was that whatever report he produced on his experiences would be anecdotal rather than forming part of a critical scientific paper. This is my own experience from attending public physical mediumship demonstrations over the past few years (including the sitting in Mansfield mentioned in the introduction) where the sitters are invited to attend under strict conditions, ostensibly put in place to ensure the protection of the medium's health, but, at the same time, effectively limiting any kind of investigation and reducing any psychical researcher to the role of a passive observer. Even at Scole, although the relationship between the SEG and the visiting independent

SPR members achieved unprecedented levels of co-operation between mediums and scientists, the investigators were still, as Arthur Ellison commented, "invited guests" and that "[t]he experiments carried out were not necessarily to our choice, and the suggestions we made to tighten conditions were not usually adopted either because they were apparently in conflict with the conditions required to produce the phenomena reliably"[56].

However, despite the restrictions, Price was going to be allowed a level of control far above anything he had been granted previously when attending a public séance on a medium's home turf and, even today, I know of no demonstrating physical medium who would agree to this kind of arrangement. Price himself describes the set up in *Fifty Years*:

> And now came the surprise. If I accepted their invitation, I would be allowed full control of the room and the sitters *up to the beginning of the séance* [Price's italics]. I could search the house from top to bottom, seal all external windows and doors, search the séance room (the drawing-room), all doors and windows of which I could lock and seal, I could move – or remove – any furniture, ornaments, etc., from the séance room which I thought fit ... I could search the sitters or any person in the house immediately before or after the séance. But once the sitting had begun, I was to remain passive and ask permission if I wanted to do anything, or make any alteration during the séance.[57]

Price was informed that the séances began at eight o'clock each Wednesday evening and that, if he accepted the conditions imposed, he was to arrive at Mrs X's house around seven o'clock on a date to be agreed beforehand. According to his account, Price told his caller he was impressed with the conditions and, after considering the matter, would write to her with his response.

Richard Stanton Lambert (1894-1981) was a close friend of Harry Price and, by his own admission, knew him well for fifteen years up until Price's sudden death in 1948. During the ten years that Lambert held the editorial reins of *The Listener*, which ended in 1939, several articles by Price on occult and magical subjects were regularly published in the magazine. In 1935, Price's book *Confessions of a Ghost-Hunter* was serialised in thirteen weekly instalments and, the same year, Lambert and Price made what was their most famous collaboration when, on 30 July 1935, they travelled to the Isle of Man to investigate a lonely farmhouse on the windswept slopes of Doarlish Cashen. There, according to a local family, the Irvings, a mongoose named Gef, sang hymns, recited poetry and travelled around the island on a bus. Unfortunately, Gef, the talking mongoose, failed to appear but the adventure provided enough material for the two men to write an account of their experience which was published by Methuen the following year as *The Haunting of Cashen's Gap – A Modern 'Miracle' Investigated*. For Lambert this proved somewhat unfortunate as, shortly after the book appeared, he was involved in "painful litigation" after taking out a libel action against Sir Cecil Levita, a former London County Council chairman. Levita had complained to Gladstone Murray, the BBC's Assistant Programme Controller, that Lambert was mentally unstable for involving himself in the occult and should be sacked from his post as editor. The court found in Lambert's favour (he received damages of £7,500) but the furore that the case created resulted in a Parliamentary Board of Enquiry into relationships between the BBC and its staff and led to internal reforms within the organisation. As Melvin Harris later commented, "Not bad for a mongoose – real or imaginary, talking or not"[58]. Despite the trouble with his employer, Lambert kept his job and remained on good terms with Harry Price, who happened to be his lunch guest on the morning of the extraordinary telephone call from the mysterious Mrs X.

Over their meal, Price evidently discussed his recent conversation and it seems, with some levity, gave a few details about the 'Rosalie' circle. Despite the free hand that he was being given to control the location and the participants before the séance began, Lambert's later remarks, when recalling their conversation, show that Price tended to regard the proposition as another Spiritualist sensation which, in all probability, would fall flat like the many others which had come his way. Despite getting his fingers burnt over Gef, Lambert realised that another possible collaboration could be achieved if handled correctly and urged Price to make an appointment to witness the 'Rosalie' phenomenon. Either Lambert or Price seems to have made a suggestion during their meal that it would be a good idea for an independent witness to take part to review the proceedings, the obvious candidate being Lambert himself.

After considering the matter over the weekend, Price returned to Berkeley Street the following week. On Monday 13 December 1937 he looked through his correspondence, made his customary beginning of the week telephone call in connection with his business work with paper manufacturers, Edward Saunders & Son Ltd, and dictated some letters: one to Sidney Glanville in connection with the ongoing Borley investigation, one to a Major Huth of Breslau concerning recent newspaper reports of Price's offer to establish a Chair of Psychical Research at Bonn University, and another to Mrs X. A carbon copy of this letter survives in the archives of the University of London and runs as follows:

> Dear Madam,
>
> I am taking advantage of your kind offer to attend a sitting at your house, and propose being with you on Wednesday next the 10th inst. [*sic*], about 7 o'clock. If there is any difficulty about this I shall be grateful if you will kindly let me know immediately.
>
> I am wondering whether you would be so kind as to allow Mr R. S. Lambert, the editor of *The Listener* (a journal which I know is read by you) to accompany me on Wednesday as a sort of witness. He would conform to all the conditions which you outlined to me last week, and I would personally vouch for him. If you can possibly see your way to grant my request, will you kindly telephone me or send me a telegram some time tomorrow (Tuesday) morning in order that I can communicate with Mr Lambert, who would then make the necessary arrangements?
>
> Thanking you for your courtesy in this matter,
>
> Yours faithfully,
>
> Harry Price.

The error of the date would appear to have been corrected on the top copy as the evening that Price visited the 'Rosalie' circle was two days after his written reply. In *Fifty Years*, he states that, when responding, he wrote expressly agreeing to all the conditions as did Richard Lambert, but, as Richard Medhurst, who enters the 'Rosalie' story later on, has commented[59], these are minor slips which probably crept into Price's later account when he was trying to paraphrase his correspondence from memory. As will be seen, Price wrote *Fifty Years* at his home in Pulborough where his files and psychical material were not readily to hand. This letter gives the only possible clue to the identity of the organisers of the 'Rosalie' sittings as the carbon copy carries the type-written heading 'Mrs Mortimer'. However, to the frustration of all subsequent researchers into the case, the address is not included.

Price also wrote to Richard Lambert the same day informing him that he had decided to attend the séance in order to "witness the marvels" for himself. The main body of his letter contains the following confirmation:

> I have asked the lady concerned if she will permit me to include you in the invitation, as a witness. I have asked her to telephone or telegraph tomorrow (Tuesday morning) in case they are agreeable. If you do not hear from me by 1 o'clock tomorrow, you will know I cannot manage it.[60]

Unfortunately, Mrs X did not respond. If she had, and Richard Lambert had been allowed to accompany Price to her home circle, I have no doubt that the outcome would have been completely different from what Price later reported in his *Fifty Years of Psychical Research* although, what this would have been, is difficult to say.

At Borley, on the evening of Wednesday 15 December 1937, Joseph Burden and Thomas Stainton, both from Christ Church, Oxford, were settling down for a joint observational period in the lonely and neglected rectory; while, over fifty miles away, Harry Price was journeying alone to what he later described as "the most amazing séance that even I have experienced"[61].

THREE

A MYSTERY HOUSE AND ITS PEOPLE

From this point onwards, we are virtually reliant on Price's account, as set down and published in his *Fifty Years of Psychical Research,* as to what allegedly transpired during a period of approximately five hours on a winter's night nearly eighty years ago. Where the requirement of anonymity is concerned, our psychical researcher followed this stipulation to the letter and went to great lengths to ensure that the séance venue and its sitters remained anonymous. As will be seen, there are a number of possible places where Mrs X and the 'Rosalie' circle may have held their meetings. Surprisingly, the Brockley of Harry Price's youth is a major contender and South Kensington, home for several years of the National Laboratory of Psychical Research, has also been suggested. At a meeting of the Ghost Club in 1939[62] (see Chapter 7) and also writing in his autobiography *Search for Truth* about the 'Rosalie' case, Price qualified things slightly by saying that the séance took place in South London[63]. In *Fifty Years* he describes the close of his outward journey that night by saying: "I arrived at M------- just after seven o'clock and made my way to Mrs X's residence"[64]. Correspondence of the time adds fuel to the mystery as the location is referred to by the capital letter 'B'.

In *Fifty Years*, Price gives a reasonably detailed description of the house where the séance was held. Sworn to secrecy, he was unable to give the exact address but, as he himself confessed, he wanted his readers to visualize what sort of place it was. He indicates it as being 'a typical, largish, mid-Victorian, double-fronted, detached suburban home' situated in 'a good-class road'. The house itself and its location will be looked at in some detail in a later chapter but, for now, this is how Price himself described the mysterious house in his 1939 book:

...I found [the house] was a large double-fronted, detached house... with a flight of twelve stone steps leading to the front door, on each side of which was a large room with bay windows. It was at a corner of another road, and had an area. There were three entrances (four, including the French window leading to garden) to the house: the front door, an area entrance (seldom used, except when coal was delivered, the coal cellar being under the front steps), approached by a flight of steps, and a door at the back of the house reached by a path running parallel to the side road. There were seven windows facing the main road: two on ground level, two above, two small attic windows at the top, and a small window (guarded by iron bars) in the area room. At the back of the house were four windows, and a French window giving access to the long, narrow garden, which was reached by some iron steps. On the side of the house facing the transverse road were two smallish windows and a lavatory window, and in the wall opposite the next-door house were two windows, a bathroom window and another lavatory window.

Clearly this description, although superficially quite exact, could fit that of hundreds of such period houses in the South London area, if the south of the river location was simply given as a cover when Price recalled the incident in later years. Its accuracy is also open to speculation as evidence exists that the published version differs in certain ways from a description recorded immediately after the sitting took place. It should be remembered that it would have been completely dark when Price arrived at Mrs X's house and the time available for studying the building would have been limited. Price also gives no indication in his account that he went outside, after being initially introduced to his hosts, to explore the garden or examine the building externally and his recollection of the number of windows and their locations would have been based on his internal tour of the house. However, it is conceivable, given that he claimed to have pressed the family for further sittings, that he may have returned at some later date in daylight. His brief description of the garden would more than likely have been gained from looking out of the ground floor French doors during his later tour of the house.

Rather than quote Price's account in its entirety as other authors have done, I have paraphrased the description of the build-up to the sitting, as well as the subsequent séance itself, and included a commentary on the various features as set down in *Fifty Years* on pages 134-144[65]. On arrival, the front door was opened by a 'trim' parlour-maid who showed Price through into the dining room where he was greeted by Mrs X and her husband. They in turn introduced him to their teenage daughter who was also present and whose age, Price states, was nearly seventeen. Given the charges of licentiousness made against Price by Richard Morris in his 2006 biography, which include accusations of affairs with a fellow psychical researcher and a medium, as well as his former secretary, Miss Lucy Kay, one can only guess at how 'trim' Price found his hosts' domestic! A light supper had been prepared by Mr and Mrs X's cook, apparently their only other employee, and over the meal Price was told background information about his hosts as well as the story of their experiences of the 'Rosalie' materialisation.

In *Fifty Years*, Price states that Mr X was a City businessman, the inference of which suggests that he was involved in banking. However, in a typescript copy of the book which survives in the archives of the University of London, Mr X's occupation is given as being that of a "hop merchant", a somewhat unusual and perhaps revealing profession. Later, when the report was prepared as a chapter for his book, Price changed Mr X's occupation, perhaps to provide a greater degree of anonymity for the family. Whether it was in fact Mr X's true occupation remains to be seen. Despite holding an apparently highly successful home circle for materialisation, Mr and Mrs X stated that they were not in fact Spiritualists but did have a passing interest in psychical research and had read a few books on the subject as well as Price's own articles in *The Listener*. According to his hosts, the history of the 'Rosalie' circle was as follows.

Several years previously, Mrs X had met and befriended an anonymous French lady (given the title Madame Z by Price in his book) while helping out at a local church bazaar. Madame, by profession a nurse, was a widow who had lived in England for a number of years. She had married an Englishman around 1914 and they had had a child together but the young family was not to last as in 1916 her husband, an officer in the British Army, was killed in action in the trenches. Five years later, more tragedy befell Madame Z when her six year-old daughter, 'Rosalie', a sickly child, contracted diphtheria and died after only a few days. This was in 1921 and little 'Rosalie' passed away in her mother's arms. Whether the loss of her husband or later her child (or both) turned Madame toward Spiritualism, or whether she was a Spiritualist prior to her marriage, is unclear, but she is described as being one in Price's account although she apparently did not attend either a local church or one of the recognised organisations of the day such as the Marylebone Spiritualist Association, founded in London in 1872.

Following the death of her daughter, Madame continued to live alone. In the spring of 1925, she began to be awakened at night by the sound of a child's voice calling out "mother" to her in the darkness. Price notes that this occurred with such frequency that she got into the habit of lying awake at night waiting for the sound of her daughter's voice. Over an unspecified period of time, 'Rosalie' began to make herself visible and Madame gradually became aware of the outline of what she took to be her child's form moving about in the room, as well as hearing the sound of her footsteps. One night it appeared that 'Rosalie' had managed to materialise fully, as Madame, putting her arm out to one side of the bed was able to feel a small child's hand holding on to her own.

It is not known when Mrs X first met Madame at the church function but it would seem to have been sometime during 1928 or possibly the year before. The two became friendly and their relationship developed to such an extent that the French woman felt confident enough to tell Mrs X about her nightly experiences. Mrs X obviously broached the subject to her husband and between them they suggested that they should hold a home circle at their own house in order to encourage 'Rosalie' to visit them. As her own home comprised simply two rented rooms, which were apparently unsuitable for holding séances, Madame agreed, and the first sittings were held toward the end of 1928. By this time, 'Rosalie' had been visiting her mother during the night hours for approximately three and a half years and she continued to do so as the circle sat weekly on a Wednesday evening in the drawing room of Mr and Mrs X's house, which was suitably blacked out for the purpose.

Nothing occurred at these séances for nearly six months until the late spring of 1929, the time that Harry Price first became involved in the Borley Rectory case. Madame Z felt her hand being held in the darkness by the small hand of a child and, from that time onwards, 'Rosalie' began appearing regularly. As the sittings progressed, subtle illumination was introduced, according to established Spiritualist protocols, by painting the glass of ordinary cheap hand mirrors with luminous paint and charging them up prior to the commencement of the séances by holding the objects close to an electric light. These makeshift plaques were placed glowing side down on the floor and were then picked up at suitable moments to allow the silent materialised figure of little 'Rosalie' to be observed briefly. Price was told that four plaques were sometimes used at the same time during the course of a single sitting.

Eventually, after much encouragement, the materialised figure began to speak and started answering simple questions put to her by her mother, her replies being confined largely to monosyllables. She appeared to be "extraordinarily shy" but, despite this, was alleged to have answered a large number of questions during the many séances held at the house. It seems that Price was given a good idea what kind of information was obtained through this questioning but none of the information imparted was included in any of his published accounts.

When Harry Price visited the Rosalie circle for his one and only sitting in December 1937, it would appear that these séances, which seem not to have varied in terms of procedure and phenomena other than the impressive materialisation of the little six year-old child, had been taking place regularly on a weekly basis for what amounts to a seemingly unbroken period of just over eight and a half years. The original circle members comprising Mr and Mrs X plus Madame, out of sight and sound of the world, had been producing the ultimate proof of the reality of survival after death and were content to keep the matter more or less privately to themselves. Occasionally, trusted guests were allowed to sit in the circle but they were few and far between and were obviously sworn to secrecy. The presence of guest sitters, it seemed, did not affect the quality of the phenomena and 'Rosalie' always materialised on these occasions.

It is important to make clear at this point that the materialisation phenomena, alleged to have been taking place for nearly ten years in the 'Rosalie' circle between 1928 and 1937, and described as such to Price, was completely at variance with the mainstream physical mediumship of the day. The amorphous ectoplasm issuing from the bodily orifices of the medium and from which the materialised spirit forms were fashioned, *de rigueur* at physical séances for over two decades since the publication of Schrenck-Notzing's *Phenomena of Materialisation*, was at variance with the materialisations being achieved in the home circle of Mr and Mrs X. This was clearly more closely associated with the phenomena of such impressive and extensively investigated mediums as Eusapia Palladino and Rudi Schneider, as well as physical mediums of our own time like Rita Goold of Leicester and Bill Meadows, whom I saw at Mansfield, as well as that of the Scole Experiment. All the well known physical mediums demonstrating in this country and elsewhere in the inter-war years, such as Jack Webber, Arnold Clare, Helen Duncan, 'Margery' Crandon and Einer Nielsen, as well as more unfamiliar mediums such as the Hungarian, Ladislaus Laszlo (a protégé of Schrenck-Notzing later exposed as a fraud), and the Austrian, Hubert Ferihummer, were seen and photographed producing their materialisations using (in red light) visible extruded ectoplasm. The 'Rosalie' materialisations did not, and, with his extensive experience of séance room phenomena, this fact would not have been lost on Price as he sat listening to the experiences of his hosts.

With the meal over, Price was shown into the drawing room where the remaining two sitters who were to make up the evening's circle were waiting, having arrived while the hosts and their guest were eating their supper. They were Madame Z herself, whom Price describes as being 'a pleasant French lady' with the impression of being in her late forties. The other sitter was a young man in his early twenties, a city bank clerk and friend of the family, whom Price calls 'Jim' although this is clearly not his real name. The occupation seems to tie in with that of Mr X with the inference being that possibly he was an associate or junior member of his host's business, although Price does make clear that he felt Jim was in the line of being a potential suitor for Mr X's daughter and was more interested in her than the séance itself. When speaking to Price, Madame apologised for not permitting Richard Lambert to attend the sitting, the reason given that they as a group had not risked allowing two strangers to attend on one single occasion in case their presence in some way scared 'Rosalie' away. This suggests that 'Jim' had attended the home circle on previous evenings although how many times it is not possible to say.

The only other people present in the house during the evening were the two members of staff, the parlour-maid and the cook, whom Price met briefly during his subsequent tour of the house. They apparently knew that séances took place regularly on a Wednesday evening but were unaware of the nature of what actually went on. Both were given instructions not to answer the front door during the time that the sittings took place and callers on the telephone were asked to ring back at a later time. The fact that the mystery house had a telephone line was one avenue of investigation that, as we will see, was explored quite thoroughly when the 'Rosalie' case was investigated during the 1960s. The fact that they were not allowed to go home early, or were given the night off, seems to suggest that they were live-in servants, particularly as the séance itself finished quite late in the evening.

With the introductions over, Price asked to be shown over the house and, in accordance with his prior agreement with Mr and Mrs X, made an attempt to control various parts of the building. This took the form of sealing the doors and windows to prevent accomplices from entering while the séance was in progress, together with a search of the various rooms, and, it seems he brought along his 'ghost hunter's kit' especially for the purpose. This was a suitcase full of equipment, the contents of which had been photographed as an illustration for his *Confessions of a Ghost-Hunter* issued the previous year, and which were subsequently described in detail in the opening pages of his first Borley book that appeared in the autumn of 1940. From his kit bag, Price produced a small hand drill or gimlet, screw-eyes, white tape, surgical (adhesive) tape, a dredger of powdered starch and a pocket torch and began putting them to use.

We have already looked briefly at the type of house that Harry Price now found himself exploring and was trying to make as secure against deception as was possible under the circumstances. It was a decently sized four-storey Victorian building and, from Price's description, appears reasonably square on plan. There was a central hallway leading from the front door and, from the account in *Fifty Years*, the right-hand front room, as viewed from the road, was the dining room in which Price was initially received and the left-hand room was a drawing room which also doubled as the séance room. Both these rooms had bay windows. There appears to have been a room at the back of the house, also used by the family, which was the room with the French doors giving access to the rear verandah and the garden. The rest of the ground floor would have been given over to staff areas including the kitchen and possibly a scullery. As the house had a lower area at the front there was a basement or lower ground floor but, how extensive this was, is not given. The upper floors obviously comprised bedrooms with the attic being sleeping accommodation for the live-in staff. Accompanied by Mr X and young 'Jim', Price toured the house with his bag of tricks:

As I came to a window, I closed and fastened it and stuck a strip of tape (which I initialled in ink) across the join where the sashes met. In the case of two "dormer"- type windows [i.e., the attic rooms], I twisted the tape round the fasteners, and secured the initialled sticky ends to the window frames. I sealed the three external doors and the French window of the house with screw-eyes, through which I threaded adhesive tape, tied in three knots, which I initialled.

Although he doesn't mention it, one assumes he was at liberty to carry out a reasonable search of each room and open and inspect any cupboards and wardrobes. Controlling a whole building like this effectively cannot have been an easy task, but Price seems to have been satisfied under the circumstances that no one could have entered or left the building without disturbing any of his seals and his being aware of it. Once all this was completed, only one area remained to be examined and controlled and Price left the most important room until last – the séance room itself.

FOUR

CHECK AND DOUBLE CHECK

———————⟫●⟪———————

I n his subsequent report on his experience in *Fifty Years*, Harry Price
bemoaned the fact that the 'Rosalie' séance did not take place in
his own psychic laboratory. In its heyday from 1926 through until
the early 1930s, Price's National Laboratory of Psychical Research had
contained one of the most sophisticated séance rooms in Europe, designed and equipped for the purpose under his own direction, for the
investigation of mediumistic phenomena. It was in a league of its own
then and there is nothing like it in existence today.

As well as the electrical controlling apparatus mentioned previously
in connection with Rudi Schneider, the séance room boasted a setup of
seven cameras including one capable of taking stereoscopic pictures; a
sophisticated lighting system including a 500-watt spot light, a 1000-
watt daylight flood light, and filters for ultra-violet photography; as well
as mechanically or electrically operated magnesium flash-lights with
facilities for trapping the smoke. There was a recording thermograph, a
dictaphone, and an illuminated note-taker's table constructed in Paris
to Price's own specification. The medium's 'cabinet' was formed with
two lined velvet curtains on roller bearings; a mahogany shutter, also
on ball bearings, created light-tight blackout conditions; and the séance
room was wired for sound with a microphone connected to a separate
wax cylinder recording apparatus sited in an adjacent room. A large
cabinet gramophone and a weighing machine completed the setup.

Clearly, Price took the investigation of physical psychic phenomena very seriously and, rather than being simply a room filled with gadgets or gimmicks, it was part of what he described with some pride in his memoirs as 'the most modern laboratory methods ... employed in putting upon a permanent footing in Great Britain this most important science of Psychical Research'[66]. It was an arena into which, with no uncertainty, fraudulent mediums entered at their peril.

In the field, however, things were very different. During the inter-war years, many people who called themselves 'psychic investigators' and published books on their experiences in the séance room had become, or were already, convinced Spiritualists. Their accounts lacked the objectivity of the independent researcher, like Price, who knew that Spiritualism was open to abuse by charlatans and that elements within the movement were capable of putting sophisticated fraud into practice. As has been mentioned previously, in 1922, Price and Eric Dingwall had collaborated on a facsimile reprint of a rare book exposing mediumistic fraud in America entitled *Revelations of a Spirit Medium*. The book, written by a phoney psychic with a conscience, described in detail how many of the marvels of the American séance rooms in the 1870s and 1880s were created. These included sittings for the direct-voice and materialisation using techniques which were still being employed forty years later. Price was well aware of what tricks and effects were possible and, despite the co-operation and apparent openness of his hosts, he had to be on his guard at all times if his investigation was to carry any kind of credibility. The fact that, following many encounters with fraudulent phenomena and years of wrangling with the Spiritualists – who by his own admission he had become tired of associating with – Price still took on the challenge of carrying out the investigation, shows how determined he was to try to find the likes of a modern D.D. Home or a Palladino.

In *Fifty Years*, Price gives the following comprehensive description of the improvised séance room where 'Rosalie' would allegedly manifest:

> It was nearly square, measuring twenty-four feet by twenty-one feet, by nine feet six inches high. In the bay of the window was a settee and against the opposite wall was a long mahogany sideboard with eight drawers. On a square occasional table near one corner was an electric transportable 'Pye' radio, plugged into a socket near the floor. From this same socket a wire led to a small electric stove in the opposite corner, the flex trailing across the hearthrug. In another corner was a round

occasional table, supporting a work-basket. On the mantlepiece were a clock and some ornaments. Six solid mahogany chairs completed the furniture of the room – with the exception of an Airedale dog, which was now lying in front of the electric fire, having just shifted his quarters from in front of the grate. There had been a big fire in the grate, but it had been allowed to go out. One element of the electric fire was switched on. The ceiling of the room was of plaster and there were six pictures on the walls, which were distempered. The curtains, which screened the windows, had been purchased specially for these séances. They were of thick, heavy material, suspended on rails, and the edges overlapped, effectively preventing any street light from entering the room. On the floor, composed of polished hardwood boards, were spread four large Persian rugs.[67]

As it is claimed that this passage was written, I estimate, around three hours after Price left the house at the close of the sitting, it is fair to say that it would appear to be an accurate representation of the 'Rosalie' séance room. The scene easily mirrors that of the many home circles that at one time were common in Spiritualist households up and down the country, particularly in the first half the twentieth century, and which still take place today. A detailed history of one such circle, which allegedly achieved an astonishing level of materialisation, is given by the late Tom Harrison in his book *Life After Death – Living Proof* (2004) which charts the story of the physical mediumship of his mother, Minnie Harrison.

The presence of the not only house-trained but seemingly séance-proof Airedale was apparently explained to, and accepted by, Price as the dog was allowed to remain in the room for the duration, and did not stir or react at all to any of the proceedings throughout the evening. Evidently it was used to the gatherings and was trusted not to interfere with or interrupt the materialisation. This is somewhat remarkable given the ample evidence for the behaviour of animals, particularly cats and dogs, reported in haunted houses throughout the world over many years. Price was obviously aware of this, particularly as in 1931 he had contributed a long foreword to F.M. Archer's *The Soul of a Dog* which included a chapter that discussed several accounts of authenticated cases of canine reaction to the presence of the paranormal. Price makes no comment on the issue of the dog other than stating that it was present in the séance room. In later years following Price's death it was suggested that the Airedale was a fake and concealed an accomplice who emerged under the cover of the blackout to create the child materialisation. However, Price does mention fondling the dog before the séance took place and observing it move from in front of the open hearth to a new position by the electric fire. It is, therefore, difficult not to accept that it was a real animal, albeit an unusual addition to a meeting of this kind.

Clearly with this kind of investigation, then as now, the psychical researcher is faced with three main issues: securing the séance room in order to prevent an accomplice from entering during the course of the demonstration; ensuring once the room has been sealed that no accomplice has been hidden inside and can subsequently come out of hiding to play tricks; and to control the sitters and the medium in such a way that they stay in their places and are unable to produce phenomena fraudulently.

With the servants given their instructions not to disturb the family and their guests for the remainder of the evening, the party assembled in the drawing room and Price set to work. His first decision was to remove all the loose ornaments including the mantlepiece clock, the wall pictures and the work-basket, and store them in the dining room opposite. When Eric Dingwall examined the 'Rosalie' case twenty years later in the company of Trevor Hall (see Chapters 9 and 10), the two researchers found the reasons for this procedure 'obscure' and were unable to work out why Price carried this out. I find this attitude rather surprising given Dingwall's extensive experience of the literature of séances and physical mediumship. Price had been told that a materialisation took place at the Wednesday meetings but he had no idea what would, in reality, take place or what Mr and Mrs X actually considered to be a full materialisation. We have already seen how Cecil Husk had been found faking a materialised face by simply leaning over a phosphorescent slate. Price was quite within his right to assume that there could be materials secreted in any of these items which, at a suitable moment, could be used to create 'phenomena' and was, therefore, removing them from the equation.

Once this was done, Price sprinkled starch powder on the hall floor outside the drawing room door, which he then locked, keeping the key in his pocket for the duration of the sitting. He then sealed the door by sticking surgical tape in four locations, across the gap between the door and the frame, and initialled each one. For good measure, two screw-eyes were fixed into the architrave each side and a length of tape threaded between them and knotted into position. The windows were controlled in the same way. The illustration of the séance room on p.139 of *Fifty Years* shows the usual angled bay window arrangement common in Victorian houses, with a large central sash window and two smaller windows on each side. As with the other windows of this type in the house, Price stuck his surgical tape across the line where the top and bottom sashes met and initialled each one.

Satisfied that the door and windows were controlled, he then turned his attention to the fireplace. In his account, Price states that he was initially unsure what to do but, on the spur of the moment, came up with a solution. Having an evening newspaper with him in his bag, he placed a sheet on the top bar of the grate below the opening into the flue and covered the paper with a thick layer of starch powder. He then drew with his finger his initials so that the newsprint was visible in the letters. We are told that this make-shift arrangement ensured that no one could tamper with the fireplace without his knowing about it afterwards.

It might seem somewhat over the top to consider the possibility of someone either entering the room via the chimney or in some way using the fireplace to fake phenomena, but Price was aware of the precedents set by charlatans over the years, and their methods used to create ghostly effects were well known to him. Having reissued the *Revelations of a Spirit Medium* for a post-World War I audience, Price would have been familiar with the account given in the book of a remarkable and audacious scam perpetrated by a bogus materialisation medium in San Francisco. Assisted by an entourage of helpers, the medium was able to create an impressive range of materialised figures (including the 'spirit' of Abraham Lincoln) in a locked and sealed séance room by using a trap door concealed in the wooden panelling of a false ceiling[68]. In the mid-1950s, psychical researcher Tony Cornell was convinced that the materialisations he witnessed at a séance with the Welshman, Alec Harris, in Cardiff were created by the medium dressing up in suitable ectoplasmic garments that he surmised were secreted in the fireplace next to the medium's 'cabinet'[69].

Price next turned his attention to the heavy furniture in the room and, with the help of Mr X, moved and examined the settee and the sideboard. The settee was up-ended and Price punched the canvas and webbing on the underside to ensure it was secure and nothing was hidden inside the base. He also trod on the loose cushions; no doubt an alarming sight for Mrs X to see her furniture interrogated in such a forthright way despite her agreement to allow Price free rein in his investigation! The drawers in the sideboard were opened and Price looked through their contents, which included table napkins, gramophone records (the player being in an upstairs room), as well as 'the odds and ends that accumulate in every house'.

Here is a slight anomaly in that the contents of the sideboard were allowed to remain in the room whereas the loose ornaments were not. Perhaps Price realised that he should have checked the sideboard earlier as, by this time, he had carried out his elaborate sealing of the door, which would have had to have been opened and the controls reinstated in order to remove the items from the room. Rather than delaying things (as well as breaking the seals), he allowed them to stay after satisfying himself that the contents were innocuous. It would have been a simple matter to seal each drawer with lengths of initialled tape once the contents had been checked, but Price does not mention doing this and we cannot assume it was carried out.

Despite the fact that the radio set was to be used during the séance, Price opened the back of the wireless and saw nothing unusual inside. Finally, he pulled back the rugs on the floor and closely examined the floorboards for signs of anything suspicious. Given the history of fraudulent mediumship, this could have been anything from a trapdoor for a confederate to a secret compartment for storing props. Price found that the boards were securely fixed and concluded that the building was 'a well-built house, and I was unable to get my penknife blade between the boards, every one of which appeared as solid as a rock'.

Having inspected the séance room, Price turned his attention to his fellow sitters. With the men he was able to run his hands over their clothing and they also readily turned out their pockets, which contained nothing that 'could be used to simulate a phenomenon'. With the ladies, common decency prevented a similar examination and Price was forced to compromise by requesting that Mrs X and Madame sit on each side of him during the course of the séance, to which both women agreed. Their hosts' daughter, however, took the bull by the horns and, without any request, promptly pulled up her skirt to prove that she didn't have anything hidden there. Her forthright action, which no doubt set Price's pulse racing for a moment, was due to the fact that she had attended a 'health and beauty' class earlier in the evening and was wearing her gymnasium clothes (Price describes 'a pair of tight-fitting dark knickers') under her skirt. 'I was convinced that she had nothing concealed on her person' was Price's polite conclusion.

No curtained 'cabinet' or table was used during the séance, the sitters' chairs being arranged in a circle in the centre of the room. Although he doesn't mention it, given his knowledge of the séance room fakery of Charles Eldred, whom we have already encountered, Price would have satisfied himself that the chairs themselves did not offer any opportunity to conceal props or other suitable items. He mentions them as being 'solid mahogany chairs', which gives the impression that their seats and backs were not upholstered in the way that Eldred's 'magnetised' chair was constructed.

Price notes that he made a sketch of the séance room, prior to the commencement of the sitting, on which was included a layout of the room, its contents and the position of the sitters in the circle. He gives the following seating arrangement in *Fifty Years* which, he informs us, was of his own design: Price sat with his back to the fireplace with Mrs X on his right and Madame on his left; the daughter of the house sat to the left of Madame, with young 'Jim' on her left, with Mr X completing the circle between 'Jim' and his wife. Four of the sitters (Price, Mrs X, Madame and 'Jim') had been given the luminous plaques made from improvised hand mirrors and these, having been charged up next to the electric light earlier in the evening, were placed on the floor, face downwards, by the side of their respective chairs.

With everyone in their seats, Price completed his control by sprinkling more starch powder in front of the door and the fireplace. He then switched off the electric fire and the lights (four wall-lights and one central ceiling light). This whole preparation, including the introductions, the supper meal with its history of the 'Rosalie' circle, and the controlling of the building and the séance room, had taken just over an hour and a half to complete. At ten past nine, by Price's watch, the 'Rosalie' séance began.

FIVE

THE 'ROSALIE' SÉANCE

A well-organised séance, or experimental sitting for physical phenomena in black-out conditions, is a unique experience, best described as amounting to a suspension of reality. There can be a sense of complete detachment with the outside world, which carries on oblivious to whatever is unfolding within the confines of the séance room. A true arena of the emotions that I consider to be one of the most exciting aspects of contemporary paranormal investigation, as relevant today as it was to the likes of Crookes, Richet and Harry Price.

How many physical séances Price attended in his career in organised psychical research is difficult to say. Over fifty were held under Price's direction with Rudi Schneider alone, and this figure doubles when mediums like Willi Schneider and other National Laboratory mediums like Stella C. and Helen Duncan are included. If these, Price's most important sittings, are considered together with the many he attended abroad during lecture tours and conference delegations, as well as those from the early years at Manor Road, I feel it is not unreasonable to suggest that Price was a veteran of at least 250 physical séances. These would have been in all manner of varying conditions, both as regards to control and to content. By his own admission, with the 'Rosalie' séance, he saved the best till last.

The protocols for the production of physical séance room phenomena – Spiritualist tradition in other words – are very much the same today as they were in Price's time. These include the need for darkness and/or subdued red light for materialisation using ecto-plasm, and singing and lively music in order to 'raise the vibrations' and create a harmonious atmosphere in which the spirit world can interact with our own. The disadvantages for psychical researchers trying to carry out objective studies under these situations are obvi-ous and promote not only the abuse of physical mediumship by the unscrupulous but, as Donald West has commented, 'scepticism by imposing conditions that impede investigation, such as darkness, rules that cast the investigators in the role of "sitters" who must not move or touch without permission, and the supposed necessity for music and chatter which distracts attention and further limits ob-servation of varied happenings that occur without prior warning'. In conclusion, '[m]agicians and illusionists could hardly devise better circumstances for their tricks'[70].

Price was used to the trappings that séance work normally involved. Even 'Olga', the trance personality of Rudi Schneider, insisted on a bab-ble of meaningless chatter from all the sitters present throughout his physical sittings. This was something which Price found exceeding-ly tedious, although the phenomena he experienced with Rudi clearly made up for the effort involved. Where the 'Rosalie' circle was con-cerned, 'the pandemonium which often accompanies a séance' as Price put it, was for once set aside. There were no opening or closing prayers or hymn-singing, and constant forced talking or banter was also not required, nor was hand-holding in the dark. Mrs X, who acted in the capacity of circle leader throughout the evening (an important role in any home circle and one whose duties normally involve giving in-structions to the sitters and responsibility for the general well-being and safety of the medium), informed the group that quiet conversation was permitted unless they were told otherwise.

N.B. The following timings are my own, based on the report pub-lished in *Fifty Years*; an asterisk indicates my own interpretation based on Price's written account.

[9.10 pm] In his account, Price makes it clear that despite the black-out, which was complete, he could accurately determine the position and identity of each of the sitters by their voices and was also able to pick up the sound of their breathing. This is an important point to note as it effectively means that, for the duration of the séance, there was little or no chance of anyone's using the cover of singing or loud con-versation to mask the sound of potentially fraudulent activity.

[9.30 pm] After approximately twenty minutes, during which time the group had been 'chatting quietly', Mrs X asked everyone to stop talking and her husband announced he would switch on the radio set for some background music. Getting up from his seat he made his way, in the dark, round the back of Price's chair and across to the small corner table to the left of the fireplace, and switched on the wireless. The Pye set had an illuminated dial on the front and the small amount of light given off while the radio was in operation was enough for Price to be able to see each of the sitters in their respective chairs. Price notes that, at this point, Madame had become very emotional and appeared to be crying. Mr X, after some difficulty in finding what he considered suitable music, settled on a foreign station and returned to his seat.

[9.35 pm] After a short time, Mr X rose and, switching off the radio set, returned to his chair. His wife asked everyone not to speak and the group sat in silence for a period of time, after which Price heard Madame softly whisper the name, "Rosalie!". This she continued to do at intervals, accompanied quietly at times by Mrs X. Price notes that both women were sobbing softly by this time and the display of emotion he found quite surprising. 'I had been warned that the séance was of a sacred character, but I had not anticipated such a display of emotion' is how he notes it at this point in his account.

[10.00-10.05 pm] A few minutes (in Price's estimation) after he had heard the hall clock chime the hour, Madame gave a choking sob and, in the darkness, said something which Price thought sounded like 'my darling'. At this moment, Mrs X leant towards him and whispered, *"Rosalie is here – don't speak!"*: a profound announcement that I am sure would have quickened Price's pulse despite his years of séance room experience. Almost simultaneously, he had the impression of something being close to him in the darkness. In his account he states:

> I neither heard nor saw anything, but the sensation was an olfactory one – I seemed to *smell* [Price's italics] something that was not there previously. It was a *strange* [Price's italics], not unpleasant smell ... I sensed, rather than knew, that she [i.e. Madame] was fondling her child[71].

Everyone was silent except for Madame who was crying, it seems, almost uncontrollably. It will be remembered that she was very close to Price on his immediate left. In between her sobs he heard 'a sort of shuffling of feet' and, at the same moment, felt something soft and warm touch the back of his left hand, which was resting on his knee. It would appear that 'Rosalie' had 'materialised' in the gap between their two chairs. Price sat completely still and made no attempt to reach out at this stage. The mother gradually regained control of herself but continued to whisper tenderly to her 'child'.

[10.10 pm*] At this point, Mrs X asked Madame whether Price could touch the materialisation and permission was given. The investigator stretched out his left arm 'and, to my amazement, it came in contact with, apparently, the nude figure of a little girl ...' Price passed his hand over the form, invisible to him in the darkness, which he estimated was approximately three feet, seven inches tall and whose breathing he could hear distinctly. He moved his hand across her chest up to her chin and cheeks, laying the back of his hand across her right cheek before returning it to her chest where he clearly felt the rise and fall of her breathing. Price then passed his hand over her thighs, buttocks and back where he could feel long soft hair falling over her shoulders, before moving down her legs and over her feet. 'They were the normal limbs of a normal six-year-old' was his impression at this time. He also had the notion that the skin temperature was 'not so warm as one would expect to find normal human flesh', but felt that this could, in part, have been due to imagination.

Despite his years of séance room investigation, Price's account gives the impression that he was clearly stunned at what he was experiencing. 'There are no words to express how I felt at the appearance of the form before me' he wrote at this point. 'A supreme scientific interest, with a feeling of absolute incredulity, would best describe my reactions. I had not bargained for anything so wonderful (or so clever!) as this'. What he also makes very clear is that he felt the show of intense emotion by 'Rosalie's' mother was a genuine one and that, if the whole materialisation was a fraud, she had been taken in by it over a long period of time, fully accepting she was being reunited with her dead child.

[10.15 pm*] Still in complete darkness, Price asked Mrs X if he could move his chair closer to where 'Rosalie' was standing and this was allowed. Using both hands he again felt the small silent figure and carried out another examination. With his right hand he lifted 'Rosalie's' right arm and felt for and counted her pulse, estimating a rate of 90 to the minute. Following this, he put his ear to her chest and was able to hear her breathing distinctly. For all intents and purposes, the impression was of a real living child present in the room with him.

Price then took both small hands in his own and requested that Mr X, his daughter, and young 'Jim' speak in order to confirm that they were still sitting in their respective chairs. They did so and Price was satisfied that they had not moved or were trying to impersonate the 'spirit' child in the darkness. He also seemed confident that Madame and Mrs X had not moved either but did not ask either to acknowledge themselves. Mrs X had only spoken a few minutes before to confirm he could make a closer examination.

[10.25 pm*] At this point, Price made an important decision. He asked Mrs X if he could examine the figure using one of the luminous plaques. Harry Price, the veteran of dozens of physical séances knew that it was still possible he was being deceived. Although it may seen highly improbable that an adult could carry out an imposture in this way, the forced conditions of the physical séance room, combining (as was the case in the 'Rosalie' sitting) a highly charged emotional atmosphere with the disorientation of complete darkness, can fool sitters and guests into believing they are experiencing physical effects, such as touches and the movement of objects, which are nothing of the sort. For example, Tony Cornell has described how one physical medium, whom he investigated in the early 1980s, was allegedly able to create the effect of a materialised child by kneeling on the floor using her bare arms to impersonate the legs of a young boy[72].

Mrs X spoke with Madame and they agreed that two plaques would be used, one held by Mrs X and the other by Price, the stipulation being that the illumination of the figure should start initially with the feet and then gradually brought higher up. Phosphorescent plaques have a variety of uses in séance situations. One I have seen on several occasions was used to demonstrate the silhouetted outlines of allegedly materialised hands as it moved around the circle of sitters. At a distance the illumination can appear fuzzy and show very little, but, at close quarters, a reasonable amount of detail in silhouette is achievable. The most common use however, particularly in inter-war séances for full-form materialisation with mediums of the likes of Arnold Clare (who used a large-sized plaque), was to illuminate the faces and robes of spirit communicators by passing the plaque close to the figures which were made visible in the soft light.

[10.30 pm*] Price picked the modified hand mirror up from beside his chair and, on turning it over, was no doubt amazed to see the small naked feet of 'Rosalie' picked out in the glow. Mrs X, who must have got up from her seat and moved past Price in the darkness, held her plaque to the left side of the figure while Price positioned his in front. The illumination was of sufficient quality for him to see the soft texture of the skin, which appeared to be without any blemishes. As they gradually raised both their plaques up from the floor, the small figure was revealed and, as Price reports in his account, 'we beheld a beautiful child who would have graced any nursery in the land'. The face appeared pale but this, as Price admits, may have been an effect of glow from the luminous paint. He describes the features as being 'classical' with bright, intelligent and what appeared to be dark blue-coloured eyes. 'Rosalie's' lips were closed in a set expression and he noted that the child 'looked older than her alleged years'.

[10.40 pm*] After a short time, Madame spoke to say that Price's examination must be brought to a close as 'Rosalie was wanted' and it seemed was about to leave them. Clearly wanting to prolong the experience as much as he could, Price asked as a special favour if he could ask the child some questions. Her mother agreed, although she remarked that it was unlikely that the child would speak on this particular occasion and only a minute would be allowed for him to carry this out.

'If the reader were suddenly faced with an alleged spirit, what questions would he ask it?' This comment is as relevant today as it was when Price included it in his 'Rosalie' chapter in 1939. *What would you have done in Price's situation and what would you have said to the small silent figure of the spirit child 'Rosalie'? Remember you have only got a minute in which to act.* As Price notes, with some preparation it would have been possible to put together a list of useful inquiries, but, on the spur of the moment, I think anyone would struggle to make good use of what amounts to an astonishingly unique opportunity.

Price, to his credit, was aware that the alleged 'spirit' was 'young and unsophisticated' and he states that he 'must have subconsciously imagined that the child was a real one; that it lived in a real place; and that it understood perfectly what I was saying'. He goes on to say, 'I found myself asking "Rosalie" what I should ask any other little girl, who had come from some strange place and whom I chanced to meet'. Deliberately and with pauses between each, Harry Price concluded one of the most astonishing encounters in the history of psychical research by asking the following five questions:

'Where do you live, Rosalie?' (No answer.)
'What do you do there?' (No answer.)
'Do you play with other children?' (No answer.)
'Have you any toys there?' (No answer.)
'Are there any animal pets?' (No answer.)

To each one, the softly illuminated figure gave no response and simply stared ahead as if not understanding.

[10.45 pm*] Realising that his window of opportunity was rapidly coming to an end, Price spoke out again. 'Rosalie, do you love your mummy?' was his final question. This time the fixed expression changed and the little girl's eyes seemed to light up. *'Yes,'* she said in a soft lisping voice. This single response provoked an intensely emotional reaction from Madame who cried out and hugged the small figure to her. Mrs X quickly took the plaque from Price's hand and placed both of the mirrors down on the floor, with a request that everyone remain silent. By this time all three women sitters in the room were crying openly. Price found himself responding to the emotion generated by the love and grief displayed by the French woman for her discarnate daughter – 'a touching and pathetic scene' was how he described it.

[11.00 pm] The group sat together in the darkness for what Harry Price estimated was around a quarter of an hour during which time 'Rosalie' left or 'dematerialised'. Price gives no indication of being aware of any change in the room and neither heard nor felt anything take place. It was only after the hall clock had again chimed the hour that Mrs X announced that the séance was over. Her husband got up and switched on the lights with a request to the investigator to make whatever search or examination he required. Everything was as he had left it just under two hours before – the door and window seals were unbroken, the control on the fireplace undisturbed and there were no tell-tale marks or footprints in the starch powder by the room door or in front of the chimney breast. Amazingly, the Airdale dog was still asleep in front of the switched-off electric fire and had apparently not stirred the whole time. To satisfy himself, Price again examined the furniture, including the sideboard and the settee, and found nothing had changed.

Unsealing the door to the hallway, and accompanied by young 'Jim', he toured the house, again examining each of the rooms together with his seals on the doors and windows. None had apparently been disturbed or tampered with. While Price was concluding his inspection, well-earned refreshments were brought through and, on his return, he joined the group in the drawing room. We can only speculate what was discussed as Price gives no indication in his account.

Having packed away his ghost hunter's kit, just before midnight Harry Price eventually took his leave. His one and only sitting in the 'Rosalie' circle had come to an end. It was an experience that I feel sure was to haunt him for the rest of his life.

SIX

AFTERMATH

———————————

'Deeply disturbed, almost distraught' is the impression a colleague is said to have had of the appearance of Harry Price on the morning following his visit to the London suburbs, and that he seemed to have been 'shaken to the core by his experience' of the previous night[73]. It is easy to see why. If the 'Rosalie' séance took place in the way that Price describes in *Fifty Years*, here, seemingly, was what appeared to be first-hand evidence of genuine materialisation by a competent investigator. It was something he had devoted almost the best part of his life in researching and hoping to encounter.

A first-time exposure to physical materialisation phenomena can be overwhelming. I attended a public demonstration of materialisation mediumship for the first time in June 2007 at a village hall in Wroxton just outside Banbury. The 'phenomena' included direct-voice, materialisation in both red and white light, the movement of control objects and, ultimately, the supposed de-materialisation and re-materialisation of the medium outside of the 'cabinet'. Although I considered myself quite well read in the subject and knew what to expect, my own reaction at the time was one of astonishment and incredulity. However, subsequent sittings with the medium at the same and another venue have made me revise my opinion of the particular 'mediumship' I witnessed, although that is something for another time.

Bristol businessman Michael Roll has spoken of his own experiences in the early 1980s with the Leicester-based physical medium, Rita Goold[74]. His initial response to the apparent materialisation of solid spirit people (whom he calls the 'Etherians') was a sense of shock combined with excitement and happiness at the possibilities for humanity that the reality of the phenomena contained. As a student of psychical research, Roll had been reading the subject of survival on and off for thirty years and in no way felt nervous during the séances he attended. Harry Price had been a dedicated researcher for just as long and, as has been made clear previously, was able to combine years of academic enquiry with enviable practical experience. His reaction was undoubtedly equal to, if not more profound, than Roll's.

The 16th of December 1937 is an important day in the history of the 'Rosalie' case, but, before we look at it in some detail, the closing pages of his visit need to be set down. If the account given in *Fifty Years* is accepted as following reasonably accurately the sequence of events, the statement that Price appeared drained the following day was also due, no doubt, to the fact that he had apparently been awake and working into the small hours.

The investigator had arranged to stay overnight in London to avoid a long late-night journey back to his home in West Sussex. Price gives no indication as to how he travelled to Mr and Mrs X's house although the most obvious being, as in David Halliwell's dramatisation (see Chapter 14), that he drove there himself. Paul Tabori also thought this was so when writing about the case in the early 1970s. Price had been a motoring enthusiast since his youth – Rolls Royce cars being a particular favourite – and, during his lifetime, he owned two such vehicles. In 1936, he bought a Mulliner Weyman Rolls Royce saloon for £300 and owned it for the rest of his life, often driving from Pulborough to Felpham near Bognor Regis where his sister-in-law and their family rented holiday houses. However, Lucy Kay, Price's secretary at the National Laboratory from 1926-1931, stated in an essay in Paul Tabori's *Biography of a Ghost-hunter*[75] that Price refused to drive himself in London during the time she knew him. He preferred getting his regular train to and from Victoria when travelling to his office, which would have been a fifty mile journey each way by car. It seems likely then, bearing these things in mind, that he took a taxi from Berkeley Street to the 'Rosalie' séance and arranged for one to pick him up once the sitting was over.

Despite the impressive guarantee by Mrs X of the certainty of being able to witness a genuine materialisation at the Wednesday meeting, one factor which ultimately contributed to Price's attending the séance was the fact that it took place in London and not elsewhere. By this time Price was disinclined to accept engagements that disrupted his weekly routine to any great extent. Unless meetings or experiments could be held at his London office (or were within a convenient travelling distance of his Pulborough home) then, often as not, despite the opportunity for self-promotion, he turned them down. This is made clear in correspondence not long after the 'Rosalie' sitting with a Mrs Rickey of Messrs. Lecture Management Ltd of EC4 over an enquiry into giving talks on psychical subjects[76]. Price confirms that, when lecturing in London, he was able to stay over at his Club, whereas with no late train to Sussex any talks (or séances) further afield in the provinces meant devoting two days to the event, which he considered counterproductive.

Price had been a member of the Royal Societies Club in St. James's Street, Piccadilly, since at least the beginning of the 1920s (his successful appointment as a member of the Society for Psychical Research in July 1920 gives this address), and it was here that he returned after his 'extraordinarily interesting and puzzling evening'[77]. At the time he appears also to have been a member of the Savage Club (resigned 1947) as a photograph, taken during the 1936 Meopham radio broadcast, shows him wearing the Club tie. He was also a member of the Reform Club from 1943 to his death.

In bed around one o'clock in the morning, Price immediately set to work drafting an account of the séance he had just experienced, the contents of which were eventually used as Chapter VIII, 'Rosalie' in *Fifty Years of Psychical Research*. The text of the report runs to around 4800 words. Exactly how much was written at the Royal Societies Club is impossible to say but if the entire account was written in one sitting, as Price implies, it would have taken him, I estimate, around two and a half hours to complete. That the account was finished by the end of the same day (i.e. 16 December) is corroborated by correspondence, which we will get to shortly.

For publication, Price added a short introduction to his account and there is also a concluding paragraph headed 'December 16, 1937' which is worth quoting in its entirety as it gives what amounts to Price's immediate reactions to his 'Rosalie' experience:

> I began writing this report (which is printed verbatim and uncorrected) within two hours of the termination of the séance, in bed at the Royal Societies Club. I purposely wrote the report at once, while

my impressions were still fresh. I feel I have not done justice in this report to the amazing events of last night, and I am still wondering if "Rosalie" was a genuine spirit entity, or whether the whole thing was an elaborate hoax. If the latter, then the "hoax" has been going on for years and no actress in the world could simulate Madame Z.'s poignant emotion. And where did the "spirit" come from? These are questions which I shall have to think about, and answer. If I had witnessed the materialization of "Rosalie" *in my own laboratory* [Price's italics], I should not hesitate to proclaim to an incredulous world that *survival was proved* [Price's italics]. It is possible – though very doubtful – that last night's historic (as far as I am concerned) séance may be repeated under better conditions in a laboratory. But Madame Z. is convinced that "Rosalie would be frightened away." The sitting I have just attended is at least distinguished by the complete absence of blasphemous humbug and hymn-singing, which characterize so many pseudo-spiritualist séances run by rogues for profit. Looking at it in retrospect, I can think of several things I ought to have done that I did not do, and one of these is the taking of "Rosalie's" finger-prints. I had ample opportunity, but no materials. Another thing I might have done was to have ascertained who the "medium" was. Madame Z. herself denies that she is mediumistic, but I can think of no one else. Apparently, there was no medium.[78]

My impression is that this was written later on the same day when Price had had time to collect his thoughts. It also suggests that, in the refreshment period following the close of the séance and the final tour of the house, he had pressed Madame for a second sitting but she had refused. The statement that the report was printed 'verbatim and uncorrected' is not strictly true because, as will be seen, editing of some sort did take place. The comment that there appeared to be no medium present is also very interesting in the light of the publicity given to the 'energy' based séance room phenomena of the Scole Experiment during the 1990s. This, it will be remembered, was achieved through a harmonious blend of the individual energies of a group of sitters, rather than one dedicated psychic.

After snatching what little sleep he could, Price left the Royal Societies Club and returned to Berkeley Street where the realities of the previous night's adventures began to sink in. The effect of the experience was to be witnessed by two people that day (and possibly a third – see Chapter 12 and the testimony of Clarice Richards) as Price sat in his office finishing the first draft of his report.

Ethel Beenham was Price's secretary for most of the 1930s until September 1939 when, following the outbreak of hostilities, Price closed his London office and released her from his service. She later married and became Mrs English. Price famously photographed her with a roll of cheesecloth in her mouth as part of his published 'exposure' of Helen Duncan, and, in the same year, she accompanied her employer and members of his Council to Braunau for a sitting with Rudi Schneider. Later in August 1943, Mrs English briefly resumed her old duties when, in the ruins of Borley Rectory, she acted as note-taker during Price's successful search for human remains. Lamentably, Ethel Beenham was never interviewed in detail in connection with Price's 'Rosalie' experience by later investigators. Her only comments were limited to a few brief responses to questions posed at the very beginning of the 'Borley Report' investigation by the SPR, a year after Price's death, and again after another considerable length of time had elapsed in 1958. 'I remember that he was *terribly* [original emphasis] excited the morning after the sitting,' she recalled in a testimonial dated 29 August 1949. 'He appeared exhausted and said he had been transcribing his notes sitting up half the night,' adding, 'If this was all play-acting, it was certainly very marvellous acting!' The fact that she was worried about her employer and was clearly aware that, by his appearance and manner, something was amiss was confirmed several years later by a visitor who called in to Berkeley Street later the same morning.

Kathleen 'Mollie' Goldney (1893-1992) was an important figure in Harry Price's long career in organised paranormal research. Twelve years his junior, she became, without doubt, the most well known female psychical researcher of the twentieth century. Brought up in India, where both her father and future husband were civil servants, she qualified in midwifery but, in the late 1920s, became caught up in the English psychical research scene. The catalyst was a correspondence with Sir Oliver Lodge on the topic of fire-walking – something that, as we have seen, interested Harry Price not long after. She joined the Society for Psychical Research at the end of 1927 and, following a permanent return to England, was involved with various aspects of the SPR for the rest of her life. As well as being a Full Council Member and Vice-President, she also served on the Finance Committee and, for a period in the 1950s, was Organising Secretary. Her many papers on psychical subjects were published over the years in the Society's *Journal* and *Proceedings*. As a researcher, Dr Nandor Fodor famously referred to her 'steam-roller personality' when interviewing witnesses or claimants to paranormal activity[79], and she has also been described as being someone who 'wanted to be where the action was'[80], particularly where the physical séance room phenomena of the 1930s were concerned. This inevitably drew her into an association with the SPR's main rival, Harry Price and his National Laboratory.

In his biography, Richard Morris describes 'Mollie' Goldney as being 'at first an admirer of Price, then an enthusiastic lover and later still a reluctant detractor'[81]. Each of these roles can be, and, in some respects, have been used when assessing her albeit minor, but in my view, significant role in the 'Rosalie' case, to discredit Price's experience. To put these descriptions into context, Mrs Goldney was the Honorary Treasurer of the National Laboratory for Psychical Research for a period between 1931-1934 and later occupied a similar role when Price revived the Ghost Club in 1938; she is one of Morris's three surmised sexual conquests mentioned previously; and she was also co-author, with Eric Dingwall and Trevor Hall, of the critical 1956 SPR 'Borley Report' that attacked Price's most famous case, and his overall reputation as a sincere and dedicated investigator.

During her time as a Council Member of Price's organisation, 'Mollie' Goldney quite literally found herself in the thick of the psychic action. 'He obtained the services of many world-renowned mediums; and scientists whose names are household words were among his guests at his investigations,' Goldney recalled many years later, 'Certainly, like the early Ford car, he "got you there" more quickly than any other investigator I know.'[82] These were exciting times and, with Price at the wheel, any investigation was likely to be controversial and unpredictable. In May 1931, Goldney assisted in the high-profile séance room experiments with Helen Duncan, the outcome of which was a dramatic chase out of the National Laboratory into the street where the medium, still clad in her voluminous black séance outfit, spent half an hour clinging, screaming, to a set of iron railings. In his *Helen Duncan: The Mystery Show Trial* (2007), Robert Hartley suggests that Goldney sabotaged an earlier sitting that Mrs Duncan held for the London Spiritualist Alliance at Queensberry Place in order to drive the medium away from the LSA and into the arms of Price and his investigating Council. Goldney appears to have stepped on purpose on a materialised 'pseudo-pod' that was moving along the floor near her chair and later 'openly boasted'[83] to SPR colleagues that she had trod on the Scottish medium's ectoplasm.

Later the same year, as has been mentioned above, Goldney accompanied Price on an eventful trip to Borley Rectory where she seems to have fallen foul of the then Rector's wife. The two women clearly disliked one another, the result of which was that Price and Goldney, at the time, accused Marianne Foyster of playing the ghost. Later, Marianne herself claimed[84] she had caught the psychical researchers in a compromising situation behind the pantry door, thereby creating the rumours subsequently put into print by Richard Morris that the two were lovers.

Despite her close association with Price, his subsequent 'exposure' of Rudi Schneider following a lengthy series of sittings the following year was something that even Goldney was unable to condone. She was one of the six signatories to an open letter to the Austrian medium dated 16 March 1933, published the following month in the Spiritualist newspaper *Light*, which distanced the writers (all National Laboratory Council Members) from Price's published report and supported both Schneider's integrity and his mediumship. Several Council Members of Price's organisation resigned over his conduct, although unlike other colleagues she remained on more or less friendly terms with him afterwards. It was suggested by critics following Price's death (see Chapter 10) that the result of this whole episode was his decision the following year to wind up the National Laboratory and enter into discussions with the University of London over his future in English psychical research. These events were to cast shadows over future events, namely later interpretations of Price's claims to have encountered little 'Rosalie' in the winter of 1937.

It must be said that, although she courted Price's friendship and took an active part in his work, 'Mollie' Goldney's true allegiances were always to the Society for Psychical Research, and particularly William Salter, who held the Presidency in the late 1940s and with whom she got on well. She assisted Salter, a somewhat formidable figure, with the Society's administration during the time that he was Honorary Secretary, and he in turn sponsored (with George N.M. Tyrrell) her successful election to the SPR Council in September 1945. Salter was openly hostile to Price and later recruited Goldney and Eric Dingwall to audit Price's working methods at Borley, a case he had the opportunity to investigate in 1931 but turned down.

Goldney remained on good terms with Harry Price for the rest of his life. She assisted with the administrational side of the Ghost Club, which he operated as a society dining event for over ten years, and was also the recipient of one of his last letters, posted shortly before his sudden death, in which he reminisced about the politics of the Schneider investigation. This association made her a natural choice, along with the likes of Sidney Glanville and Lucy Kay, together with René Sudre and Hereward Carrington (two psychical researchers with whom Price never managed to fall out), to set down some personal reminiscences when Paul Tabori was compiling his biography in 1950. Too critical for the type of book Tabori was writing, Goldney's piece went unused but, despite its less than flattering tone, there is something quite touching about the comments, written as they were before her work on the SPR 'Borley Report' changed the landscape forever. 'For, with all that can be said against him, he still has this to his credit,' she wrote. '[H]e put psychical research on the map for the man-in-the-English-street; to many, indeed, the words "psychical research" suggest one investigator only, and that investigator is Harry Price. If he gave his public an erroneous view of what psychical research ought to be, at least he aroused their interest, and should they go further and consult the *Proceedings* of the [SPR], they will get a wiser outlook and a better appreciation of the subject; but it would be Harry Price that had led them there.'

Leaving aside the allegation that the relationship between the two was at one time more than simply professional, although she may have liked him as a person, Goldney subsequently revealed what she considered to be the true reason for her continued association with Price (at least during the 1930s when he was active in investigating Spiritualist phenomena). This was during the course of a rather acrimonious published correspondence on the very case in hand in the late 1950s. It clearly demonstrates the, at times, intense rivalry that existed between psychical researchers and their various organisations, and that on occasion each party was not opposed to fifth columnist-type activity. Regarding the bust-up that took place among Price's National Laboratory Council, Goldney wrote:

> I decided not to resign because it was suggested to me by colleagues that someone should remain in close contact with Price in order to know what was going on in his laboratory. I did not know at that time as much about him as I have learned since his death, but I made then no secret of my adverse opinion of some of his views and activities.[85]

One of the 'colleagues' that immediately springs to mind is William Salter who, at the time Goldney was assisting on a regular basis and as has been said, disliked Price and his methods. Rather than publicity-inspired investigations, such as the Talking Mongoose and Black

Magic escapades on the Brocken, the SPR were keen to know whether Price had got one up on them and was experimenting with a new star medium in his séance room in South Kensington. The activities of Lord Charles Hope and Lord Rayleigh behind the scenes when Price was holding his eventful Schneider sittings in 1932 show that when the secrets of eternity were potentially at stake, ethics went out of the window and both psychical societies were quite capable of going behind each other's backs.

As we have seen, the opportunities for serious physical mediumship investigation began to fall off as the 1930s progressed and both parties started to look elsewhere for suitable areas of study. Price concentrated on spontaneous cases like Borley while the SPR followed the new happenings at Duke University and began to devote its energies to the more fashionable subject of ESP. Despite the inevitable reduction in séance room action, Goldney, who lived in London, when passing in the vicinity of Berkeley Street would often call in to see Price and, in her own words, 'ask what the news was in the psychical world'[86]. As luck would have it, one of these impromptu visits occurred on the morning of 16 December 1937 as Harry Price was coming to terms with his adventure of the previous evening. To quote Paul Tabori from his *Beyond the Senses* (1971):

> She was received by Miss Ethel Beenham, Price's secretary who appeared to be greatly worried about her employer. "You'd better go in and see him," she said. "He's in a rare state! I have never seen him so upset in all my time with him..."[87]

Much of the recorded account of Goldney's encounter with Price that day is included in a letter she wrote to Trevor Hall in 1954 during the time that they were working on their Borley investigation for the SPR. In later years she also discussed the incident with other people including David Cohen of the Manchester Psychical Research Society and ghost hunter and author, Peter Underwood. To Hall, Goldney described Price as looking 'drawn if not haggard' and she was confident that she had 'not seen him so affected before'. The slight stutter that the psychical researcher always effected was more pronounced and, clearly perturbed, he gave her an account of his experience with the 'Rosalie' circle, including the control of the séance room and his examination of the 'materialised' child. Goldney was able to hear fresh and vivid personal testimony as the sitting had taken place only twelve hours previously. Price also spoke about his agreement with Mr and Mrs X and the stipulation laid down by Madame Z that there was to be no further investigation of any sort.

When writing his biography of Price in 1949, Paul Tabori made a point of speaking to Goldney, personally, about her encounter on that morning. In his book he included his impressions of the way she described Price's demeanour during the time they were together. Importantly, her unused contribution of reminiscences quoted from previously contains a lengthy passage about just this meeting and is included in its entirety as follows:

> His account of the single séance he attended at which he could detect no fraud and at which what appeared to be a fully-formed materialisation of a child ("Rosalie") occurred, is one of his most sensational reports. But he was the sole investigator present and never achieved a second sitting. I happened to call in on him at his office in Berkeley Square [sic] the next morning, and found him with his hands full of a sheaf of papers; he told me he had sat up a great part of the night writing out an account of what had occurred. He was more excited and shaken than I had ever seen him, and yet – over and over again in the succeeding months I was puzzled, and asked myself why, if he really thought it possible he had achieved being present at a genuine fully-formed materialisation, he did not press much harder than he was doing for another sitting! The pressure was sufficiently weak to allow months to go by and then the war intervened and "Rosalie's" mother was no longer in England to give the promised repetition, we were told.

In later years, Mrs Goldney attempted to distance herself from her encounter with Price over the 'Rosalie' séance. Her audit of his work at Borley, which had an effect on her later views as to his character and qualities as a genuine researcher, she felt made 'superfluous further elaborate examination of his activities'[88]. The importance of including mention of her statement here is that it gives good confirmatory evidence that Price did attend a séance in the way he describes in *Fifty Years* and, being unable to explain it in rational terms, was shaken by the experience. Goldney's testimony cannot, however, be used to support the true nature of the account as related by Price, or 'Rosalie', as a genuine example of materialisation phenomena. 'Mollie' Goldney was a highly intelligent woman with a strong personality who, as a psychical researcher of some note, amongst other things, was given to 'uninhibited questioning of unsatisfactory evidence'[89]. David Cohen, who met her during the course of his 'Rosalie' investigation in the early 1960s (see Chapter 12), called her 'one of the toughest persons to convince about the supernormal'[90]. A single conversation with Price, whatever their true relationship, even if he appeared to have been profoundly affected by the experience, would in no way be enough for her to accept and make a professional judgement on the claims, even if she did believe that the séance occurred in the way Price described that morning.

This is made clear by her initial reaction on hearing Price's account. After Price had finished telling his story, Goldney made the suggestion, in a jocular manner she later admitted, that if he, as one of the most well known investigators of the day, was convinced he had encountered genuine phenomena, with all the implications it presented, and despite the demands of the 'Rosalie' circle for secrecy, he should go to Cosmo Lang, the Archbishop of Canterbury, 'and MAKE HIM [original emphasis] come with you to these people and tell them the happiness of the whole human race is affected, and they MUST [original emphasis] allow further investigation'[91]. Price's reaction to this is not recorded but Goldney made efforts in later years to point out that it was intended as a joke. She could easily have substituted the Pope or the King of England for the Archbishop. After this, Goldney evidently took her leave, seemingly having had enough of the psychic news for one day.

Despite her adventures with materialisation mediums like Helen Duncan, Mrs Goldney did not treat all claims of physical mediumship in the same light-hearted way. In later life she considered Rudi Schneider – during the time he was being examined by Price at the National Laboratory – to be the most impressive medium she ever sat with, and that his phenomena were the most striking things she ever witnessed in a séance room. She also leapt to the defence, with Richard Medhurst, of allegations of impropriety made by Trevor Hall in his 1962 book *The Spiritualists* against Sir William Crookes during his investigation of physical medium Florence Cook in the 1870s[92]. The impetus for this was that, despite their collaboration on the 'Borley Report', she and Hall were by this time (the mid-1960s) not on particularly good terms, due in part to Hall's later involvement with the 'Rosalie' case (see Chapters 9 and 10). Rather than championing the genuineness of the famous 'Katie King' materialisations, this was more a forthright critique on Hall's working methods and his evaluation of evidence[93].

One person who was surely waiting for news of Price's mystery séance was Richard Lambert. He wasn't to be disappointed and his later testimony, both written and anecdotal, provides the strongest evidence for Price's version of the 'Rosalie' sitting taking place when he said it did. Over twenty years later he was able to recall, in a letter to the Editor of the *International Journal of Parapsychology*, his own experience of the morning of 16 December 1937. After a brief account of his luncheon appointment with Price, the week before, Lambert wrote:

> My next memory is of the morning of December 16, when I was called up on the telephone in my office by Price, who was obviously in an excited state of mind. I remember clearly his opening words: "Lambert, I don't know at this moment whether I am standing on my head or my heels!" He subsequently gave me a detailed description of what had taken place the night before at the apartment of "Madame Z." [*sic*] This description was essentially the same as that which Price published in 1939 in his *Fifty Years of Psychical Research*[94].

Lambert went on to say that Price's attitude over the 'phone 'was that of a man completely flabbergasted by his experience' and that '[h]e would neither accept the phenomenon as genuine, nor admit that he had been the victim of deception'. Despite Madame's complete resistance to any kind of follow-up investigation, Lambert recalled that Price said at the time that he intended to try to arrange a second sitting as soon as he could, and, if successful, would take Lambert with him as a witness. Not surprisingly, the 'Rosalie' séance formed the subject of many discussions between them in the ensuing weeks, and the incident of the telephone conversation obviously made a strong enough impression for the BBC editor to recall at a much later date.

Later the same day, Price dictated a letter to Lambert addressed to his office at Broadcasting House, the carbon of which is held at the University of London, as follows:

> Dear Lambert,
>
> Herewith is the "Rosalie" report, which I am sure you will read with great interest. I have added a foreword to the report, in case I use it as a chapter of my new book. I am hoping that some day I may be able to add additional matter, should I be fortunate enough to get another sitting.

Will you kindly let me have the report back, when finished with, as, as I have said, it is part of the MS "Fifty Years of Psychical Research".

Trusting to see you soon, and with kind regards,

Yours sincerely,

Honorary Secretary.

This shows that an initial version of Price's written account of the 'Rosalie' séance, comprising more or less what was later published in 1939, was complete by the end of the following day. Commenting in *Beyond the Senses*, Paul Tabori felt that the phrasing of this letter showed that the writer was under a considerable emotional strain at the time. This, I feel, is open to interpretation and what clumsiness may exist in the text could be due to the fact that Price had other business to attend to and was simply rushing to catch the post. The same day he also wrote a lengthy letter to Samuel Soal, a Council Member of the ULCIP, in connection with the publication of recent research work (see Chapter 15), the wording of which is straightforward and unambiguous.

What Price actually means by 'a foreword to the report' is, however, somewhat unclear. As mentioned previously, there is a lengthy paragraph, which begins the 'Rosalie' chapter (p.130) in *Fifty Years* that is clearly intended to be an introduction to the main narrative which begins 'December 15, 1937'. However, parts of this contain references to correspondence with Price's publisher, which had not yet taken place (see Appendix A). Price also says that the séance 'was held fifteen months before these introductory remarks were written' so it seems that whatever 'foreword' Price preceded the account he sent to Lambert on 16 December, it was revised at a later date for final publication. It seems likely that the concluding paragraph quoted above, containing Price's thoughts and reaction to his experience, could in fact be this original foreword which, containing useable material, he later put at the end of his account.

Lambert responded with a letter dated 17 December on BBC headed paper:

Dear Price,

Many thanks for the Rosalie Report, and your letter of the 16th. I shall read the former during the weekend with great interest, and very much hope that later on you will get another sitting and be able to reach a conclusion about the phenomena. It is ever so good of you to let me see the Report, which I will return early next week.

Yours sincerely,

pp. R.S. Lambert.

The 'Rosalie' report was duly returned and joined the growing amount of material Price was assembling as his next published work. It was to be the one in which the story of the spirit child would be finally presented to the public, and set in motion what was later described as 'perhaps the greatest mystery left by that enigmatic psychical researcher'[95].

SEVEN

FIFTY YEARS OF PSYCHICAL RESEARCH – THE STORY OF A BOOK

―――――――⟫●⟪―――――――

" *Fifty Years of Psychical Research* is an epitome of all the important developments and experiments which have taken place during the past half-century.'[96] So said Harry Price at the beginning of a press release drafted, at his publisher's request, in the spring of 1939 promoting the book which ultimately was to bring the enigma of 'Rosalie' to worldwide attention. As the 'Rosalie' story is inextricably linked with this, Price's sixth substantial publication dedicated to the study of the paranormal, I feel it necessary to look at the development of *Fifty Years* in some detail as it highlights several interesting and highly relevant aspects of the case.

After the publication of *Confessions of a Ghost-Hunter* in 1936, Price settled into a routine of researching, writing and publishing full-length works for the remaining twelve years of his life. The five books completed in this period were the ones that brought him the most public acclaim and he had immediate plans for two more, the completion of which were only interrupted by his sudden death. These were to be a third book on the Borley case, plus the journal of English writer and literary critic Emily Alice Haigh (1879-1943), better known by the pen name of Mrs Beatrice Hastings, bequeathed to Price who intended to edit and issue it under the title *Diary of a Split Personality*. Stricken with cancer, Mrs Hastings had posted the manuscript to Price the same day she purposely gassed herself to death at her Worthing home with the kitchen cooker.

At the beginning of 1937, Price entered into discussions with the publishing firm of Ivor Nicholson and Watson concerning the commissioning of a new book. The time was right to get to work on what he clearly felt was to be his magnum opus which, as has been discussed, had its inspiration in Frank Podmore's *Modern Spiritualism* (1902), considered to be one of the standard works of Victorian psychical research. The importance that Price placed on what would become *Fifty Years* is evident from the outset and made clear in a letter to Ivor Nicholson and Watson's commissioning editor, Graham Watson, dated 25 February 1937 discussing royalties:

> I have never accepted less than 15% for a major book – and as my next will be the most important I have written, and will take very much longer to write than any I have done, I do not feel like dropping down to 10.[97]

Both sides eventually climbed down with Price agreeing to accept a 15% fee for the first 300 copies and 10% for all those sold thereafter; but another problem quickly raised itself, that of the cover price of the finished book. Simple economics dictated this was related in the main to manufacturing costs such as the price of paper for printing and the proposed length of Price's manuscript (which eventually weighed in around 120,000 words), but Price was keen to make the book affordable by offsetting the high cost of printing against the increased number of copies that an attractive price would hopefully generate. Early in March 1937, he wrote to Watson with the firm suggestion that the book should not be sold for more than 10/6d a copy and backed this up by citing his experience with Victor Gollancz who, in his opinion, had over-priced his *Leaves From a Psychist's Case-Book* four years earlier. At 15 shillings, it had only sold in the region of 1100 copies rather than the 10,000 which was Price's estimate of sales at a more reasonable price. This proved to be a stumbling block and the discussions with Watson ultimately came to nothing. Price's subsequent trip to Germany, the move to Berkeley Street, the Carshalton fire-walking experiments, and the organisation of the Borley investigation, resulted in his psychic history being put on the back-burner and it was not until much later in the year that he was able to get the project up and running again.

On 22 September 1937, Price invited Allen Drinkwater of Longmans, Green and Co. to lunch, with the specific intention of discussing both *Fifty Years* and the potential fruits of his ongoing psychical stake out at Borley Rectory. Price's hopes of securing a two book deal with the publisher rapidly came a step closer when, immediately after their meeting, Longmans' commissioning editor, Ken Potter, wrote the following day expressing much interest in both projects with a request for a précis of the contents of Price's psychic compendium. Price responded by return:

> I have prepared a synopsis of my proposed "Fifty Years of Psychical Research" and have most of the material to hand. I should like to see you about it, and I could then hand you the suggested scheme. The work would not be a mere "history" of the movement, but a comprehensive epitome of the work done, and progress made, with details of many experiments.[98]

Price and Potter were evidently two men who saw eye to eye and much of what is perceived as the popularising of Price's later output clearly dates from the time of their first association. Price had made a name for himself over the preceding fifteen years or so as a clear-headed psychical researcher who, at the same time, was not adverse to publicising his exploits, thereby educating the public at large on the fledgling subject of psychic science through the popular press. By the early 1930s his talent for writing had developed to the point that he was able, given the opportunity, to pursue a career as a writer on a subject of which he had both first-hand experience and academic knowledge. The furtherance of such a career, however, depended on being able to sell enough books to survive.

Critics who rubbish Price's contributions to twentieth-century psychical research by accusing him of being nothing but a psychic journalist (a phrase which Paul Tabori dismissed as being 'a grave understatement of his merits'[99]), penning sensational but dubious accounts of his adventures for the Sunday papers, seem to forget the fact that even academics and professors have to earn a living. A case in point is that of Stephen Hawking's successful *A Brief History of Time* (1988), which apart from satisfying the respected scientist's desire for the ordinary layman to have access to his academic work, was also written to put money in the bank. Apart from his popular books Price, like Hawking, also contributed technical papers to specialist institutes and publications, albeit in the main on his own terms. Mind you, I am not for one minute suggesting that the academic output of Harry Price can be compared in any way with the achievements of the former Lucasian Professor of Mathematics at Cambridge. As well as the journals of his own organisations – the *British Journal of Psychical Research* and the later *Bulletins* of both the National Laboratory and the ULCPI – Price had many articles on psychical subjects published by the American SPR, and papers in translation also appeared in the French *Revue Métapsychique*.

It goes without saying that, as a commissioning editor for a major publisher, Ken Potter would have been on the lookout for a promising author who could shift copies, and the two works on offer from Price clearly showed potential. However, to imply that Potter was instrumental in changing the quality of Price's output from scholarly papers to sensational copy is being overly simplistic and does not fit the facts. Price had always been keen to present the subject of psychical research to the layman whenever he could, particularly when it was an aspect of psychic science with which he was personally involved. In the Introduction to his *Rudi Schneider: A Scientific Examination of his Mediumship* (1930), he made the sweeping statement that '[t]he British public has learnt more about scientific psychical research in the last few months than it did in the previous fifty years'[100] – the kind of one upmanship that no doubt irritated his contemporaries in the SPR no end. Despite writing for the popular market, Price was also keen to present clear and technically accurate records of his work, as the published protocols of his mediumistic experiments with not only Rudi Schneider, but Stella Cranshaw and Helen Duncan clearly show.

The main arguments of the Price bashers is that the quality and accuracy of his later books, particularly from *Fifty Years* onwards, deteriorated due to the fact that, owing to his precarious financial position, the author was more concerned with money-making than with useful contributions to science. This attitude not only seems to begrudge a man from using his talents to earn a living, but to my mind is not borne out by the content of the works written, both during and after the war years. Sidney Glanville, a close colleague of Price during the 1937-38 Borley tenancy, felt that, out of all his published works, *Fifty Years* and the later *Search for Truth* (which, despite being a book of autobiography, contains a vast amount of historical background to psychical research in general) were his best efforts. The following comment from the posthumous tribute that Glanville penned for Tabori's 1950 biography, sums up, in my view, the approach of not only the books in hand but also Price's later output as a whole:

> Neither of these are scientific works nor were they intended to be. They are the result of some thirty years of intimate connection and observation of an absorbing but difficult subject and written for the attention of those who have not the time, inclination or opportunity for making a study of supernormal phenomena.[101]

Rather than being a dumbing down exercise, the quality of *Fifty Years* shows that Price was keen to present a concise account of the developments in psychical research, a discipline with which he was proud to be associated, while his penultimate and longest work, *Poltergeist Over England*, does not deserve the snobbish sniping or inaccurate comments that both Trevor Hall and Richard Morris have respectively bestowed upon it. Where Ken Potter is concerned, correspondence in the University of London Library shows that he viewed not only the 'Rosalie' aspect of Price's book with a publisher's eye for book sales, but was also the source of one of the most famous and oft quoted comments concerning Harry Price's overall attitude to the paranormal.

During the time that Price began working on *Fifty Years*, he was approached by an English writer, J.R. Sturge-Whiting, who had written a lengthy – but then as yet unpublished study – debunking the famous Versailles time slip case which had appeared several years previously as *An Adventure* (1911). Price agreed to try to get a suitable publisher interested in Sturge-Whiting's book and also felt sufficiently confident in the quality of the author's writing to contribute a foreword in the event of its getting accepted. Early in January 1938, Price sent the typescript of Sturge-Whiting's *The Mystery of Versailles* to Potter at Longmans with the request that he look the piece over. This Potter did but felt that, although the material was of good quality, it was not the kind of book that would generate the sales that, as a publisher, he and his particular firm needed. In a letter to Price dated 13 January 1938 rejecting Sturge-Whiting's critique, Potter included the following phrase that later commentators such as Hall, Morris and Borley sceptic Robert Wood[102] have laid as a legendary Freudian slip at Harry Price's door: *'We think that there is always a much bigger market for the "bunk" than for the "debunk"'*.

The comment evidently caught Price's attention and, when *The Mystery of Versailles* was finally published the following year by Rider and Co., it found its way into print in the following way as part of Price's brief introductory remarks:

> The solving of the Versailles puzzle was long overdue, and psychical researchers are indebted to Mr. Sturge-Whiting for devoting so much time and trouble to its elucidation. He will not be thanked for his pains. *An Adventure,* the record of the Trianon visit, is one of the classics of psychic literature, and even the most sceptical student of the alleged miraculous has been almost forced to accept a paranormal explanation of the "visions", failing a rational solution to the mystery. Well, here it is. The more credulous will not accept Mr. Sturge-Whiting's answer to the Versailles legend, and shouts of "Iconoclast!" will be raised. So *many* [Price's italics] people prefer the "bunk" to the "debunk"! The fact that *An Adventure* has stood its ground for nearly thirty years without being seriously attacked is proof of how strong a *prima facie* case was made out for the "phenomena". It is also proof of what an excellent piece of work Mr. Sturge-Whiting has accomplished.[103]

At this time, *Fifty Years* was the number that Price was actively promoting as any potential book on Borley Rectory was, out of necessity, a work in progress. Despite the experience of sharing a law court with Gef the Talking Mongoose, Richard Lambert, who, as we have seen during the 1930s, was one of Harry Price's closest associates, was keen to involve himself in some way with Price's style of psychical research. It came as something of a surprise to me, when researching for this book at the University of London Library, to find that, during this period, Lambert was in fact a potential co-author of what was to become Harry Price's most famous book, '*The Most Haunted House in England*' in the same way that he had contributed to the Gef investigation and shared the title-page of *The Haunting of Cashen's Gap* the previous year. The two men kept an appointment with Potter at Longmans' Paternoster Row offices at 2.30 pm on Thursday 7 October 1937, where both projects were to be discussed. Where *Fifty Years* was concerned, this was a resounding success as Potter gave the green light to a book of between 70-80,000 words from Price's pen and set the wheels in motion to prepare a contract.

As for Borley, Potter felt unable to commit to a project which was still ongoing and it was agreed to set this aside until after the investigation had ended, following which it would be possible to assess if the results of the enquiry were up for publication. This was, no doubt, a disappointment for Lambert who had already visited Borley himself as a temporary observer[104] and, in Price's own words, was 'willing – even anxious – to put in some work on the book'[105]. Lambert's enthusiasm was, however, tempered by strong opposition on the home front as his wife, having had enough of the effects that her husband's involvement in the supernatural had had on their lives during the Gef libel case, was strongly opposed to any other collaboration involving the subject and Lambert reluctantly had to withdraw from the project[106]. Potter eventually commissioned a full-length book on Borley once the on-site tenancy investigation finished in May the following year, but it was only Price that received a contract from Longmans on 18 August 1938. Despite this and his later differing views on the Rectory case as a whole, Lambert and Price remained on friendly terms. As will be seen, the former BBC man had no hesitation in coming to Price's defence more than twenty years later over the controversy that the 'Rosalie' case would bring to the researcher's posthumous reputation.

The interest shown by Longmans in his new book clearly galvanised Price into action and by the time that a draft contract come through on 27 October he had 4,000 words complete in typescript. Among the points that Price insisted on addressing was again the issue of the cover price, which earlier proved to be the stumbling block with Ivor Nicholson and Watson, but, on this second attempt, Price was successful and a clause stating that the book would not be sold for more than 10/6d was inserted into the agreement. He was also keen to let Potter know the efforts (both academic and financial) that he was going to, to produce his latest and most important work, with the comment:

> As my library and all our records are at the University, I have had to engage my old secretary to look up these records, collect data, etc. It is impossible for me to do this work in the limited time I am in London.[107]

A revised contract was issued on 2 November, which both parties duly signed and, on 5 November 1937, just over a month before 'Rosalie' entered his life, Price received a cheque for £100 as an advance on future sales. Although a healthy figure for 1937 (just over £6000 in today's money), Price was quick to bemoan the fact to Potter that a reasonable proportion of his advance would be spent, out of necessity, in paying Ethel English's additional wages!

With the deal secure, Price gathered his thoughts and settled down in his West Sussex home to create his modern continuation of Podmore's classic. Despite the startling and clearly unnerving distraction of the 'Rosalie' experience the following month, plus the need to oversee and collate information from the ongoing Borley investigation, work on the new book continued apace throughout December and into the New Year. Indeed, by 25 January 1938, Price was able to report to Potter that he currently had 40,000 words under his belt. However, the nature of the project, together with the fact that much of his research material was not immediately to hand at Pulborough, meant that the completed contents were not consecutive and remained this way for some time.

Work on the project slowed, in the following months, due to the fact that Price was forever casting his psychical researcher's net as wide as possible. In March, and with the assistance of 'Mollie' Goldney, he continued to keep a high profile on the social psychic scene by reviving the Ghost Club, which had its first meeting at the Royal Societies Club on the 15th. For the inaugural gathering (which included dinner for 7/6d a head), Price decided to look at the possibilities for deception in Rhine's card-guessing ESP experiments and arranged for debunking demonstrations by vaudeville 'telepathists' Madame Zomah and her husband, together with William Chinn, an 'eyeless sight' performer in the mould of Kuda Bux. On 19 May 1938, the tenancy of Borley Rectory came to an end while, in July, Price returned to Carshalton to supervise another experiment in Eastern mysticism when Indian fakir Rahmen Bey was 'buried alive' for a short while in front of an enthusiastic crowd of onlookers and newspaper reporters.

By this time, Ken Potter was keen to see how work on his new book was shaping up. A timely reminder on 12 July 1938 prompted the following reply from Price by return of post in which, to keep on the good side of his editor, he was keen to emphasise the labours involved in producing a new classic:

> I am making headway – slowly – with "Fifty Years of Psychical Research" and have written about 63,000 words. The fact that my library (to which I have to refer so often) is at the University, makes the writing of the work a little more complicated. However, *I am forging ahead* [my italics].[108]

Early in November the end was in sight, with Price again informing Potter that he would finish as soon as he could, and the whole book was eventually complete by the end of January 1939. The summation of five decades of international investigation into the supernormal had taken him nearly a year and a half to produce. In a letter to Potter, dated 3 April, Price agreed to publish his *Fifty Years* in the autumn and, later the same month, by which time he had begun working in earnest on his Borley book for Longmans, a provisional date for publication was set for 18 September 1939.

But what of 'Rosalie'? Despite the huge demands of writing his psychic history, as well as the diversions of other projects such as Borley and the Ghost Club, the astonishing experiences of that December night were surely never far from Price's thoughts? Specifically there was the importance of trying to obtain another sitting with the 'Rosalie' circle. As we have seen, the letter that Price wrote to Richard Lambert on 16 December 1937, enclosing his initial version of the 'Rosalie' report, clearly shows that he intended to include the material in some way in his new book. Harry Price was by nature impulsive and did not, on occasion, hold back from immediately giving accounts of his latest adventures to eagerly waiting pressmen. It is difficult to see a person in his position who, after having such an astonishing experience (and with a firm book deal with a major publisher in place), not wanting to capitalise on it, and clearly 'Rosalie' had the potential to be the most important and ground-breaking event of not only his entire career in psychical research, but that of any other psychical researcher then and now. Price could have called a press conference at any time after his sitting with Mr and Mrs X and filled the newspapers with sensational headlines of his spirit child encounter. The fact that he didn't, that he in fact waited nearly two years before publishing his account and did this, as will be made clear, against his better judgement, shows he knew that if 'Rosalie' was to have any credibility there had to be further scientific investigation under controlled conditions. Even with an agreement to anonymity, a Barnum and Bailey approach would hardly have encouraged the members of the 'Rosalie' circle to allow Price to have further access to their séance room.

At this distance of time it is difficult to establish just how much effort and to what extent Price did try to negotiate another 'Rosalie' sitting. The 'Mrs Mortimer' letter is the only one of its kind extant in the University of London Library that appears to be a direct communication with Mr and Mrs X, but the absence of further correspondence does not preclude the fact that further letters were not written and sent. Copies of later letters may have existed at some time amongst Price's records but were subsequently lost. Price may have sent enquiries using post-cards (as did many of his correspondents including Eric Dingwall and Cyril Joad), or, as the family were on the telephone, simply called them up. A more likely explanation is that Price wrote to the family from Pulborough where *Fifty Years* was written and, being a handwritten letter, no copy was taken. Price disliked using a typewriter and much of his correspondence from Arun Bank was carried out in longhand.

On 17 December 1938, when putting the finishing touches to the *Fifty Years* manuscript, he included reference to the 'Rosalie' incident in a section on 'Full-Form Materialisations' in the concluding chapter, and made the following statement:

> It is now more than twelve months since I wrote the "Rosalie" report in bed at my club, and several unsuccessful attempts have been made to induce the mother to consent to further experiments. But she is terrified at the thought that our arrangements might have the effect of driving her "daughter" away.[109]

In the published book, this is immediately followed by the brief sentence 'But I am still persevering' which, a footnote says, was added in May 1939. There is an additional note that runs: 'There is now a possibility of my attending another séance during next winter.' As this note does not appear in the typescript held at the University of London, it would seem that he was still attempting to hold another séance well after the book was finished. Price concludes his last reference to 'Rosalie' in *Fifty Years* in the following way:

> I am trying to work out a technique which will be acceptable to both mother and those scientists to whom I hope to exhibit the phenomenon. In particular, I want Professor C.A. Pannett to apply certain tests, which would, I am sure, elucidate the mystery. A medical examination would not be difficult under the conditions which obtained when I saw the girl.[110]

Charles Pannett (1884-1969) was a Fellow of the Royal College of Surgeons, a former Registrar of St. Mary's Hospital and, through being Professor of Surgery at the University of London, became a Council Member of Price's ULCPI. A distinguished pioneer of rectal surgery, he applied his talents ever lower down in 1935 when he carried out observations on Kuda Bux's feet, during the Surrey fire-walking experiments, and wrote a report on the event that was published in *Nature*. Despite having such distinguished colleagues as Pannett standing by, the second séance that Price hoped to attend in the winter of 1939/40 never took place. I see no reason to doubt Price's word that he did in fact try, on more than one occasion, to continue his work with the 'Rosalie' circle. However, for various reasons, the principal one being the resistance of Madame Z, but also apparent events which Price made public at a much later date (see Chapter 8), he was never able to meet 'Rosalie' again – at least not in this world.

On Tuesday 24 January 1939[111], the Ghost Club convened in the new Hall of India at Over-Seas House, Park Place, St James's Street, SW1, for a social evening of psychic discussion. Harry Price, who shared the top table on this occasion with Ernest Maggs the bookseller and actress Mabel Constanduros, was himself the after dinner speaker following a full stage demonstration by the Czech vaudeville 'psychic' Fred Marion (real name Josef Kraus), and decided to test the water by giving an account of his experience with the 'Rosalie' circle over two years previously. According to Paul Tabori, he was 'closely questioned'[112] afterwards by several of the Club members and a brief report of the evening was included two days later in early editions of *The Times*. The Spiritualist newspapers, *Psychic News* and *Light*, also picked up the story the following week and, not surprisingly, made much of the fact that Price appeared to have at last admitted to experiencing genuine phenomena.

Under the bold headline "Price Sees a Materialisation!" on the front page of *Psychic News*, Maurice Barbanell easily took him to task for his previous scepticism of physical mediums such as Mrs Duncan and Frank Decker. 'What a dilemma for Harry Price!' he beamed, 'After all the publicity for his "explanations" that materialisations were caused by regurgitated cheese-cloth and chewed-up tooth paste, he now has to admit that he saw a materialisation under test conditions!' Quoting from its source, the *Psychic News* reported that Price had had 'a remarkable experience' and, following a brief description of the sitting, continued by saying, 'after many years of psychical investigation he was forced to believe that he had witnessed a case of "genuine spirit materialisation."' Despite the triumphant tone, Barbanell had ultimately to qualify his account in the following way:

> He left himself, however with a loop-hole, for the "Times" went on to quote Price as saying "as a scientist" he could not admit that there was absolute proof until he had tested the phenomena in a laboratory. He

THE ENIGMA OF ROSALIE

was afraid that would not be possible as he had given his word not to proceed with an official investigation. Surely the "Times" has made a mistake. Price could not have described himself as a scientist, for he possesses no scientific degrees.[113]

The final remark can be taken as being either a provocative snipe or a howl of despair.

George Lethem, the Editor of *Light*, who, as one of the invited guests, saw Price give his account first-hand, similarly felt this 'wonderful psychic experience' was the point of no return where belief in the reality of survival was concerned. 'Very widely Mr. Price is regarded as an enemy of Spiritualism and as a very candid critic of some phases of Psychical Research,' he noted, 'and it is probable that at least a proportion of the members of the new Ghost Club look to him for "exposures" of Mediums and the elucidation of alleged "hauntings" as due to trickery, rather than for evidence showing that psychic phenomena can be very real and that sometimes they point emphatically towards Survival ... Such was the effect of the story he told to an astonished gathering last week.'[114] In closing his piece, Lethem reiterated the fact that Price was unable to condone his experience without reservation as offering proof of the afterlife, but he stressed the fact that, according to Price himself, efforts were still being made to secure a second sitting in the presence of other members of the ULCPI.

The idea that, at last, Price had embraced the tenets of Spiritualism was bound to throw the cat among the pigeons where his associates were concerned. 'Whatever has happened?' asked a shell-shocked J. Sturge-Whiting, who, as well as writing to Price on 3 February 1939, also penned George Lethem an incredulous but ultimately unpublished letter. 'Has Crookes come back with his phosphorescent lamp and his perfectly formed child in a dark room – later to be described as test conditions? There must surely be a mis quotation [*sic*] regarding your conclusions.'[115] Price, however, was quick to allay any fears that he had joined the ranks of the converted. 'I thought you would get a shock!' he replied somewhat reassuringly, 'However, you have heard only half the story, and a garbled version at that ... Naturally, *Light* printed the portion of the story most pleasing to its readers.'[116]

Not surprisingly the articles came to the attention of Eric Dingwall who, on the same day as Sturge-Whiting, wrote Price a sarcastic letter, the following extract from which shows the disregard he subsequently held for much of Price's later activities:

I see your after dinner story of the materialization has had a wide publicity. It seems very odd that you never told me a word about this miracle, if it occurred. It is also very odd that in all these remarkable tales there are no names, addresses, or means of checking. I have another one now. One of the most eminent lawyers in the provinces tells me that at a séance at which he was present (no details, of course) a white horse materialized and walked round the circle. I will suggest to him that your circle should meet his and that we should be treated to the first materialized Lady Godiva...[117]

Dingwall, who claimed that Price never responded, ended his letter with the Parthian shot, 'What is the real object of telling these tales?'

Although the Ghost Club discussion was an informal one, Price obviously knew his talk would be controversial and is a clear example of how, at times, he could be his own worst enemy. When Dingwall's letter was published in 1958, both he and his co-author, Trevor Hall, considered Price's silence spoke volumes in showing that the 'Rosalie' story was just that, a fanciful accompaniment to the cigars and brandy of Price's Ghost Club diners, but it is difficult to see how he could, in fact, have defended himself at this point. The annoyance he obviously felt at the younger man's Smart Alec comments would have been compounded by the fact that he knew his hands were effectively tied. By his agreement to the protocols of the original séance, the situation would remain until at some time it was possible to carry out another sitting, either with an assistant or at a location of his own choosing. As we have seen, Price later the same year invited Dingwall to attend some public sittings with Jack Webber. If a second sitting had been on the cards he may have invited Dingwall to come along, although, given the friction that existed between Price and the SPR, it is more likely he would have involved someone he knew he could trust. After all, this had the potential to be the most important piece of paranormal investigation he would ever be involved with. Richard Lambert was the obvious choice, although by this time he was making preparations to leave the country and relocate to Canada.

Another possible collaborator was Cyril Joad (1891-1953), the Head of the Department of Philosophy and Psychology at Birkbeck College. A member of Price's Ghost Club and by this association 'another sharp journalist reviled by purist colleagues'[118], Joad had previously been involved with some of his publicity orientated investigations in the early 1930s. These included the Black Magic experiment in the Brocken and being photographed with Price in an allegedly haunted bed in a Chiswick museum in September 1932. Joad was on close friendly terms with Price for over twenty years and had followed the writing of *Fifty Years* to the extent that he was allowed to read the book in typescript prior to publication. On 10 October 1938 he wrote:

> I have read your chapter on Rosalie. It seems to me to be the most exciting thing that has happened in the course of your career and, therefore – for you have described it vividly and well – the most exciting thing that appears in any of your books. Personally, I am still incredulous. Of course, I know (a) that it was exceedingly unlikely that you were hoaxed and (b) still more unlikely that you are lying. Nevertheless, the view that little girls' bodies, complete with larynxes, are suddenly materialised out of nowhere, and that they have some important relation to some other body which is now, presumably, a bundle of bones in a coffin, where it has been for some years past, seems to me so totally fantastic that, unless I were myself to see and to feel, I do not think anything would persuade me that this had in fact really occurred.
>
> This I daresay is a statement about me, to the effect that I am grown incredulous and prejudiced; yet that is how I feel about it. Is it quite impracticable to persuade these people to let you go again, and inconceivable that they should permit me to go with you? ... Whatever be the true interpretation of what took place, the chapter itself is thrillingly exciting.[119]

As a scientific report, Price knew that his account of the single 'Rosalie' sitting was incomplete and unsatisfactory. It is true that from the outset, when writing to Richard Lambert enclosing the draft report, he was decisive enough to state that the material was likely to form part of his new psychic history for Longmans. To my mind this shows two things. The first is that, on the 16th of December 1937, Price clearly believed that he may well have experienced genuine phenomena. If he had realised he was being fooled during the sitting, why spend several hours writing up such a detailed report and bothering to send it to Lambert at all? Unless of course he *did* realise the trick but felt it was too good a mystery to pass over in print. If Madame Z did genuinely believe 'Rosalie' was real then the X family were carrying out a cruel deception, which would give some degree of protection from being made to look stupid if Mr and Mrs X subsequently went to the papers and told how they had fooled the great 'psychist' with their tricks. Yet given Price's well known dislike and long-standing crusade against charlatans and their abuse of the bereaved, if he did suspect fraud, why not simply expose it then and there, or write a report which described how the clever fakery was carried out? The second point I feel is that his decision on the 16th to include the 'Rosalie' material in the forthcoming *Fifty Years* was based on the confidence he had in his own ability to persuade the 'Rosalie' circle to allow another sitting to take place under better conditions of control. Although he himself may have been at a loss to explain 'Rosalie' in rational terms, his experience at the Ghost Club, the provocative comments of Dingwall and the Spiritualists, together with the well meant but astonished reactions of Sturge-Whiting and Cyril Joad, would have made him realise that more evidence was needed to support its publication being valid. Ken Potter, on the other hand, viewed it in a completely different light and was the one that persuaded Price to throw caution to the wind and publish his experience. This view is supported by correspondence, which survives in the University of London Library.

On 26 January 1939, two days after the Ghost Club dinner and soon after work on *Fifty Years* was complete, Price sent the manuscript to Frank Whitaker, the Editor of the *John O'London's Weekly* newspaper, in connection with a possible deal to serialise the book, with the following observations:

> As promised, I am herewith delivering, by hand, the complete MS. of my next book. I shall be so grateful if you will make any alterations in the preliminary remarks to the "Rosalie" chapter, as you suggested. I think you know my real views about the matter, but probably I have not expressed these very well, or have not made them strong enough. But I know that you realise my attitude in the matter. As I told you yesterday morning, it was never my intention to include the chapter in the book, though Mr. Potter of Longmans thought it should go in … It is very good of you to glance through the MS., and I shall be much interested to hear what you think of it. Of course, the "Rosalie" chapter should be read in conjunction with other chapters dealing with "materialisation".[120]

This shows that ultimately 'Rosalie's' debut before the general public was a publisher's decision and that Price was unhappy about it. What

Whitaker's comments actually were concerning the introductory remarks (see Appendix A) are unclear, but, given the comments that Price follows on with, it would seem likely that even the experienced newspaperman felt that the séance, as reported, was so extraordinary that it should be backed up with some kind of explanatory statement. The following week, Whitaker wrote to Price suggesting some clarification to the beginning of the report section of the 'Rosalie' chapter. This was in connection with the description of the house itself:

> I have glanced at the Rosalie chapter again, and I now see how the misapprehension about the rooms occurred. On Page 180 you say that "a flight of stone steps led to the front door, on *either side* [original emphasis] of which were *two* [original emphasis] rooms with bay windows". This suggested to me that the two rooms were on the ground floor, whereas what you really mean is that the two rooms were one above the other. It is only a small point, but, as the pheasant said, "You can't be too careful when people are out to shoot you."[121]

As can be seen by referring to the published version the suggested changes were made. Interestingly, what was also amended was the description of the steps leading up to the front door: the version sent to Whitaker mentions a single flight whereas the final version in *Fifty Years* specifically states there were twelve in number. This shows that Price's overall description of the mystery house may not be as exact as has previously been accepted. If this was a journalistic invention, inserted to impress readers with his powers of observation, it is conceivable that other external features could also be suspect. These minor revisions are particularly relevant to the later investigation of the case, during the 1950s and 1960s, which are discussed fully, later in this book. Despite looking through the work as a whole, Frank Whitaker ultimately declined to make an offer for the serial rights.

That Price did make alterations to the opening of the chapter is shown in a letter to Ken Potter, dated 17 March 1939, written after Whitaker had made his comments. 'I have made the "Introduction" to the Rosalie chapter *a little stronger* [my emphasis]' he wrote, 'so I think we will let it go now.'[122] Without the original drafts for comparison it is impossible to state for certain what part or parts of the published introduction Price revised. The bound typescript held at the University of London does contain some handwritten amendments, which were incorporated into the finished book, but the introduction is not altered in any way. I suspect that Price may be referring to the opening line where he notes '... *the most remarkable case of materialization* [my emphasis], or rather alleged materialization, I have ever witnessed' as being the part made as he says 'a little stronger'.

At the beginning of May 1939, a Mr McElroy of Allied Newspapers contacted Longmans expressing an interest in serialisation but Price turned it down. In a letter to S. Belton Cobb, one of his publisher's publicists, he remarked:

> I consider it most unsuitable for serialisation in any paper owned by Allied Newspapers. They want snappy, sensational stuff – and not a sober history which I have tried to make my work.[123]

When Eric Dingwall and Trevor Hall published their critique of the 'Rosalie' case ten years after Price's death (see Chapters 9 and 10), the main thrust of their argument was that, because Price had indeed written 'a sober history', he needed the sensational spirit child story in order to generate publicity to sell his book. With this in mind I decided to look through the surviving correspondence between Price and the staff at Longmans during the period that *Fifty Years* was being written, as well as the time leading up to its publication in the autumn of 1939, to see if the philosophy of Price's critics could be substantiated.

Rather than the incomplete investigation of 'Rosalie', what is apparent from the extant letters at the University of London Library is the importance that Price places on his new book as a vehicle for publicising what he considered to be one of his most important (and controversial) contributions to the contemporary psychic scene: his *Psychic Practitioners (Regulation) Bill*. This was a proposed Parliamentary Bill, which the barrister and M.P. for Central Edinburgh, James Campbell Guy, had suggested Price put together for the regulation of contemporary mediumship. Price had drafted the paper with the assistance of another barrister, Gordon Alchin, and Guy had promised that he would sponsor it as a Private Members' Bill and see it through Parliament. Given his extensive experience and antipathy towards the blatant fraud he had encountered over many years of paranormal investigation, the proposed Bill was a logical thing for Price to involve himself with. Ultimately it did not become Law, but clearly was the inspiration and forerunner to the Fraudulent Mediums Act 1951, which Price did not live to see put in place.

Price knew that his Bill would be controversial, particularly where the rogue element in the Spiritualist movement was concerned, but the thinking behind it was sound and logical. 'The Bill is by no means anti-spiritualistic' he said in a letter to his friend Clarice Richards, a former Honorary Treasurer of his National Laboratory of Psychical Research, on 28 July 1939 during the time that *Fifty Years* was in preparation. He added 'it is definitely anti-fraudulent medium and will be supported by all good spiritualists'[124]. When the full text was eventually published he justified it in the following way:

> The purpose of this Bill is to amend the law concerning psychic and occult practices; to regulate the activities of those purporting to be, or calling themselves "mediums"; and to safeguard the public from the frauds of those pretending to possess an occult or psychic faculty, at the same time protecting the genuine medium and the genuine enquirer, and furthering the interests of scientific psychical research.[125]

Price emphasised the importance of his Psychic Bill throughout his dealings with the publisher of *Fifty Years* and considered it to be a highly newsworthy item in the book's promotion. In a letter to Ken Potter dated 11 August 1938 he wrote:

> This Bill is *very important* [Price's italics] and will create a stir when it is published. Jimmy Guy, the barrister and M.P. for Central Edinburgh, has promised to sponsor it in Parliament for me. I want first publication of it to appear in my book, but I shall have to submit it to a Parliamentary draughtsman for his opinion, in case there are any snags in it. It is the first constructive Bill for the regulation of occult practices.[126]

On 6 May 1939, Eileen Kelly from Longmans wrote to Price requesting a short piece of between 200-250 words, which could be incorporated into promotional leaflets they were preparing as press notices. Price complied and part of his synopsis, as well as demonstrating he was acquainted with the new and fashionable developments in ESP, shows the way his proposed Psychic Bill would, if brought onto the Statute Book, sweep away undesirable elements in the Spiritualist movement:

> The positive results achieved in psychical research are given in full and the history of "extra-sensory perception" is traced from the early experiments of Sir William Barrett to the latest university tests with hundreds of subjects...The seamy side of spiritualism is unveiled and the "mechanics" of the fakers are described, together with accounts

of the many prosecutions and *causes célèbres...* In an Appendix to his book is the full text of Mr. Price's Bill for the regulation and registration of mediums, which will be shortly presented to Parliament.[127]

When the proof came back, Price returned it with the last part corrected to give it even more clout: '*The text of Mr. Price's Bill to regulate mediumship, which is being presented to Parliament this autumn, is published in full*' and ordered a 1000 copies of the notice for his own use. A month before *Fifty Years* was due to be issued, when Eileen Kelly was organising review copies to be sent out to various newspapers and periodicals, Price wrote to her with final instructions:

> Especially, must my forthcoming Bill be mentioned as it is a news item which the papers will seize upon.[128]

Amongst all this 'Rosalie' is nowhere to be seen. Rather than being the focus of attention, the report of Price's incomplete investigation was being included as one of many interesting examples of his work as a modern psychical researcher. In fairness to Price's detractors, it must be said that, up to a point in the production of his book, he could have withdrawn the 'Rosalie' material and asked for it not to be included. That he didn't does not automatically mean he saw it either as a sensational news item or a gimmick to sell his book. However, he must have recognised that it was an astonishing account that would cause a certain amount of comment and criticism, particularly where the Spiritualist press was concerned.

For Price, *Fifty Years of Psychical Research* was a record of the many developments in a difficult and controversial subject that he was determined to show he was at the forefront in making a respectable scientific discipline. This was probably the reason he ultimately turned down the idea of including what amounted to a 'free gift' with each copy of the book, a possibility which was discussed in June 1939 around three months before publication. At this time Price had been attempting to conduct his own ESP experiments in collaboration with Frank Whitaker and his *John O'London's Weekly* and had produced his own version of Rhine's 'Zener' cards specifically for the investigation. These were called 'Telepatha' cards, the design and production of which Price considered superior to the ones being used at Duke University, and a set was given away to anyone who entered what amounted to a national telepathic test. Unfortunately the experiment was something of a damp squib – only four hundred people entered the competition and the results were inconclusive. Mr Ridge of Messrs Newnes, Whitaker's printer, who was landed with a surplus stock of 4,600 sets of 'Telepatha' cards, was keen to see them put to some use and floated the idea to Price that they could be given away with copies of *Fifty Years*. Price wrote to Ken Potter on 19 June 1939 mentioning the idea but it came to nothing.

On 30 June, Price returned his corrected proofs to Messrs. Western Printing Services and, by the end of the following month, the index had also been checked and approved. The book eventually went to press early in October 1939 as British newspapers were becoming blackened with news of impending international disaster. On the 18th of September, two days after the complete encirclement of Warsaw by the advancing German forces, Price's new work, his fourth for a major publisher and resplendent in its lacquered purple and black dust-jacket, was released. It was against such a dramatic background that little 'Rosalie' finally made her published debut.

EIGHT

WHAT THE PAPERS SAID

————————

S omething of Harry Price's attitude to the role he played in psychical matters in Britain during the first half of the twentieth century – and in particular the way he viewed his own importance in the developing discipline of psychical research, not only in this country but abroad – can be seen in the thirty-four hard-bound and numbered scrapbooks he accumulated between 1921 and 1945 held in the archives of the University of London Library. They contain several thousand press cuttings, notices, hand bills and articles on psychical matters, from the early exposure of William Hope through to *The End of Borley Rectory*, that in some way mention Price either in whole or in part. Each article is neatly clipped and pasted in with a handwritten note on the source (if this isn't apparent from the material itself) and, in the volumes I have inspected myself, Price has tellingly underlined the appearance of his own name throughout in his characteristic red pencil. For me it shows that Harry Price took his work, and himself, very seriously. An entire volume (No. 31) is devoted to reviews of *Fifty Years of Psychical Research* together with promotional papers connected with the book, and some of this material spills over into the next numbered scrapbook which covers the period of *'The Most Haunted House in England'*.

Despite the outbreak of war in Europe, *Fifty Years* received a wide coverage in many newspapers and periodicals during the autumn and

winter of 1939. Press interest was not limited to this country and re-
viewers and newspapermen in South Africa and America picked up
the story. Longman's publicity department did their job well, helped
in no small way by Price himself who put his thousand copies of Eileen Kelly's flyer to good use amongst his many media contacts who
covered the psychic scene and all things supernatural.

The response to *Fifty Years* as an addition to the standard literature
was generally very positive and several reviews picked up the attempt
that Price had made to link his work with the classics of the past. 'An
excellent summary of modern attempts to investigate an elusive subject' was how the *Manchester Guardian* described Price's new book,
adding, 'This comprehensive and well-documented record is a fitting
supplement to Podmore's older history': an observation which must
have pleased the author no end; while Price, the educator of everyman,
no doubt appreciated the *Western Mail* who commented, 'Mr Price's
erudite, critical, yet vastly entertaining survey has robbed the common
reader of every vestige of excuse for not knowing something about psychical research.' 'A stimulating and very interesting volume' was the
cautious, but nonetheless positive, view of *Light*, the Spiritualist newspaper in whose pages Price had often traded blows with researchers
and mediums alike, but Martin Tindall in the political weekly *Time
and Tide* (18 November 1939) gave him a resounding pat on the back
when he reported that *Fifty Years* was a 'sporting record of a life's devotion to an obscure cause' with the additional comment, 'I hope Mr
Price's entertaining book will be widely read.' For *The Listener* (26 October 1939), prominent psychical researcher C.D. Broad (see Chapter
13), knowing something of Price's career over the past two decades,
was quick to point out the author's somewhat unsubtle inclusion of his
own activities where the history of psychical research was concerned,
but overall was appreciative of the book's merits. 'I suspect that some
readers may be repelled by the rather egotistical tone of the book,' he
noted. 'Mr Price does not suffer from a shrinking modesty and is not
inclined to wait for others to blow his trumpet. But this is a minor defect of manner; he has rendered very valuable services to the subject
and this book is a most useful introduction to it for the general reader.'

The popular press were equally enthusiastic, due, no doubt, to the
opportunities that a book, devoted to the spooky subject of ghosts and
séance rooms, provided in taking attention away, albeit briefly, from
the growing international troubles. 'Rosalie' did help in this respect,
but, on looking through the many cuttings pasted into Price's album,

it is clear that, with five decades of material from which to choose, the reporters and news writers were spoilt for choice. Although the case did feature in some way in most of the popular papers, it was just *one* case, one aspect of Price's work in the arena of mediumistic investigation, that was reviewed alongside the phenomena and activities of people such as Mrs Duncan, Annie Eva Fay, Franek Kluski and 'Margery' Crandon, and was not singled out of proportion with the many controversial topics that were presented. That some newspapers did make it a headline cannot be denied.

The *Aberdeen Journal* picked up on both 'Rosalie' and the Borley investigation in a banner for its edition of 30 October 1939, boldly stating: *'Science is baffled by the Ghostly Nun in the Haunted Rectory. By the Dead Child Who Reappeared in her Mother's Arms'* and preceded an account of 'Rosalie' with the following statement:

> But in the catalogue of charlatans and humbugs, unproven phenomena, unsatisfactory tests and unexplained mysteries that Mr Price gives you in his book there is one astonishing story that stands out above all others.

A two-page article in the *Sunday Dispatch* for 15 October 1939 headlined its review of Price's adventures by saying: *'Harry Price, The Psychic Investigator went to a Séance in a room he had made "Trickery-Proof". A Child Came Back...Her Head was Warm...Her Pulse Fast'*. *Reynolds News* asked the question *'Was She a Real Ghost?'* in its issue for Sunday 22 October 1939 and subsequently serialised the 'Rosalie' chapter in order to help its readers make up their minds. 'If you are a spiritualist there is much in this book that will anger you' commented a reporter for the *Yorkshire Telegraph* in part of a review dated 18 October 1939, adding that, for the 'layman in these things, there is much to fascinate, indeed there is not a dull page'.

Clifford Bax, the playwright whose brother, the composer Arnold Bax, received a knighthood the same year that Price encountered 'Rosalie', reviewed *Fifty Years* in a lengthy article "Exploring the Spirit World" for Frank Whitaker's *John O'London's Weekly* on 17 November 1939. Bax had been a member of the Society for Psychical Research for several years and was ideally suited to give an informed opinion. Despite his evident appreciation of Price's dedication to the cause of scientific paranormal enquiry (Price is described as a '[f]irst rate investigator'), the section on 'Rosalie', titled "The Kensington Ghost Girl", gives the distinct impression that his review copy was not to hand when at least this part of the article was written, as the following extract clearly shows:

> And there is still "Rosalie"...Mr Price feels so uncertain about this little ghost-girl – whose pulse he took and to whose heart he listened – that he asked his publisher whether the account should be printed. The story of his meeting with this little girl, in a house in Kensington, under very stringent "conditions", is so extraordinary that, like Mr Price, I am still wondering what really happened. It seems, however, that he touched and even saw the body of a six-year-old girl who had been dead for, I think, three years.

Bax's clear pinpointing of the séance would appear to be a confusion with the fact that Price's National Laboratory of Psychical Research, and the later ULCPI, had both operated previously out of two addresses, Queensberry Place and Roland Gardens, in South Kensington. Surprisingly, despite the obvious mistake, David Cohen (see Chapter 12) was more inclined to accept Bax's location when he assessed the case in the 1960s but made no attempt to follow up this very tenuous lead[129].

Cyril Joad, on the other hand, who knew what was coming, gave 'Rosalie' the briefest of mentions in the November 1939 edition of *First and Last* in what he found to be 'the most entertaining book on the subject of psychical research known to me.' Summarising, Joad cautiously noted that, 'Mr Price also believes that he has witnessed at least one living full-form materialisation' but with his earlier views unchanged by any further investigation, either on Price's part or his own, felt obliged to state that 'no single case of ectoplasm, materialisation, hauntings, or poltergeists ... has been demonstrated to the satisfaction of science', 'Rosalie' included.

Not surprisingly Price's merciless exposure of all that was bad in mediumship, both past and present, was given a cool reception from parts of the Spiritualist press as, by association, the rest of the movement was tarred with the same brush. Maurice Barbanell kicked off by devoting a large Editorial in his *Psychic News* to ridiculing Price's crusading *Psychic Practitioners (Regulation) Bill* and was of the opinion that the movement had not only to root out the fakers itself, but should not be dictated to by either Parliament or, even worse, by psychical researchers, particularly those like Price who, he felt, 'thrived on publicity'. What drew the most comments from writers and readers of the Spiritualist newspapers was the fact that, faced with such an experience as the appearance of 'Rosalie', Price still would not embrace the Spiritualistic cause and finally come out in support of the reality of survival after death. For many, the 'Rosalie' chapter, coming from the pen of an investigator like Harry Price, was the ultimate proof.

In this respect *The Two Worlds* called *Fifty Years*, '[a] contentious book', simply because Price 'seems absolutely beyond conviction' in his dealings with mediums and their phenomena. For *Light* in the edition for 26 October 1939, novelist and former war correspondent for the *Morning Post*, Henry F. Prevost Battersby, a Spiritualist himself, realised that, for a psychical researcher of Price's reputation to put his name to such an account, the incident was of great importance. In a front page review, which also carried a portrait of Price himself, he commented:

> The case of Rosalie supplies the most interesting chapter of the book, not because there is anything out-of-the-way in the happenings, but on account of the author's reaction to them.

This view was followed up in an Editorial by George Lethem entitled "Problems for Mr Harry Price" on 2 November 1939 which made reference to the Ghost Club dinner, at the beginning of the year, during which Price had told colleagues about his remarkable experience:

> Questioned about the appearance and disappearance of the form when he first told the story at a meeting of the Ghost Club, Mr Price admitted that there was no possibility of a normal child having been smuggled into the room and smuggled out again without his knowledge; so that the only reasonable explanation was that he had seen and handled and spoken to a veritable materialised spirit-being.

> Now, here is a "ghost story" vouched for by a thoroughly competent observer – to wit, Mr Harry Price himself. Why does he hesitate about proclaiming that story as "veridical" and "convincing"? Does he expect ever to get evidence from a better or more trustworthy witness. Surely that is impossible.

Price trod a fine line in respect to his relations with scientific orthodoxy and the Spiritualist movement throughout his psychical career and this kind of response clearly put him into a corner. The 'Rosalie' sitting had, for a period of time afterwards at least, stunned him but he knew he did not have the crushing proof, the independent testimony or the vital repeatable experiment, that was needed. After all, the concept of survival after death shakes the materialist and religious establishments to the very core. Clear proof of this is shown much nearer to our own times by the following statement that Adrian Berry, a former Science Correspondent for the *Daily Telegraph*, gave when writing in the early 1990s:

> Few subjects more infuriate scientists, physical scientists in particular, than claims of "paranormal" events, such as spoon bending, levitation and communication with the dead. They are resented because, if confirmed, the whole fabric of science would be threatened.[130]

Michael Roll, who, as the head of the Campaign for Philosophical Freedom, has lobbied for over twenty-five years for a fair presentation in the media and educational outlets for what he describes as the 'secular scientific case for survival after death', describes it in the following way:

> The whole of scientific teaching across every discipline, including psychology and philosophy, is locked into death being the end of everything – the mind dying with the brain. Any scientist who challenges this is immediately destroyed by their peers. These orthodox scientists have as allies their sworn enemies, the professional priests from all religions. The priests are fighting to keep their monopoly on the lucrative life after death industry.[131]

Price was in a no-win situation because any silence or inaction on his part was construed by the critics as the realisation that a tall tale had now got out of hand. George Lethem continued to turn up the heat in a subsequent Editorial, this time headed "Mr Harry Price's Progress", which appeared three months later on 15 February 1940, again painting a picture of Price as a man on the brink of joining the Spiritualistic cause:

> On more than one occasion we have expressed the hope that Mr Harry Price may yet admit publicly that the spirit-hypothesis is the only one which *completely* [original italics] covers the psychic facts to which he has borne witness in his various books.

> It is evident to anyone who has followed Mr Price's work during the past twenty years that he is veering more and more toward the

spiritistic hypothesis as the result of his own investigations. This is interesting in that he must be conceded to be a cautious and well-balanced investigator.

Despite the goading, Price stood firm. He was also under fire from the other side of the fence in the form of Eric Dingwall who, irritated as we have seen by Price's 'after dinner story', had reviewed *Fifty Years* for the Society for Psychical Research. 'It appears to be made up of scattered articles, papers and notes, with little attempt to co-ordinate the mass of material or evaluate the historical sequence of development' was how he dismissively summed up the book in the SPR *Journal*, and, in the Supplement to *Nature* dated 30 December 1939, rubbed salt in the wound in the following way:

> Although this work purports to be a critical survey of the work undertaken by psychical research workers during the last fifty years, and even to be a continuation of the late Mr Frank Podmore's history of modern spiritualism, it is, if the truth be told, nothing of the kind. It consists of a miscellaneous collection of material, written in a popular style and forming more than anything else a kind of abstract digest of some of the more sensational cases of recent times.

Clearly one of the recent 'sensational cases' that Dingwall had in mind was a certain spirit child from the London suburbs. Things eventually blew over and, having achieved his desired contribution to the annals of contemporary psychic literature, Price began focusing his attention on compiling his second paranormal offering for Longmans.

Three years were to pass before he returned, albeit fleetingly, to 'Rosalie' again. By this time *Fifty Years* had suffered from the production problems which became common for publishers throughout the war years. Two years after publication, the book was still in print but out of binding[132]. Five hundred copies were bound early in 1942, but labour shortages and the effects of enemy air raids caused delays. At one point, Longmans binding works received a direct hit by German bombing with the result that, during this period, the publisher had close to a million copies of various books out of covers[133].

In September 1942, with a change of publisher, Price issued his autobiography *Search for Truth*. As part of a concluding chapter titled 'Work in Hand', covering various projects, with which he hoped to involve himself after the war had ended, he gave details of an experience brought to his attention by a correspondent. Mrs Beatrice Cooper claimed to have experienced the materialisation of her young daughter – who also died prematurely of diphtheria but aged fourteen – in her bedroom in the way that the spirit child had appeared to Madame Z in the days before the coming together of the 'Rosalie' circle. Price reported that he intended to try to carry out some kind of controlled experiments with Mrs Cooper, in the hope that he could encourage the development of the phenomenon, but nothing came of it. Out of necessity he made reference to his benchmark case but restricted himself to a brief paragraph. Later, critics felt this reticence was due to the embarrassment that the 'Rosalie' story had become, but Price stood his ground:

> I was not – and still am not – entirely satisfied with the phenomenon, striking as it was. I was persuaded to publish the report against my inclination, as the "case" was incomplete and full investigation was unwelcome and difficult.[134]

As we have seen, this statement can be supported and cannot be dismissed out of hand.

With his memoirs complete and issued, Price turned his attention to one of his favourite paranormal subjects, the poltergeist, and spent the remaining war years compiling a lengthy survey of their antics. During this period his postbag came to be dominated, more and more, by responses to the Borley investigation to which he actively returned in the autumn of 1943, while working on *Poltergeist Over England*, but correspondence still continued to reach him, both critical and open minded, about the unresolved 'Rosalie' case. Dr C.E. Douglas of St Andrews, writing on New Year's Day 1941, showed the way that Price's account bucked the trends, not only of theology, but his own chosen profession:

> Has anyone before found evidence of a spirit with a respiratory and circulating system in working order? ... Now observers, from Jesus of Nazareth onwards have taken it for granted that "A spirit hath no flesh and blood, as ye see Me have", and the ordinary term, "discarnate" is universally applied.
>
> Perhaps as a doctor I am unduly impressed with this fact in the case but I venture to suggest that it might be considered to fix it as one of definite and rather brazen fraud. The child you examined was alive

and I suggest further that the conjuror element might busy themselves with the question as to how it was done.[135]

Although well meant, the fact that Price was well acquainted with the 'conjuror element' seemed to have passed the doctor by.

The one 'Rosalie' enquiry that travelled the furthest distance came from Raymond F. Hale, who described himself as an 'American sailor somewhere in the Pacific'. His letter, written on 12 November 1944 and forwarded from San Francisco, was a request for news of any further developments in Price's investigation. In fact, Hale and all those interested in some way with the spirit child encounter had to wait a further two years before Price eventually provided some kind of closure for the case as a whole.

In 1946, Price contributed a four-page article entitled "Is this a true ghost story?" to *Help Yourself*, a small private society annual, and as well as a résumé of his encounter with 'Rosalie' in the winter of 1937, gave, for the first time, details of the events which led up to the end of his investigation. This publication is now an exceedingly rare item and the copy I have been able to examine was from the collection of the late Alan Roper, a former member of the Ghost Club and the SPR. A typescript copy also survives in the University of London Library.

After covering the background and particulars of both the 'Rosalie' circle and the séance itself, Price closed his involvement in the following way:

> I kept in touch with Mr and Mrs X, who acted as intermediaries between the French lady and me. At the end of August 1939, Mr X took his family for a motor tour of the Continent. As Madame Z wished to see her French relatives, he dropped her at Paris on the outward journey. Then came the war. He was in Zürich at the time and made a dash for one of the ports. He was unable to get to Paris to pick up "Rosalie's" mother and, in fact, had to leave his car at Ostend. At the time of writing, nothing more has been heard of Madame Z.[136]

As with the account of the séance itself in *Fifty Years*, we are reliant on the *Help Yourself* essay as providing Price's last word on the 'Rosalie' case. We have seen that Price said he hoped to attend another sitting in the winter of 1939 but, ultimately, the reluctance of Madame to commit to further investigation together with the outbreak of hostilities made things permanent. Given the later criticisms (see Chapters 9 and 10) and however unsatisfactory this explanation may be – however convenient it might appear to a sceptical mind as providing a means of shutting the door on the spirit child episode once and for all, particularly as there is no supportive evidence or surviving correspondence – it does not automatically mean that Price was telling bare faced lies. In fairness, this may well have been what he himself was told by the family themselves. There may be no truth in it, but, if that was what Price was told then that was what he had to report at a later date. In 1965, David Cohen attempted to address this issue by showing that, as late as the end of August/beginning of September 1939, travel agencies and hotels in Paris were still advertising as normal and, as such, the trip by the X family was not as reckless as it might seem to be at a later date.

The remaining part of Price's *Help Yourself* article reinforced aspects of the séance that set it apart from the usual Spiritualistic meeting whereby members of the public pay to experience either communication or phenomena. Price remarked:

> Is this a "true ghost" story? At the time I was convinced that it was. Then, next day, I began to wonder if "Rosalie" was a genuine spirit entity, or whether the whole thing was an elaborate hoax. If the latter, then it had been going on for years and no actress on earth could have simulated Madame Z.'s poignant emotion. And why should they cheat? No one was getting anything out of it. Neither money nor publicity nor kudos. And would any sane family fool one another every week for years on end? Hardly! And where did the "spirit" come from? Was there a revolving wall in the drawing-room or a trap-door in the very solid parquet floor? If so, could it have survived my minute and systematic search of the apartment? I suppose that this is possible, but moving floors and sliding walls imply costly, elaborate and silent machinery to operate. And what could possibly be the motive for such a stupendous fraud?[137]

Even after the passage of nearly ten years, Price appeared still to be frustrated and unable to come to terms with his experience.

What was still tantalisingly out of reach in 1946 became permanent on Easter Monday, 29 March 1948. After posting letters to 'Mollie' Goldney and the British peer Charles Henry Wyndham, Price retired to his study to enjoy an after-lunch pipe and was killed almost instantly by a massive heart attack that left him dead in his armchair.

Early the following year, Paul Tabori was approached by Price's executors, the Midland Bank Trustee and Executor Ltd of Brighton, to take on the management of his published works and his literary estate as a whole. Tabori, as a member of Price's incarnation of the Ghost Club, had met the psychical researcher on a number of occasions and his father, Cornelius, a writer and journalist, had investigated several paranormal cases himself in Europe before the war.[138] Tarbori accepted and in order to inject some fresh capital into the estate penned *Harry Price – The Biography of a Ghost Hunter* which was issued in 1950.

Tabori became fascinated by 'Rosalie' after coming across what meagre correspondence does still exist in the University of London archives early on during research for his biography. He was disinclined to believe that Price had made the entire story up and, in an attempt to provoke interest in the case, republished the *Fifty Years* chapter in full with an appeal for more information. Tabori wrote:

> Was he lying? I do not think so. He was not good at inventing tales. The few pieces of fiction (all unpublished) which I have read from his pen all show that he was utterly incapable of spinning a convincing plot. And why should he lie? What possible motive could he have had for risking the reputation of a lifetime? Psychologically and morally, this theory will not hold water...I believe that Harry Price was speaking the truth and that he was both frightened and shaken by his experiences. If Mr X – whom Harry Price has described in a letter to his publisher as a well-known City businessman – realises that he owes a duty to psychical research and to Harry Price's memory, perhaps he will come forward after reading these lines. But unless he or some other sitter at that remarkable séance twelve years ago comes to our aid, the riddle of Rosalie must remain unsolved forever.[139]

The 'Rosalie' chapter of Tabori's book was syndicated in America and published by *Fate* magazine but, despite the publicity, there was no response.

A similar appeal had appeared a year earlier in the correspondence column of *Light* from a reader, Alex Baird. 'Would it be possible for any of the ladies or gentlemen who attended this circle to write an article about that intriguing phenomenon?' Baird asked, 'I feel it would be a great pity if, with the exception of Price's version, this valuable case is lost to the world. I can sympathise with the mother who fears that through the intervention of strangers, however well meaning, she may lose contact with Rosalie, but I would plead with her that there are thousands of mothers who have never had such a glorious experience, and that her story would comfort them.'[140] It was a heartfelt request that went unanswered and seemingly showed, as Tabori commented at a later date, that the spirit child enigma 'must remain one of the many unsolved mysteries and inconclusive cases of psychical research'[141]. Behind the scenes however, efforts were being made to prove him wrong.

NINE

MR HALL AND
THE 'BORLEY REPORT'

———————➤●◄———————

Although the posthumous attacks on Harry Price's reputation as a reputable and sincere investigator of psychical happenings date from only a few months after his sudden death, the seeds were in fact sown some twenty years earlier. In December 1948, the *Inky Way Annual (Book 2)*, the second instalment of a seasonal fund-raising publication in aid of several journalistic charities, was published. Amongst its many light-hearted and entertaining articles and cartoons was a short self-penned essay chronicling the adventures of Fleet Street reporter Charles Sutton. In his article, Sutton made an uncorroborated statement that he caught Price pretending to be a poltergeist in Borley Rectory in July 1929 and was only prevented from publishing an exposure at the time by the intervention of his newspaper's legal advisor.

Sutton's *Inky Way* accusation came to the attention of William Salter who, as has been mentioned briefly, disliked Price as a person and was dismissive of Borley as a genuine haunting. Salter decided that Price's investigation needed some close auditing and, free from the threat of a libel action, in January 1949 a reappraisal of his published accounts of the Borley Rectory case was instigated under the auspices of the Society for Psychical Research. Salter was the Society's President at the time of Price's death and his long run as Honorary Secretary had come to an end the same year. During this time he had built up a good working relationship with the enthusiastic 'Mollie' Goldney who witnessed Price's initial reaction to the 'Rosalie' séance back in December 1937. Goldney, as a former associate, was a natural choice to reinvestigate Price's Borley activities given her time as a Council Member of the old National Laboratory. Another was long-standing SPR man, Price's former literary and séance room collaborator, Eric Dingwall.

Although the qualifications of both Goldney and Dingwall may have looked good on paper, they were made in many ways superficial by the nature of their past associations with the man whom they were now investigating. Because of this the Borley enquiry could never have been, in the best sense, a dispassionate evaluation as there were too many personal issues involved. Both researchers began the somewhat formidable undertaking of re-examining the evidence for the 'most haunted house in England'. This involved taking statements from participants in the Borley drama, including former residents of the rectory and Borley village itself, as well as examining the mass of unpublished papers and material which Price had gathered and left for posterity at the University of London. It was an onerous task which occupied the two investigators on and off for the best part of the next two years.

As well as a fascination with the paranormal, common threads among the interests of at least some mid-twentieth century psychical researchers were an abiding interest in conjuring, together with the history of legerdemain and a love of book-collecting. Eric Dingwall and Harry Price shared all these qualities. Around the time that he first became involved in the SPR's Borley reappraisal, Eric Dingwall met another kindred spirit through a mutual association at the Magic Circle.

Trevor Henry Hall was a thirty-nine-year-old chartered surveyor from Leeds who was about to embark on what was to become a highly controversial part-time career in British psychical research. Hall's interest in conjuring began when, as a boy, he was taken to a Maskelyne magic show by his father. This was, as he later recalled, something of an 'immediate antidote'[142] to a meeting with Sir Arthur Conan Doyle who, at his London bookshop, had given the youngster a lecture on the wonders of Spiritualism. In the mid-1940s, Hall published three short books on card magic and other conjuring techniques and began to frequent the Magic Circle. He later claimed that reading Harry Price's *The End of Borley Rectory* was the event that kindled his subsequent interest in paranormal phenomena, and, when he became friendly with Eric

Dingwall, the opportunity presented itself to make a mark on the world of psychical research. In November 1951, he was invited by Dingwall and Goldney to assist in their Borley investigation and Hall joined the SPR in order to collaborate officially in the enquiry.

Hall threw himself enthusiastically into the task in hand, travelling around the country interviewing witnesses, corresponding with Price's former associates, and compiling information to such an extent that, when *The Haunting of Borley Rectory* eventually appeared in 1956, the result was that two-thirds of the report were written by him alone. It was the first of eight books (two in collaboration) on 'critical psychical research'[143] issued at intervals over a thirty year period, although, as John Randall has stated, Hall's published works were more 'aimed at "debunking" many of the most famous cases in the history of psychical research and undermining the reputations of some of the most respected researchers'[144] rather than examining the mechanics of the paranormal itself.

Where the 'Borley Report' was concerned, Hall later stated it 'was written in the public interest to correct the sensational and inaccurate presentation of the case by the late Harry Price'[145]. In Hall's mind-set Borley Rectory, in the words of Professor Anthony G.N. Flew, who reviewed the Dingwall, Goldney and Hall book for *The Spectator* shortly after publication, was 'the house of cards which Harry Price built out of little more than a pack of lies'[146], a quote that pleased Hall so much that he included it in practically everything else he later wrote on the case. Opinions were divided on whether the SPR report was a fair and accurate appraisal of Price's presentation of the Borley case, especially as he was no longer around to defend himself. It was, however, a tremendous blow to Price's posthumous credibility and the public at large – and especially those new to psychical matters – could not be blamed for thinking that, as a reviewer for *The Economist* stated at the time, 'Harry Price emerges unmistakably as a rogue, a falsifier and manufacturer of evidence'[147]. As if this wasn't enough, there was more to come.

During the 1950s, Hall was something of a rising star in British psychical research and, through his SPR membership, he was able to take part in a handful of investigations on behalf of the Society. Between 1954 and 1956, he was awarded the Perrott Studentship in Psychical Research at Trinity College, Cambridge. This involved studying ESP under the supervision of parapsychologist Alan (George) Owen, whose wife, Iris, took part in the famous 'Philip' table-tipping experiments in Canada in the 1970s. Hall never published a report or a thesis on his work although some of his subsequent ghost hunting was done under the terms of the Perrott scholarship.

In January 1954, by which time the Borley reappraisal was practically complete, he visited the Yorkshire Museum in Museum Street, York, where a caretaker claimed to have seen an apparition and a book was mysteriously propelled from a bookshelf during a visit by local newspapermen. Hall later held a night-time vigil, in the museum, accompanied by a group of ghost hunters from the SPR that included Eric Dingwall and Roland Winder, the Librarian at the Magic Circle. Although no phenomena were experienced, Hall did come across, at first hand, the problems that the involvement of reporters and the media can have in hampering serious paranormal investigations. In this case, members of the local and national press were kept at bay 'only by resolute and fairly plain speaking'![148] Two years later, in February 1956, he did much of the leg-work in travelling to Selby where strange poltergeist-type noises had been heard in a local doctor's surgery. The two practice physicians clearly felt he was the man for the job and had been prompted to contact Hall for help after reading a review of the 'Borley Report' in the *Yorkshire Evening Post..*

Harry Price's Vice-Presidency of the Magician's Club[149] and, more importantly, his membership of the Inner Magic Circle, gave Hall some common ground to work on when taking part in the Borley investigation. In the early part of 1952, he corresponded with Douglas Craggs, a renowned ventriloquist who, as Secretary of the Magic Circle, knew Price reasonably well and, during the 1940s, had a passing interest in investigating mediumistic phenomena. Hall quizzed Craggs over aspects of Price's character and, in a letter dated 16 April 1952, he gave his opinion on the subject of 'Rosalie' séance. Craggs had previously commented publicly, in a somewhat belated review of *Fifty Years*, in the Magic Circle's own members' magazine, *The Magic Circular*, in April 1941. I have already discussed at length the issues and Price's own feelings on the inclusion of 'Rosalie' in the book, but Craggs was of the opinion that the account of the séance was spurious and Hall later enjoyed quoting the following extract from Craggs's letter to support this:

You will remember my review of his book in which he described the Rosalie materialization. This, in my view, was a complete invention and unworthy even of Price. When I sent him an advance copy of my review in which I criticised the Rosalie chapter, he forbade me to publish it and instead of the usual "Dear Douglas" he began his letter with "Dear Sir". I ignored his letter and the review duly appeared. About five months after the publication of the review he wrote me in a very friendly strain saying he was sure I was right and that he should never have put Rosalie into print.[150]

Interestingly, despite promoting the magician's negative opinion of the 'Rosalie' case, Hall never quotes or makes reference to any other part of Craggs' review in any of his writings, the simple reason being that, apart from the brief reference to the spirit child case, it was wholly supportive of both Price and his work. In his opening statements, Craggs comments:

> In *Fifty Years of Psychical Research* Harry Price, a distinguished member of the Inner Magic Circle, traces the history of Spiritualism and the varied phenomena by custom associated with it up to the outbreak of this war. After paying generous tribute to Podmore's *Modern Spiritualism* which, published in 1902, "is still the standard book of the period with which it deals," Harry Price draws from his own unrivalled experiences to paint a colourful and fascinating picture of modern psychical research.[151]

The reason that the writer was unable to endorse Price's 'Rosalie' experience was that, as a professional magician, he represented the view of the conjuring fraternity to whom the whole concept of materialisation was preposterous and therefore impossible. He himself admitted this. The conjuror, '[s]ecure in his knowledge of the principles of magic and confident in his ability to detect trickery in the presence of any phenomenon, he will read with something akin to shock that skilled and competent investigators have witnessed phenomena produced under the most stringent test conditions.' That Craggs was shocked by Price's account is clear but his rejection of it was also due to the fact that, as Price admitted and bemoaned the fact, he had neither been allowed to carry out further repeatable experiments, nor was able to support his statements to the satisfaction of critical orthodoxy. Craggs writes:

> If the reader has not heard of "Rosalie" he should make her acquaintance in this book. The reviewer, for one, would like to know more about her, for he finds it beyond him to comment upon an episode so extraordinary and so lacking in corroborative evidence that it stands out in a book which is otherwise remarkable for its careful documentation.[152]

Craggs himself may not have believed for one minute that materialisation was possible, but the lack of supportive evidence was the thing he was most concerned with when reporting the account for the Magic Circle and this is made clear by his comments; the only reference to 'Rosalie' in the entire article. Like all of us, he simply wanted to know more. Without further information he was unable to accept it: the only negative point in a volume he found to be 'critical, stimulating and provocative, a veritable landmark in a field of research where the pioneer can expect little in the way of recognition or reward.'[153] This selective use of his source material characterises much of Trevor Hall's work where psychical research is concerned.

Whether this was Hall's first introduction to 'Rosalie' is difficult to say as, through his association with Eric Dingwall and working relationship with 'Mollie' Goldney, he would have had ample opportunity to hear and talk about the case. As a student of psychical research, Hall would also have been familiar with the majority of Price's books including *Fifty Years* which followed in the footsteps of similar books by Podmore, Carrington and others. Whatever the origins, with the Borley investigation more or less complete and, seemingly having got the measure of the man and his motives, Hall considered other aspects of Price's work fair game in the name of 'critical' psychical research. It was to be something of a personal crusade, bordering almost on obsession, and was to occupy him on and off for the next three decades. In *The Borley Rectory Companion* (2009), Peter Underwood, Eddie Brazil and I describe Hall as being one of Price's 'most persistent opponents'[154], a title which, we felt, summed up his continued attempts to discredit Price's role and character. This was a man whom he never knew nor associated with, but who had no scruples about later using his important collection of magic books at the University of London as research material for a successful PhD thesis from Leeds University obtained in 1970. I don't intend to devote more to Hall's activities, except where they are concerned with the case in hand, other than to state that one possible motive for Hall's continued actions was the fact that his collaboration with Dingwall and Goldney did not succeed in demolishing for good what the SPR report dismissively termed the 'Borley legend', the one case that seemingly got him interested in psychical research in the first place.

In 1954, Hall began to take an active interest in 'the Rosalie affair'[155] as he later described it. The results of his enquiry were published much later in 1958 as part of another collaboration with Eric Dingwall, entitled

Four Modern Ghosts, issued by Hall's favourite publisher, Gerald Duckworth. Much of the material presented in the book stems from Hall's active but short-lived participation in paranormal investigation for the SPR in the preceding years. The *Four Modern Ghosts* themselves are the York Museum investigation from 1954; an alleged poltergeist outbreak at a house in Runcorn, Cheshire in 1952, which was known to the two researchers at the time but, due to work commitments and the Borley case, they were unable to investigate; the Selby poltergeist that occupied Hall during the early months of 1956 (disguised for publication under the pseudonym of the 'Ousedale Haunt'); and finally the case of Harry Price and 'Rosalie'. The two authors state that the purpose of their book was 'to assist students [of psychical research] to evaluate material submitted to them for scrutiny and to obtain useful results when dealing with actual cases which they are called upon to investigate'[156] and, in the main, the material presented is useful and still relevant today. The York Museum ghost, the Runcorn poltergeist and the investigation at Selby/Ousedale, all contain factors which should be taken into account when a serious investigation of alleged paranormal activity is undertaken.

At York, the authors felt that the mixed nature of the reported phenomena was a clue to the probable, and, in their view, non-paranormal, cause of events and demonstrated the importance of carefully assessing witnesses, particularly with regard to their state of mind and possible motives in reporting 'phenomena'. Here they imply that the movement of the book from the library shelf was carefully staged (Hall surmises a hidden thread was employed to pull the book free) by a relation of the museum caretaker in order to make the latter's claims to witnessing an apparition inside the building more credible.

The Runcorn case (at a small terraced house in Byron Street) showed the need for careful study by competent investigators during the period when disturbances were taking place, rather than attempting to make an enquiry at a later stage when the phenomena has either waned or ceased altogether. In this instance, objects were said to have been thrown and furniture, in a bedroom shared by two eighteen year-old youths, mysteriously disturbed and moved about. The exploitation and unwanted intrusion by sightseers and the media is also clearly demonstrated. At one point, when observers attempted to carry out a vigil in the haunted bedroom where the two boys were trying to sleep, the house was packed with sensation-seekers and over a hundred further people filled the street outside. Totally impractical conditions for a serious investigation and reminiscent of the Battersea Poltergeist case investigated by Harry Price in January 1929 where, at one point, police on horseback were employed to keep crowds at bay while Price and pressmen visited the house. The sensational publicity by the *Daily Mirror* during the late 1970s, when the Enfield Poltergeist was being investigated by Maurice Grosse and Guy Lyon Playfair for the SPR, is a modern example.

In their 'Ousedale Haunt', Dingwall and Hall present a fairly strong case for the mysterious noises and disturbances to be due to the tidal action of underground water (created by prevailing conditions of unusual weather), rather than a poltergeist centred around a young female employee that the reported phenomena at first resembled. The idea that the majority of haunted house cases can be explained away by the movement of subterranean streams and water courses was being revived at the time by Guy Lambert, SPR President 1955-1958, who published a lengthy paper entitled "Poltergeists: A Physical Theory" in the SPR *Journal* (Vol.38, No.684) in June 1955. The authors support this theory at Selby/Ousedale, where old brick sewers with outfalls to the River Ouse were known to exist close to the doctors' surgery, but find it unconvincing at Runcorn where Lambert had suggested it was a probable cause for the disturbances. Dingwall and Hall also emphasise the need to distinguish between place-centred phenomena (i.e. traditional haunted houses) and person-centred phenomena (i.e. poltergeists), something reasonably familiar to us today, but which at the time was not as well appreciated and still a subject of confusion. The only odd man out, so to speak, where *Four Modern Ghosts* is concerned, is the inclusion of Harry Price and 'Rosalie'.

The authors describe their chapter on the 'Rosalie' séance as 'the first detailed examination of one of the most famous cases described by the late Mr. Harry Price' and support its presence in their book by stating that modern psychical researchers 'may gather a few hints on how to appraise a story of this kind.'[157] As we will see, rather than providing practical information and advice on the difficult subject of investigating physical séance room phenomena, the whole rationale is clearly in the mould of cutting what the authors feel is a tall tale down to size. With their 'Borley Report', the two men confidently considered they had the measure of Harry Price. For Trevor Hall, here was another chance to reinforce the seemingly unassailable results of that investigation (in which we noted he played a major part) by presenting another uncompromising analysis of material from Price's psychist's case-book. As with aspects of *The Haunting of Borley Rectory*, the 'Rosalie' chapter of *Four Modern Ghosts* is a superficially impressive but ultimately flawed and prejudiced examination.

Just how much material Eric Dingwall contributed to *Four Modern Ghosts* on the subject in hand is difficult to assess. We have already encountered his candid view on the 'Rosalie' séance and he must have been in general agreement with the conclusions to allow his name to be published over them. It seems clear, however, that he was not completely behind Hall in unanimously supporting what was being presented, and a measure of how much (or little) he went along with the views of his co-author emerged a few years after publication (see Chapter 12). If the object of this section of the book had been to look realistically at the investigation of modern physical mediumship then it was a missed opportunity and Dingwall's obvious experience in this area, much of it gained during the 'Roaring Twenties' of séance room investigation, was clearly wasted. Twenty years earlier he had issued his *How to Go to a Medium: A Manual of Instruction* (1927), which covered, for the assistance of the serious-minded layman, the investigation of both mental and physical phenomena, including sections on materialisation and the control of physical mediums. Despite the change in fashion in psychical research during the 1940s and 1950s, there were still a small number of field workers, such as the soon to be encountered David Cohen, who were prepared to explore the Spiritualistic dimension, and who would have found an update of the kind of material presented in Dingwall's earlier book informative.

A former Research Officer for the SPR, Donald West, summed up the 1950s outlook of most researchers to physical mediumship in his *Psychical Research Today* (1954), a similar guide for contemporary investigators and, in my view, a more practical and objective book. This appeared in its original edition (by the same publisher) four years before Dingwall and Hall's *Four Modern Ghosts*. In a chapter covering séance room phenomena, West felt that physical mediums were 'few and more notorious than important' and that 'the average séance for physical phenomena is an uninspired performance'. He also makes the following statement, born of years of distrust on the part of mediums and researchers alike:

> Before the development of infra-red photography, physical mediums could effect the most brazen frauds. Now that the infra-red image converter enables one to see in the dark, the mediums no longer have it

all their own way. Despite the offer by some S.P.R. members of a reward of £250 for a physical phenomenon that can be watched through the infra-red telescope, no medium has submitted to serious investigation. The common-sense view is that they have all been frightened off by fear of detection.[158]

It was in such a climate as this, antagonistic and dismissive of physical mediumship and materialisation, that Dingwall and Hall turned their guns to bear on an episode in psychic history which had at its centre these very subjects. They were also being presented by a researcher who, they felt, was little more than a psychic showman himself.

TEN

THE DINGWALL AND HALL INVESTIGATION

―――――∻●⊱―――――

The Dingwall and Hall enquiry is a catalogue of missed opportunities which, if properly exploited, could have gone a long way to solving the mystery of the 'Rosalie' case. Taking place as it did at the outset seventeen years after the séance itself, it was a period when important witnesses were still available for interview and could have provided valuable testimony. They amount to lost chances that are unavailable to anyone attempting to pick up the pieces of the puzzle today.

Out of necessity, the 'Rosalie' account in *Four Modern Ghosts* begins with a résumé of the particulars of the séance as presented by Price in *Fifty Years*. To this is added the later material subsequently included in *Help Yourself.* Despite the Baird appeal in *Light* the year after Price's death and the publication of Paul Tabori's biography, no further information on the case had come to light in the intervening four years up until the time that Hall became interested in 'Rosalie'. The two researchers were therefore forced to base their analysis mainly on Price's account, together with whatever breakthroughs they themselves could make. Their initial appraisal of Price's material led them to conclude that, if the statements were taken at face value, the chances that he had been fooled were in fact slim. They comment:

In our view, *if* [Dingwall and Hall's italics] Price's account of the Rosalie séance be true, then his arguments ... against the possibility of trickery may be well founded. His description of the room is both full and precise, and it is not easy to see how a secret entrance in the walls floor or ceiling could have escaped scrutiny ... It is equally clear from Price's description of the very few pieces of furniture in the room and his ruthless examination of them, that a child could not have been concealed in the room either before or after the séance.[159]

Price's inability to discover a motive for fraud was also seen as being significant. '[It] is easier even to assume that Rosalie was a genuine materialization,' they note, 'than that the séance was an elaborate, costly and motiveless demonstration prepared and rehearsed with consummate skill by six people, including a young child, for a single performance, in conditions of absolute secrecy that prevented either reward or recognition.'[160]

The two researchers then set down what they considered to be possible explanations of Price's 'Rosalie' experience. All are logical, intelligent and clear-headed deductions and are those that anyone who cares to make a careful and unbiased examination of Price's account would reach. In their book, Dingwall and Hall only consider there to be three options and combine nos. 2 and 3 below together. However, I feel the notion that Price knew more or less from the outset that there was fraud involved is enough to make this a separate explanation. They are as follows:

1. The séance did take place and 'Rosalie' was a genuine materialisation, the 'tremendous implications'[161] of which the two researchers were well aware.

2. Again the 'Rosalie' séance did actually take place 'somewhat as described by Price, although with less careful and elaborate precautions than Price recounted', but was fraudulent in nature. During his time at the house of Mr and Mrs X, Price was taken in by the performance but later realised he had been deceived. Despite this he took the opportunity to use his adventure as the basis for 'an excellent and sensational story.'[162]

3. As 2 above but Price realised during the course of the sitting that he was being conned (a scenario that the two researchers felt to be the more probable), but again he used the experience to his advantage during the course of writing his new book.

4. Price made up the story of 'Rosalie' in order to make one of the chapters of *Fifty Years* 'a highly sensational one'[163] to boost its sales and gain reviews in newspapers and periodicals of the day.

Where options 2 and 3 are concerned, the researchers consider that the séance may have been one in an ongoing series held for the benefit of Madame, possibly to the benefit in some way of Mr and Mrs X. The suggestion that Price's invitation may have been 'bravado or a wager that the show was good enough to deceive not only the gullible Mme Z but even a well-known psychical expert'[164], shows an interesting foresight of future events (see Chapter 14 and Appendix B). However, they clearly did not consider it to be an explanation worthy of serious consideration and examination.

Of all the logical explanations available and considered by them, the co-authors of *Four Modern Ghosts*, not surprisingly in view of their time spent rubbishing Price's work at Borley, felt that the last option listed above was the only one worthy of a detailed analysis. They devote the rest of their report to proving the theory, or *fact* as it was clear to them, that Price invented 'Rosalie' for his own ends. At the outset they make a short throwaway comment which in fact amounts to a highly inaccurate and misleading statement. As the basis for their accusations, they say that 'no evidence so far has been adduced to support the hypothesis that the séance occurred at all.'[165] Some of the material already presented in the present work (see Chapter 2) clearly demonstrates that this is inaccurate, and more will soon be made apparent.

As I consider Trevor Hall to be the prime mover behind not only the inclusion of the 'Rosalie' case in *Four Modern Ghosts*, but also the main voice behind the report's conclusions, it is worth looking briefly at the way much of his 'critical' psychical research was carried out. This can be done quite easily by quoting a passage from a lengthy review by Stephen Braude of one of his later books, *The Enigma of Daniel D. Home* (1984), which appeared in the SPR *Journal*. Regarding Hall's assessment of the famous Victorian medium, Braude writes:

Undoubtedly, Hall's book will seem impressive to those who are unfamiliar with the case of Home, and who will accordingly be dazzled by the apparent breadth and depth of his scholarship. What they won't know is that Hall completely ignores evidence tending to undermine his unfavorable appraisal of the case, and that his mastery of the material is confined largely to irrelevant detail. In fact, Hall's book is simply the latest in a long line of works about parapsychology in general and physical phenomena in particular, whose persuasiveness rests entirely on certain traditional questionable tactics. Hall's favorites, evidently, are: (a) to generate suspicion about Home's character in order to cast doubt on the genuineness of his phenomena, and (b) to focus only on the weakest cases, while ignoring those in which the evidence is strongest and in which consideration of Home's personality or character is clearly irrelevant.[166]

As will be seen, much of this way of working is relevant to the 'Rosalie' enquiry that Hall undertook thirty years earlier.

In order to come to the conclusion that 'Rosalie' was an invention, it is essential to prove that *no independent testimony exists to support Price's statements* in *Fifty Years* concerning the background of the circle and his invitation to attend a meeting. Also that Price *never went to such a meeting* and that the house itself is either a *wholly fictitious location*, or a real place which has *nothing to do* with the alleged story of 'Rosalie'. Reasonable evidence needs to be presented that satisfies all of these criteria if we are to dismiss the séance as a hoax. How then do the authors of *Four Modern Ghosts* achieve this? This can be answered by dividing the above criteria into two parts, as follows:

1. Independent Testimony Supporting Price's Account

Of the two sections that can be examined in connection with the case, this area is one which contains the most convincing arguments that 'Rosalie' was a bone fide investigation. However, it is the one that gets the least attention by Dingwall and Hall, to the detriment of the quality of their investigation. Quite clearly, as has been discussed earlier, the three people who were able to support Price's statements regarding the invitation to the 'Rosalie' circle, his taking part in the séance, and his state of mind immediately afterwards are, in order of importance, Richard Lambert, Kathleen Goldney and Ethel Beenham. At the time of the Dingwall and Hall enquiry, all were alive and available to be interviewed in connection with the case. This would seem an essential thing to do given their known associations with Price and his work. In order to make the facts fit their theory that 'Rosalie' was an invention, the authors of *Four Modern Ghosts* side-step the problems that these three witnesses potentially poised by ignoring Richard Lambert and Miss Beenham entirely. They then subject 'Mollie' Goldney's contributions to a superficially impressive discrediting exercise that was good enough for publication, but could not stand up to later enquiry.

As her association with Price effectively finished with the closure of his London office in 1939, Ethel English, as she was by then, was no longer a part of the contemporary psychical research scene, and her omission from Dingwall and Hall's enquiry did not cause her to make any comment until much later. As has been noted, she was a potentially impressive witness who was never called. Richard Lambert, however, was understandably perturbed that he had not been consulted, particularly as the negative conclusions that the two researchers reached were completely at odds with what he knew to have taken place in 1937.

Following a review of *Four Modern Ghosts* by veteran psychical researcher Hereward Carrington in the Parapsychology Foundation's *International Journal of Parapsychology*, Lambert immediately wrote to the Editor and his letter was subsequently published in the *Journal's* Spring 1960 issue. In order to 'dispel the harsh conclusion of Messrs. Dingwall and Hall in their book'[167], Lambert gave a concise account of his luncheon meeting with Price over which the psychical researcher told him of his earlier telephone conversation with Mrs X. 'In our conversation,' Lambert recalled, 'Price treated the invitation with some levity, but I urged him to take up the offer and prove or disprove its genuineness. He then said he would accept the invitation, if I would go along with him as an independent witness, as I had done on the occasion of some of his earlier investigations (e.g. the Talking Mongoose)'[168]. He also mentioned Price's telephone call on the morning of 16 December during which Lambert had the distinct impression of Price being 'completely flabbergasted' as he recounted his adventure of the previous evening, and made the following comment:

> I find it impossible, in the light of the above, to believe that Price had either "spun a wilful fantasy" [a quote from Carrington's review] or was dramatising the events of previous séances, for my benefit.[169]

Lambert reiterated his feelings on the matter six years later when asked to contribute a foreword to David Cohen's book on the 'Rosalie' case (see Chapter 12). Concerning the way that Dingwall and Hall approached the enquiry, Lambert wrote:

What is unforgivable is, that the authors of *Four Modern Ghosts* knew perfectly well that I was an available witness to Price's "Rosalie" experience, because I was referred to several times by Price in the "Rosalie" chapter of his *Fifty Years of Psychical Research*. But for some unknown reason, Dingwall and Hall made no attempt to contact me on the subject. Nor have they since commented on my letter to the *International Journal of Parapsychology*, or modified their fantastic accusations.

Until they do so, I shall continue to think that the sins of which they accuse Price are reflections of their own shortcomings as investigators.[170]

I couldn't agree more with Lambert's viewpoint. The fact that he had relocated to Toronto by the time Trevor Hall became interested in 'Rosalie' could in no way have proved an obstacle as his details could have been obtained easily from *Who's Who*, a publication that Hall himself often enjoyed informing correspondents he was listed in himself.

What is interesting to note is Lambert's own view on Harry Price, someone that he knew quite well and met regularly for a period of around twenty years. It shows that rather than accepting everything at face value, Richard Lambert was critical enough to assess Price's cases on their own merits and come to his own conclusions. In his letter to the Editor of the Parapsychology Foundation's *Journal*, Lambert wrote:

In my opinion Price, towards the end of his life, became disappointed with the negative fruits of his long series of psychical investigations. Secretly, he yearned to find something *positive* [Lambert's italics] which would justify his life-long expenditure of time and money. His sceptical zeal had by this time abated, but unfortunately his scientific judgement (never more than that of an intelligent amateur) had also correspondingly weakened.

In this frame of mind Price had his Rosalie and Borley experiences. The Rosalie experience completely baffled and frustrated him. It confronted him with a hopeless dilemma. Either he, the archsceptic, must admit he had been taken in by an obvious fraud; or he, the archsceptic, must eat the words he had spoken so often and emphatically in his career against "spiritism." Price was unwilling to do either, and therefore turned his back as soon as possible on the whole unpalatable episode and tried to forget it.

Borley marked a parallel stage in the same progress. Only here the phenomena admitted of a certain interpretation (however far-fetched), and this Price, in his failing days, tried to provide. I do not for a moment believe he was consciously dishonest, but rather that he fell victim to his own weakened judgment.[171]

In my opinion this view strengthens the case for Price's being truly shaken by his experience in the 'Rosalie' circle.

One person who could not be so easily dismissed as Richard Lambert, however, was 'Mollie' Goldney whom both men knew well. As an introduction to their attempt to deal with the problem that the presence of Harry Price's former associate presented, the researchers state: 'It will be obvious to the reader that one objection to the hypothesis that the Rosalie story was wholly or mainly fictitious rests on the testimony of Mrs. Goldney.'[172] Never a truer set of words was included throughout their entire book. It was essential, therefore, to present what appeared to be a watertight case for supposing that 'Mollie' Goldney had been successfully deceived by Price on the morning of 16 December 1937 into believing that he was reeling from an encounter, which he was unable to explain away in normal terms. To do this, the authors of *Four Modern Ghosts* turned to Price's controversial investigation of Rudi Schneider in London in 1932.

We have already seen what effect the ramifications of Price's 'exposure' of Rudi had on the organisation of his National Laboratory, but also more importantly in the way that Goldney reacted and her own stated reasons for doing as she did. The need to keep tabs on what Price was involved with in the psychic world (plus whatever personal feelings she may have had for him, given the allegations of Marianne Foyster and Richard Morris), were the reasons that she maintained a friendship. She also took on an administrative role when Price revived the Ghost Club at a meeting (at which she was present) on 10 February 1938, just under two months after the 'Rosalie' séance took place.

Not being privy to the real whys and wherefores of Mrs Goldney's continued association with Price, Dingwall and Hall were free to give their own interpretations. They cited the way that she had willingly discussed her meeting with Price with Paul Tabori, as well as her official capacity as part of Price's incarnation of the Ghost Club. In their view this showed that her opinion of Price 'had improved to the point where she was willing to be publicly associated with him, and therefore might not doubt the almost incredible story of the séance'. There was also 'reason to suppose, however, remarkable as it may seem, that, between 1933 and Price's death in 1948, Mrs. Goldney's faith in him was completely if temporarily restored.'[173]

Reinforcing their view they wrote:

> That Mrs. Goldney still believed him as late as 1949 seems to us to be demonstrated beyond reasonable doubt by the fact that she allowed Dr. Tabori to include her testimony (albeit anonymously) in his biography of Price, in which it was quoted as the principal confirmation of the truth of the Rosalie story. Price's account was so incredible on the face of it that one can only conclude (*a*) that Price's "drawn if not haggard" appearance and so on deeply impressed Mrs. Goldney and (*b*) that she had no doubts whatever in December 1937 regarding Price's absolute integrity and would accept the story he told her, however incredible, as true.[174]

This was enough to create the doubt needed to remove 'Mollie' Goldney from the equation and prove that no independent testimony existed to support 'Rosalie' as a real event. With his National Laboratory seemingly in ruins after the Schneider fiasco, Price found himself 'virtually alone'[175] in the psychical world, and created the fantastic story of the séance out of the necessity to boost the sales of his new book.

As with Richard Lambert, the publication of *Four Modern Ghosts* in 1958 provoked an outburst from Mrs Goldney who had no idea that she had been used to shoot down Price in such a way. Although she knew that Hall was, or had been, interested in the 'Rosalie' case, the book and its contents came as a complete and rather unpleasant surprise. She was also unaware that sections of her letter to Trevor Hall responding to his request in 1954 for a more detailed account of her meeting with Price on 16 December 1937 (material 'privately supplied by a colleague'[176]) had been lifted and quoted as part of their critique. The balloon went up when Maurice Barbanell – who had received a review copy of Dingwall and Hall's book – telephoned to ask her views on the 'Rosalie' séance. Goldney was furious and wrote a scathing letter to the Editor of the SPR *Journal* that took the two authors to task.

In her rebuttal she took exception to the 'gratuitous suppositions' regarding her views on the 'Rosalie' case which, she felt, were 'entirely misleading' in the way they had been reproduced and included without her knowledge. Describing Hall as a 'newcomer to psychical research' during the period of their Borley collaboration, she pulled both him and Eric Dingwall up over several points. It was not an accurate description to say she evidently accepted the story that Price had told her on the morning of 16 December, while the statement that she had no doubts at that time of his 'absolute integrity' and would accept whatever story he told her as true was '[a] gross distortion'. Her letter finished in the following way:

> If my experience at their hands is a fair sample of their methods of dealing with witnesses, one cannot but have doubts as to the value of any conclusions they may have reached.[177]

Strong words from someone who, only a short time before, was happy to support the same authors in their wholesale assault on Price's work at Borley. Her response to the 'Rosalie' report may well have been due in part to the later realisation that Hall had effectively overrun the Borley enquiry using much the same tactics, sparking what has been described (by Peter Underwood in *The Borley Rectory Companion*, p.176) as her later regret in associating with the project. However, correspondence in the SPR archive at Cambridge shows that the main reason for their falling out was due to a protracted row over Hall's expenses for a lecture, on the Borley case, to the Cambridge University Society for Psychical Research. This commenced at the end of January 1956, almost immediately after the 'Borley Report' was published, and resulted in the first of Hall's resignations from the Society at the end of the following month. He subsequently rejoined four years later but left permanently in 1962 following another row, this time in connection with the publication of *The Spiritualists*.

Back in 1958, Dingwall and Hall were unrepentant and, in a frosty reply, stated that where 'Rosalie' was concerned, her statements on the matter proved to them 'beyond reasonable doubt'[178] that she believed what Price had told her on a December morning twenty years before. Despite their resolute stance, there was more criticism to come.

2. A Wholly Fictitious Location

One aspect of the 'maddening' case of 'Rosalie', as writer Robert Aickman described it in the early 1950s[179], that has occupied the efforts of psychical researchers in later years has been the search to find the house of the mysterious Mr and Mrs X, both to prove and disprove Price's story. Much of this effort has been centred on Harry Price's youthful home of Brockley as being the actual location. 'That Brockley locality',[180] as David Cohen later described it, first enters the 'Rosalie' story in 1950 with the publication of Paul Tabori's *Harry Price – The Biography of a Ghost-hunter*. On two occasions during his presentation and commentary on the séance, Tabori states that the 'Rosalie' circle met at a house in Brockley, Kent[181] and that Price was so anxious to keep the location secret that he went to the extent of using a false initial when presenting his report in *Fifty Years*. This was obviously of great interest to Trevor Hall as in order to present Price's story as a fabrication it was essential to prove that the 'Rosalie' house existed only in Price's devious mind and nowhere else.

In the early part of 1954, Hall approached 'Mollie' Goldney (who knew Tabori) with the request that she contact him and ascertain exactly where he obtained the information concerning Brockley that appeared in his book. Goldney subsequently telephoned Tabori and established that the location came from reading correspondence held at the University of London. However, in hindsight, he felt that Bromley (also in Kent but also a London Borough) was in fact the correct location and Brockley was a mistake. As Hall at the time was living in Leeds, Goldney offered (graciously it would seem given the ultimate way her involvement with Hall at this time turned out) to visit the Senate House and look for the relevant papers on his behalf. This she did but was unable to locate any letter of the kind described by Paul Tabori, despite spending some time at the University library. As Price's archive contains in the region of 20,000 letters (2000 in connection with Rudi Schneider alone) and at that time was not catalogued in the comprehensive way it is today, perhaps this is not surprising. Despite this, Tabori felt he had seen the reference in 1949 when collecting material for his biography.

At this point, Hall's enquiry stalled for lack of new material and remained in limbo for seemingly about three years. During this period he undertook his role as Perrott Scholar at Cambridge and investigated the Selby/Ousedale poltergeist for the SPR. Finally, in the early part of 1957, Dr J.H.P. Pafford, the Goldsmiths' Librarian at the University of London, provided the necessary impetus which got Hall back on track. In Dingwall and Hall's own words, he 'found the correspondence which *proved positively* [my italics] that Price had revealed that the séance was at Brockley'[182] and made copies available for study. At this stage it was necessary to consult again with Paul Tabori as this new revelation went against his belief that Bromley was the true location. Tabori subsequently retracted his statement and, in a letter to Hall dated 22 February 1957, stated 'that he had no doubts about the location and that any previous mention of Bromley by him must have been a slip of the tongue.'[183]

The correspondence alluded to (but not quoted or published in *Four Modern Ghosts*) is an undated letter written to Price around the time that he was working on his Psychic Practitioners Bill by Clarice Richards who, along with 'Mollie' Goldney, attended the inaugural meeting of the revived Ghost Club in February 1938. It was subsequently published by David Cohen in 1965 and the relevant passage is as follows:

> Surely *these people at Brockley* [my italics] when they know the lengths you are going to stabilise this subject [i.e. fraud in the Spiritualist movement] will help you, especially if they are people of culture.[184]

At this point it should be mentioned that an additional letter does exist in the Price archive, which also contains a reference to Brockley in connection with the 'Rosalie' sitting. This was not discovered by either Dingwall and Hall, or later by David Cohen, and we will examine it and its relevance in a later part of the present work (see Chapter 13).

Another point that also needs to be addressed concerns Price's former secretary, Ethel English. As mentioned previously, she had been interviewed, as part of the Borley investigation in August 1949, by 'Mollie' Goldney and the two women had, and continued to enjoy, a close and friendly relationship between then and 1958. During the course of her testimony, Mrs English specifically mentioned the 'Rosalie' case and confirmed that, although she was unable to remember details, she had, to the best of her knowledge, typed correspondence between Price and the 'Rosalie' circle. Why the authors of *Four Modern Ghosts* omit to mention this is a matter of conjecture. If either of the two men knew of her statement then it was conveniently forgotten and was unlikely to be discovered by members of the public within the private archives of the SPR. A slightly more charitable explanation is that both Dingwall and Hall were unaware of the specific 'Rosalie' references in Mrs English's Borley testimony gathered by Mrs Goldney (none of which appeared in the completed 'Borley Report'), and, as the relationship between the authors in the period after its publication had become somewhat strained (Hall and Goldney were no longer on speaking terms), any potential dissemination of the information would have been difficult if not impossible.

The remaining part of the argument presented by Hall in *Four Modern Ghosts* – that 'Rosalie' was wholly fictitious – relies completely on the assumption that Brockley *was* the location where Price said the séance took place and that this is supported by a document held at the University of London. This was given a lengthy desk-top study supported by 'many hours'[185] of field work in an attempt to prove the complete fallacy of Price's account. Anyone reading the Dingwall and Hall report at the time (or today for that matter), whether they were a reviewer, a researcher or a layman, would have been impressed with the tenacity and effort that the authors evidently went to in the name of critical psychical research. However, as will be shown, the cornerstone of Hall's debunking account rests on decidedly unstable foundations.

In a typical lecturing manner, Hall described his approach as follows:

> It will be clear to the reader that if the locality in which the house was alleged to be situated could be discovered, a search could be prosecuted for a building displaying the features which Price described [in *Fifty Years*].[186]

In order to do this, and with Brockley his chosen location, Hall obtained twelve standard 1/1250 scale Ordnance Survey sheets and mounted them together to form two large-sized maps. They covered 'the whole of the area which could possibly, and even loosely be described as "Brockley"'[187] and included not only Brockley itself but also surrounding parts of New Cross, Deptford, Lewisham and Catford. Dividing the two maps up into three hundred 3 ¼" x 3 ¼" numbered squares, Hall studied each square in the hope of finding (or more correctly being unable to find) a house that matched the characteristics included by Price in his 'Rosalie' chapter, i.e. a large double-fronted house on the corner of the junction of a main road and a side road, and with a flight of steps up to the front door.

From this study, four houses were short-listed as being potential candidates due to their size and corner location. Two were discarded as not having double bay windows on the front elevation, and, of the remaining semi-finalists, only one house showed a flight of steps leading to the entrance. The winner was located in Wickham Road, Brockley, and, presumably with a sense of unease that his plans to rubbish Price yet again were potentially under threat, Hall sent Eric Dingwall (who lived nearer to London at Crowhurst and often visited the SPR's premises in Tavistock Square), to check whether the building matched the rest of Price's description[188]. No doubt to his relief, it didn't, prompting the confidence of the following statement in *Four Modern Ghosts*:

> It seems safe to say, therefore, that there appears to be no house in Brockley which complies with the description given by Price in *Fifty Years of Psychical Research*, and that this description must therefore be regarded as probably fictitious.[189]

It only remained to give a reason why the South London suburb had been chosen in which to place the fictional séance and for this Hall turned to Price's *Search For Truth* for an explanation. The simple facts that Price knew the area well in his younger days, attended the Manor Road spiritualist meetings (on Wednesday evenings as was the 'Rosalie' séance), and that his wife Constance lived in Brockley before their marriage, all suggested that, when looking for inspiration for his tall tale, he had simply drawn on his own youthful experiences.

However impressive this circumstantial evidence appeared to be, the killer blow was the fact that, while investigating local Spiritualist circles before the Great War, Price had attended an eventful gathering at a house in Wickham Road, Brockley, and had described it in some detail in his autobiography[190]. This was a séance that never was, as the medium, a local plumber who claimed to have the gift of clairvoyance, turned up drunk along with a companion also the worse for drink. A fight broke out between the two men before the sitting began and both ended up falling out of the front door and down the entrance steps into the garden, quickly followed by the medium's jacket and overcoat which were thrown after them. It seemed almost too great a coincidence that the investigation into the 'Rosalie' mystery should lead ultimately into the pages of Price's own life story.

The loose ends were quickly and easily tied up. It was a simple matter to describe as 'incredible recklessness'[191] the way that Mr and Mrs X went with Madame on their Continental motoring holiday at the end of August 1939, just as the might of the Wehrmacht was poised to invade Poland, conveniently removing her albeit anonymous presence from any future investigation. The silence of the other circle members – young 'Jim', Miss X, together with the 'trim parlour maid' and the cook – was also explained by their non-existence, despite the subsequent appeals for information after Price's death.

Despite the uncertainties of including the 'Rosalie' report as part of *Fifty Years* that we have clearly seen existed, Dingwall and Hall felt that Price 'may have begun to realize that only very credulous people would be likely to continue to believe him' if similar material was included in future books. The success of the publication of his first Borley monograph, *'The Most Haunted House in England'*, in the following year meant that there was no need in 'presenting small thrills like that of Rosalie' in future works. The time had come 'to disown her.'[192] Contemporary readers could then be forgiven for agreeing with this, Dingwall and Hall's final word on the 'Rosalie' case.

Writing of *Four Modern Ghosts* for the SPR *Journal*, F.J.M. Stratton was clearly dazzled by the breadth and depth of the scholarship on show when he stated:

> From two writers who were joint authors (with Mrs Goldney) of *The Haunting of Borley Rectory* one would expect a careful and critical study of any case they are reporting and that is what they have provided. The wholly negative verdict that they give in the case of "Harry Price and Rosalie" is what one would expect and to the writer it seems justified.[193]

Another positive review was supplied by Simeon Edmunds in *Light*. 'The meticulous care with which the significance of each piece of evidence is assessed,' he noted, 'and the way in which the facts are marshalled in the conclusions, deserve the highest praise, quite apart from the actual cases which are of considerable interest in themselves.'[194] *Psychic News* was, however, less reserved. The passion of its front page headline "Another Attack on Harry Price – S.P.R. members debunk famous 'Rosalie' case" (7 June 1958) was due in no small part to the fact that, as far as the current editorial department was concerned this, 'one of the most dramatic paranormal happenings of modern times', was the furthest ever the famous critic of Spiritualism had ever gone to accepting the tenets of the movement. 'It is ironic that over the Rosalie materialisation, on the one occasion when Price frankly admitted himself convinced,' was the sad conclusion, 'he should be now ridiculed by a former colleague [Eric Dingwall]. For it was in the same way that he himself ridiculed so many in his own lifetime.'

Never was Harry Price's reputation as a serious and credible psychical researcher at such a low point as the absolute nadir reached in the late 1950s following the double blows, first of the 'Borley Report' and, close on its heels, the rubbishing of 'Rosalie'. Help, though, was on the way; the cavalry was coming and, surprisingly, those who moved to defend Price's posthumous reputation emerged in the main from the ranks of the Society for Psychical Research itself. Robert Hastings, an SPR member from Cardiganshire, Wales, had been lobbying to undertake a re-examination of the way that the Society had audited Price's work at Borley almost from the day that the Dingwall, Goldney and Hall report had appeared. Peter Underwood, a former correspondent of Price, was soon to revive the Ghost Club, and, as part of his own wide-ranging career in psychical research, would begin his own reappraisal of Price's most famous case. While in Manchester, a steadfast, middle-aged, working-class amateur investigator was soon to become one of Harry Price's (and little 'Rosalie's') most ardent and passionate champions.

ELEVEN

THE GHOST HUNTER FROM MANCHESTER

———⟫●⟪———

The Manchester Psychical Research Society was a small paranormal group particularly active in the late 1950s and early 1960s. This was a time when ghost hunting was looked on in the UK as an interesting hobby carried out by an eccentric minority, rather than the full-scale entertainment industry that cable and satellite television has practically reduced it to in recent years. Under the Honorary Presidency of George A. Knowlson (B.A.) of Rishton, Bradford, a retired headmaster with an interest in the supernormal, the society met on Tuesday evenings at the Milton Hall in Deansgate, Manchester, for lectures and discussions on the many aspects of psychic phenomena and Spiritualism. The organisation's Investigation Officer and leading light was David Cohen of 71, Moss Bank, Crumpsall, a machine operator in his early fifties. By day Cohen stitched raincoats in a Manchester factory while evenings, weekends and holidays were given over almost exclusively to a determined and enthusiastic study of poltergeists, mediumship and hauntings.

Apart from the obvious connection with psychical research, David Cohen and Harry Price were very similar men. Both were from ordinary backgrounds, trying to make their way in a subject that, at the time, was dominated in the main by not only academics, but also professionals from a different social level. Both were self-taught in an exacting and difficult discipline. By saying, 'My difficulty is not acquiring the true facts but in being just an ordinary unqualified "working chap" getting these facts on paper'[195] when presenting the results of his 'Rosalie' investigation, Cohen reveals the same frustrations that Price also experienced with his contemporaries. Nor were they theorists or armchair ghost hunters. Both were men of action and, by nature, independent in their approach to paranormal investigation. Despite being members of the SPR (Cohen joined in 1957 and, like Price, kept the membership until his death), the two men were constrained by its orthodoxy. They needed their own platforms and the freedom they gave with which to carry on their work – Price with his National Laboratory, Cohen with his Manchester Society. Given that they had so much in common, perhaps it should be no surprise that the younger investigator would eventually be drawn to the senior researcher's most difficult and challenging case.

Despite the similarities and hands on approach that both showed to the investigation of physical mediumship, the one fundamental difference between Cohen and Price was that of interpretation with regard to its phenomena. Cohen quite clearly favoured a Spiritualistic approach and, in that respect, was a researcher in the mould of such mediumistic investigators from the past as Edwin Bowers (Frank Decker), Edward Cope Wood (Leonard Stott), Harry Edwards (Jack Webber and Arnold Clare) and Alan Crossley (Helen Duncan and Alec Harris). Nearer to our own times this list should also include Robin Foy (Scole) and Victor Zammit (David Thompson)[196]. When summing up his own qualifications as an investigator, David Cohen gave the following justifying statement as 'my standpoint regarding the Spiritualist hypothesis' as a way of showing an apparently objective scientific approach:

> Probably, I have been present (and often taken the chair) during more Spiritualists' meetings than any other psychical researcher, and I have ALWAYS [original emphasis] tried to be as impartial as humanly possible. Yet during my participation in 1,000 séances[197], and hundreds of public meetings, I have NEVER [original emphasis] received one single veridical message that I could honestly admit came from somebody I knew very closely that had "passed over". Still personal friends of mine have had entirely different results starting (like most of us) as complete sceptics.[198]

Although he claimed never to have had any personal proof of survival, an examination of his methods shows that, for Cohen, discarnate spirits and entities were behind practically all of the striking phenomena that he claimed to have experienced, and blackout séances and table-tipping were very much part of the tools of his trade. Cohen also sat in a development circle for several years and also professed to have some form of mediumistic ability himself.

Despite his own remarkable experiences, Harry Price never publically admitted any kind of belief in survival. He only ever considered mediums such as Stella Cranshaw and the Schneider brothers as having a dormant, but latently human faculty, that was in the process of being rediscovered by reorganising the outlook of established science. Ghosts, poltergeists and ectoplasm (if the latter in fact existed), did not equate to the existence of an etheric world populated by the spirits of the departed, and Price accepted nothing that he could not control completely in his own laboratory. His numerous encounters with fraudulent phenomena during the course of a long and high-profile career was the deciding factor, but the closest he ever came to changing this worldview was with 'Rosalie'.

As for David Cohen, if it was not for his work on the 'Rosalie' case with its posthumous and passionate defence of Price, it is true to say that, as a paranormal researcher, he would be all but forgotten. No doubt his premature death is a major factor in this but what is also clear is that, despite taking an active role as an investigator and having an interest in psychical matters from the early-1930s[199] onwards, Cohen never sought publicity for himself and much of his paranormal work was provincial in nature. Apart from a slim pamphlet, *Poltergeists and Hauntings are With Us Forever*, produced through the vanity publisher Regency Press in 1965, his similarly self-published book, *Price and his Spirit Child "Rosalie"*, issued the same year, was his single contribution to the psychical literature. Even this latter work was published reluctantly, as a protest at what he considered to be the then fashionable denigration of formerly respected researchers from the past, such as William Crookes and Price. If he had lived into the 1970s and even 1980s things may well have been different. With his eclectic mix of interests and investigations it is not too far-fetched to imagine Cohen enthusiastically tackling such controversial subjects as spoon bending and the Geller phenomenon, Electronic Voice Phenomena (EVP), together with 'orbs' and crop circles.

As a psychic investigator, Cohen found more than enough material with which to keep himself busy, both locally in Manchester and in towns across the north of England, where interesting cases seemed forever to be awaiting his attention. His preferred method of reporting his exploits was to present them as lectures to his Manchester society. As he never compiled or published any official reports of his investigations, other than the half dozen cases included in *Poltergeists and Hauntings are With Us Forever*[200], practically all of his records have been lost. Although not wishing to divert too far from the subject of 'Rosalie', I feel it is important to give some examples of David Cohen's investigation work, as they provide an interesting insight into his own particular style of contemporary psychical research.

The furthest afield Cohen travelled was to Bavaria on two occasions during the early 1960s. These were holiday investigations somewhat reminiscent of the psychic vacation that Charles Richet, Julien Ochorowicz, Frederick Myers and Oliver Lodge shared on the Ile Roubaud in 1894 with Eusapia Palladino. In September 1962, Cohen visited Konnersreuth to meet the controversial stigmatist Theresa Neumann who died within weeks of the researcher's visit. Disowned by the Catholic Church in 1938, Neumann, who was born in 1898, had begun to exhibit the wounds suffered by Christ on the cross in her late twenties. This was followed by a lengthy period of poor health that included blindness, paralysis and convulsions. For many years on a weekly basis, the Bavarian woman entered a trance-like state and blood flowed freely from her eyes, hands, feet, side and forehead. Neumann herself kept a constant fast which, for over three decades from 1927 onwards, consisted of only the daily Communion wafer. Konnersreuth became a pilgrimage site but the Catholic Church never fully endorsed her phenomena and, by the time that Cohen was able to see her, the miraculous effects had been in rapid decline for around five years. 'I believe I am the only psychical researcher who has actually witnessed the stigmata', Cohen later commented, 'although of course *not* [Cohen's emphasis] under Laboratory controls.'[201]

Sufficiently impressed, Cohen returned to Konnersreuth two years later. By this time the research into the 'Rosalie' mystery, that we will look at in detail in the next chapter, was virtually complete. During this second trip he managed to interview Father Naber, Neumann's parish priest, as well as two doctors who had known her closely for around thirty years. All that was left was to carry off a copy of the stigmatist's death certificate as a souvenir. It was as part of this vacation in May 1964 that Cohen tenaciously managed to track down and carry out tape-recorded interviews with surviving members of the Schneider family in Braunau. As well as Willi Schneider and three of his brothers, he also visited Weyer where he met Mitzi Schneider, Rudi's widow. Extracts from these encounters were subsequently translated and used by Anita Gregory as part of her extensive study, *The Strange Case of Rudi Schneider* (1985)[202].

Closer to home, another former Price case that Cohen encountered, this time pre-'Rosalie', was Gef the Talking Mongoose. During 1960, Cohen travelled to Cashen's Gap and, with a combination of luck and the doggedness that he later displayed when looking up the Schneiders, managed to meet and interview Voirrey Irving (1918-2005). At the time she was the only surviving member of the family that claimed to have shared their lonely farmhouse with a mysterious talking creature. Cohen later gave a lecture on his trip to the Isle of Man but, with typical restraint, resisted from publishing an account of his experience.

The year of the Cashen's Gap vacation also saw Cohen take on what was to be for him a controversial and personally taxing investigation. It was known, for a brief period, as the Salford Poltergeist and is included here in some detail as it gives a reasonably good idea of the type of person that David Cohen was, as well as a measure of his approach to paranormal investigation. There is also a slight connection with his later 'Rosalie' work. Although the newspaper account, that eventually appeared, cast Cohen in a somewhat unfavourable light, it does highlight his sincerity where psychical research was concerned. This was something that was noted by other people who knew and met him during the time that he was involved with the 'Rosalie' case.

By this time, as well as being the lead investigator for his Manchester group, Cohen was a relatively new but nonetheless enthusiastic member of the Society for Psychical Research. On their behalf he was asked to look into apparently inexplicable happenings at a small terraced house, number 24 Tully Street, in nearby Salford, Lancashire. For a period of three months beginning at Christmas time 1959, the Hill family – Jack Hill, a machinist in his forties, his wife Olive aged thirty-eight, and their twelve year-old grandson Alan – all reported a series of loud and disturbing noises, that included what appeared to be the bizarre sound of a bouncing ball, coming from the upper floor of the building. The sounds, which typically took place between 11.00 pm and 1.00 am, caused sleepless nights and the family eventually became so distressed that they requested help from various members of the local community. In chaotic scenes not far removed from the Runcorn case eight years previously, utility workers, local authority officials, priests and later psychical researchers visited the cramped house, attempting in various ways to discover the cause of the disturbances.

David Cohen visited Tully Street regularly for several weeks but, in his own words, 'this case became very complicated and most difficult, and so I reported to an official of the SPR, that I needed help.' What problems the investigator encountered is not clear, but it may have been a conflict with two local priests who came to the conclusion that a restless spirit was at the root of the trouble. Cohen, however, considered the disturbances to be a 'typical "poltergeist" case' with young Alan Hill as the nexus or focal point 'that with luck might well have been a modern classical one'[203]. During the night of 22-23 February 1960, the priests held an exorcism, which proved ineffective as the noises continued. At Cohen's request, the Society for Psychical Research contacted the Rev. W.H. Stevens, who had brought the Runcorn case to their attention in October 1952, but the minister was unwell and could not attend. Neither could the redoubtable Trevor Hall who was also approached but, due to severe weather conditions, was unable to make the car journey across the Pennines from Leeds. Left to his own devices, Cohen decided to fall back on his own organisation and, assisted by several members, continued to visit Tully Street in the hope of experiencing and capturing for posterity evidential phenomena.

As at Runcorn and much later Enfield, news of the disturbances began travelling further afield and a national paper, in this case the *Daily Express*, became interested in the story. Two journalists, Merrick Winn and Raymond Hawkey, together with a staff photographer, spent a total of three weeks at the Salford house taking in the events as they gradually unfolded to what became an unpleasant conclusion. With growing unease, the Fleet Street men watched scenes that today we would relate with a sense of familiarity as being disturbingly close to William Blatty's 1971 horror novel *The Exorcist*. In a trance-like state, Alan Hill crawled across his bedroom floor, obliviously dragging pieces of furniture behind him. Olive Hill, who claimed to have seen the boy floating near the ceiling, desperately held him down on the bed while cold water was splashed in his face, causing the child to explode into violent rage. Knocks and rapping sounds came from the upstairs bedroom in response to David Cohen's questioning as he and his fellow investigators called out from the living room below, while neighbours and visitors claimed to have seen footprints appearing by themselves in empty rooms and spoons flying about the house.

Around midnight on Sunday 6 March 1960, the Fleet Street men called for a doctor and Alan Hill was taken to hospital. A fortnight later, Winn published a photo article entitled '"Poltergeist" Exposed!'[204] which took several parties, and David Cohen in particular, to task for the dreadful state of the young boy's health. In hospital, Alan confessed to making the noises by banging on a loose floorboard between his bed and the wardrobe. This had been in response to the alphabetic tapping code that he had learned from the Manchester ghost hunters. For Winn, the young boy was a vulnerable and disturbed child who needed medical help, not exorcisms and wild tales about restless ghosts and unquiet spirits.

Although he acknowledged that the priests, together with Cohen and his team, were well meaning, their sincerity was dangerous, causing more harm than good in what amounted to a macabre atmosphere of 'neurotic excitement' boosted by the psychic investigator's Spiritualistic twaddle. Winn commented:

> I first met Mr David Cohen, the society's investigating officer, on the night of the exorcism service though he had already been interesting himself in the affair for some time. Mr Cohen, 45-year-old bachelor, is not typical of psychical researchers. The first step in a serious investigation would have been to make sure Alan could not make the noises himself. Mr Cohen did not take this step, nor did anyone else...
>
> Mr Cohen based his investigation on, for me, unbelievable beliefs which so far as I understood him went like this :- A "spirit" was using Alan as a medium to get messages to Mrs Freda Roberts (who lives next door). This "spirit" was "Teddy Roberts," Mrs Robert's father-in-law, who died four years ago, and Mr Cohen, in order to receive the messages, had "educated" it in a tapping code...
>
> "There's no danger," Mr Cohen assured me and everyone, "because the spirit entity will leave Alan alone once it has given its final message."...
>
> The "spirit" had already, during February, delivered some messages. It said Sheffield Wednesday would win the Cup.[205]

Despite being asked by a local doctor not to see Alan for a week in order for a medical examination to be held, Cohen had continued to visit Tully Street. Finally the Hills, on Winn's urging, asked him to leave the same evening as the school boy was taken to hospital. "I've had 20 years' experience and I should know more than the doctors" the researcher was reported as saying, although Winn stated this was not in the way of a boast, but the investigator's own personal belief.

When writing about his own qualifications as an investigator in his *Spirit Child* nearly four years later, Cohen made the following observation. Here he was most likely referring to Tully Street and the case of the Salford Poltergeist:

> *From bitter experience* [Cohen's italics] I know what it means to have my reputation smeared more than a little in the National Press after working at my own expense on cases that have involved months even years of personal participation.[206]

Cohen, furious at the way he had been portrayed in the *Express* article, had made written complaints to the Editor, the Press Council and his own M.P., but his protests came to nothing. Despite what he considered a 'gross misrepresentation' of his character and methods, he later came to reflect on the incident. '[I]f I was only the "armchair" type of researcher I should have got out once this reporter was in', he commented, adding 'It is my "cussedness" but I don't like cases half finished, *I like to suspend judgment and see them through to the bitter end* [Cohen's italics].'

An example of his willingness to spend considerable time and energy in pursuit of the supernormal is demonstrated in another case. This ran concurrently with the Tully Street investigation and came to prominence the following year. As with the Salford Poltergeist, it brought Cohen into contact with another working class family and likewise ended with newspaper headlines. However, what could be described as the incident of Nicholas the ghost is in truth one of David Cohen's most intriguing psychic adventures, and one which appears not to have a satisfactory explanation. Consequently it remains something of a mystery to this day.[207]

In the spring of 1959, Cohen had been asked to visit an unassuming house in the Fallowfield district of south Manchester. The owner, a recently widowed woman with a teenage son and a younger daughter, claimed the terraced house was haunted by the ghost of an old man named Nicholas who appeared to the young boy in his bedroom at night and (in what must be a first where the paranormal is concerned) played Ravel's *Bolero* for him on the youth's own violin. Over the course of several months the mother had heard the sound of music (always the same piece) coming from the adjacent bedroom. On every occasion when she had gotten out of bed and looked into his room, her son was apparently asleep with the violin closed away in its case. Distressed by what was happening, the woman had eventually tackled the teenager about the bizarre music and he had calmly explained the reason behind the nocturnal concerts. Relieved that she was not suffering a breakdown, but understandably disturbed and in the hope that the ghostly musician could be persuaded to leave, the lady contacted the Manchester Psychical Research Society and, not surprisingly, its Investigation Officer quickly swung into action.

As at Tully Street, Cohen and other members of the Manchester PRS began holding séances in the living room of the Fallowfield house in an attempt to establish contact with the ghostly Nicholas. These experiments continued regularly for a period of two years. By early 1961 the séances had progressed to the point that, during blackout phases of the séance meetings, a pair of hands apparently began to materialise and interact with the sitters. It is at this point that the case of Nicholas changes from a *Blithe Spirit*-type scenario into something far more interesting and demonstrates the seriousness that, despite his at times questionable approach, David Cohen could show with regard to his paranormal work.

Cohen approached Tony Fletcher, then on the staff of the Finger-print Bureau of the Greater Manchester Police. Fletcher, who later rose to become Detective Chief Inspector of the Bureau, recalled his encounter with the psychical investigator in his 1986 book, *Memories of Murder*. Quite simply, and no doubt mindful of the 'Margery' exposure in the 1930s, Cohen wished to recruit the services of a professional finger-print expert to attend one of the Fallowfield séances in order to take the prints of the materialised Nicholas. These would then be compared with the hands of all the sitters in the room. If either the mother or her son were playing tricks, then the test would quickly show who in fact the violin-playing spectre really was. On the other hand, literally, there was a hope that what would be produced was physical evidence of a genuine materialisation.

Unfortunately for Cohen, Fletcher declined to co-operate (a decision he later admitted he regretted) as he didn't believe in ghosts and felt becoming involved in the affair would make him appear foolish. However, a colleague Sergeant Rowland Mason, a well-respected member of the Bureau, was less sceptical and eventually agreed to take part, albeit in a private capacity. Mason visited the Fallowfield house, accompanied by David Cohen, and attended two séances which were held on Friday evenings. He quickly became mystified by his experiences. In the darkened room the table, around which the woman, her son, Cohen and the policeman were sitting, rose into the air and practically touched the ceiling. A tambourine marked with luminous paint began moving about the room, constantly changing its direction and travelling at such a speed that it seemed impossible that anyone present could be faking the effect. As the tambourine was levitated, the table itself shook violently and loud knocks sounded across its surface.

The highlight of the second sitting was the manifestation of what purported to be the hands of Nicholas himself which, in the blackness, touched Mason on the shoulders and arms. Although Cohen described them as being 'dry and scaly' with lace cuffs over the wrists, at the time Mason was only able to feel their touch and could not confirm the appearance.

At a third séance, the policeman decided to try to catch the ghost's finger-prints by surreptitiously dusting the tambourine prior to the sitting commencing. Alone in the living room he managed to wipe the instrument clean, dust it with mercury powder, and replace it on the sideboard without anyone apparently noticing. Soon after the séance commenced, Mason was shocked to suddenly have the duster with which he had wiped the edges of the tambourine and left lying on the sideboard, thrown into his face. A recording of Ravel's *Bolero* was played on a portable tape machine and, as before, there were knocks on the table and the tambourine flew wildly about the room. When the lights came on, Rowland quickly seized the tambourine and dusted it with finger-print powder. To his astonishment the instrument was as clean as he had left it at the beginning of the sitting. On a fourth visit, he openly dusted the tambourine before the commencement of the séance and again it was found to be clean at the end of the evening, despite having been seen to rise from the sideboard and circle the room. At this séance, Nicholas was asked by Cohen whether he would consent to having his finger-prints taken and, through a series of knocks on the table top, replied in the affirmative.

At the next sitting, Mason brought a chemically charged pad and sensitized paper to the house and placed it on the séance table in front of him. During the course of the sitting, he was able to catch hold of what appeared to be a dry human hand in the darkness and, with his own free hand guide it first to the finger-print pad and then to the specially prepared paper. Despite the blackout, the policeman was confident that he had managed to bring about what appeared to be the first professional finger-printing of a paranormal entity. The next morning, Mason brought the paper to the Bureau and showed it to his colleagues. Instead of finger-prints they were able to see a strange set of marks which resembled three parallel scratches each about one inch in length. 'They could have been made by a bird's claw; they could equally have been made by three finger nails scratching the paper' was how Tony Fletcher, who inspected the marks personally, later described them.[208]

The final stage of this unofficial Police investigation into the musical ghost was an attempt to capture a photograph of Nicholas using a camera loaded with infra-red film. For this an experienced Police photographer named John Cheetham agreed to visit Fallowfield. He attended a preliminary séance where he reported experiences similar to those of to Rowland Mason – the table knocked and levitated, the tambourine danced about the room, and Cheetham and his wife, who accompanied him, were touched on several occasions by what appeared to be two hands in the darkness. It was agreed that the following week, the photographer would set up a camera on a tripod aimed and focused at an armchair in a corner of the séance room and, during the course of the sitting, Nicholas would be invited to sit in the chair and the camera would be operated using a cable-release.

The sitting took place and, at the prescribed point in the proceedings, Cheetham took his infra-red photograph. The resulting print, which was developed at the Police laboratory the following morning in front of an expectant crowd of Scenes of Crime officers, showed only an empty chair with a large cushion resting against the back. Nicholas had failed to appear, or had he? Although a simulacrum is the most likely explanation, several of the policemen, including Tony Fletcher, thought that they could see the outline 'of a very old man, bearded and turned to the right, rather like the head of the old king on a coin' amongst the creases in the chair cushion. If the photographer had been able to take his infra-red picture while either the tambourine was in flight or Rowland Mason was finger-printing the 'spirit' hands, perhaps something far more interesting would have appeared.

At this point David Cohen's nemesis, in the form of reporters from the *Daily Mail*, got wind of the happenings and an article detailing the case of Nicholas the musical ghost, including the unofficial involvement of the Greater Manchester Police, was published in the newspaper. The presence of the policemen, despite the fact that no official police time had been used, came to the attention of the Chief Super-intendent of the Greater Manchester CID who effectively brought the investigation to an end. Whether Cohen and his team succeeded in 'laying' the ghost of Nicholas is unclear as the Manchester researcher was soon moving on to other things.

The above accounts give a reasonable idea of the measure of David Cohen and his particular style of paranormal research. Peter Under-wood, at the time an active paranormal investigator, met Cohen several times during the early 1960s. 'I judged him to be a sincere and honest man,' he later recalled, 'if somewhat credulous on occasions. He spent a long time playing tapes to me on one visit which he had obtained at a haunted house and which he believed recorded the voice of a polter-geist: indeed he believed he had "cracked the poltergeist code" and was able to converse with these curious entities ...'[209].

By 1962, the year following the Nicholas enquiry, Cohen began to shift his attention away from his home town and head further south, more specifically to London. It was here that he would garner what could be described as his fifteen minutes of fame in the strange sto-ry of 'Rosalie'.

TWELVE

THE COHEN INVESTIGATION

—————◆————————

A determined researcher but an unwilling author is a way of summing up David Cohen's role in the overall story of Harry Price
and 'Rosalie'. He himself admitted this as what started out as
a data gathering exercise for a potential lecture to his Manchester society gradually developed into a passionate attempt in print, not only
to support Harry Price, but also to bolster the posthumous reputations
of other notable psychical researchers from the past. 'Because of the
unscrupulous method of HP critics distorting his life's work,' he wrote
to Paul Tabori in the early winter of 1962, 'reluctantly I have decided
to publish a book about my investigation,' adding 'This is my first attempt ... and I feel sure as an experienced author you will understand
my point of view and difficulties.'[210] Leaving aside his brief *Poltergeists
and Hauntings* pamphlet, its outcome proved to be not only his sole
major contribution to the psychical literature but, ultimately, his last
major paranormal investigation.

Prior to working on 'Rosalie', Cohen admitted to having only a passing interest in Price and his world, although, as has been made clear,
later he came to realise that, as people, they both had much in common.
'I was indifferent to his prolific psychic investigations' was how he described his initial attitude, and qualified this by saying that he (Price)
'had always impressed me as a publicity seeker "exposer" of mediums,
and always ready to *push* [Cohen's italics] any of his psychic cases into

141

the press...' This was 'to obtain self adulation for the sake of publicity.'[211] He wasn't alone in this opinion. Price was the most high profile British 'psychist' both before and after World War II, the time that Cohen became not only interested in the contemporary psychical scene but also took his first fledgling steps as a researcher. His view was, no doubt, obtained by following the last phase of Price's paranormal career as it played itself out through radio broadcasts and newspaper features. His familiarity with the senior researcher's back catalogue from this period took place only at a much later date.

In the opening months of 1962, the forty-seven year-old Manchester investigator 'for no apparent reason'[212] as he described it, became interested in aspects of Price's earlier work. He obtained and read as many books he could find including the two Borley studies, the 1930 Rudi Schneider monograph, *Poltergeist Over England, Fifty Years*, as well as the Tabori biography. True to his Spiritualist leanings, Cohen alluded this interest to a sudden and mysterious compulsion to reacquaint himself with Price's cases, as though he were being guided to pick up the reins afresh. In a letter to Paul Tabori dated 26 May 1963, by which time his work on the 'Rosalie' case was substantially complete, he went as far as to liken this compulsion to 'some unknown "demon"' which had driven him to spend almost every spare moment working on the project. The truth of the matter is that his chance encounter with Voirrey Irving two years before had no doubt provided an initial stimulus. This was continued and strengthened later at a lecture meeting at the Milton Hall in Deansgate involving a demonstration of automatic drawing by a psychic artist. The widow, whose house was frequented by the violin-playing Nicholas, was given a portrait of a man, which, she claimed, was a good likeness of her father. He had been an Army officer who had supervised POWs, on the Isle of Man during World War I, one of whom had apparently helped Voirrey's father, James T. Irving, to construct the wooden panelling of the house on which Gef would later rap his messages.

For the Easter weekend of 20-22 April 1962, Cohen travelled to London on the trail of new psychic adventures. Beforehand he had read up on Price's 'Rosalie' encounter and an idea had formed in his mind that the subject of materialisation, and specifically the strange story of the spirit child, might make an interesting talk at one of the future gatherings of the Manchester Psychical Research Society. With limited time available it was not until the Whit-week holiday, beginning 11 June, that he was able to pursue the case more thoroughly; the specific

The revival of physical mediumship in the 1990s: Robin Foy (far left) and the Scole group take part in an experimental sitting for physical psychic phenomena (*Robin Foy*)

Price and his secretary Ethel Beenham demonstrate the séance room arrangement at Roland Gardens, South Kensington, in the early 1930s. (*University of London Library*)

A Ghost Club Dinner during the Harry Price era. Paul Tabori (1908-1974), subsequently Literary Executor to the Price Estate is sitting at the table in the right foreground looking at the speaker (*Paul Adams*)

The haunted house broadcast: Watched by his friend Alex Dribbell, Harry Price makes an historic live radio programme at Meopham, Kent, on 10 March 1936 (*The Times/Paul Adams*)

'The most haunted house in England': The main entrance to Borley Rectory, as Price's observers would have found it during the year long tenancy investigation of 1937-1938 (*Paul Adams*)

Dean Manor, Meopham, Kent: Price and BBC Director Seymour de Lotbiniere relax during the preparations for the first live outside broadcast from a haunted house (*University of London Library*)

Richard Lambert (right) with Voirrey and James Irving during the
Talking Mongoose adventure in 1935. Lambert was a close collaborator
with Harry Price both before and after the 'Rosalie' séance (*University of
London Library*)

Mrs. Mortimer.   15th December, 1937.

Dear Madam,

   I am taking advantage of your kind offer to
attend a sitting at your house, and propose being
with you on Wednesday next, the 15th inst., about
7 o'clock. If there is any difficulty about this,
I shall be grateful if you will kindly let me know
immediately.

   I am wondering whether you would be so kind as
to allow Mr. R. S. Lambert, the editor of The Listener
(a journal which I know is read by you) to accompany
me on Wednesday as a sort of witness.   He would conform
to all the conditions which you outlined to me last week,
and I would personally vouch for him.   If you can possibly
see your way to grant my request, will you kindly telephone
me or send me a telegram some time tomorrow (Tuesday)
morning in order that I can communicate with Mr. Lambert,
who would then make the necessary arrangements?

   Thanking you for your courtesy in this matter.
                     Yours faithfully,

The 'Mortimer letter': Long
hidden in Price's archives it
confirms his appointment
with the 'Rosalie' circle
in December 1937 (*Paul
Adams*)

Harry Price in action, sealing the window of a haunted house in Crawley in 1946. Similar precautions were taken during the 'Rosalie' séance nearly ten years before (*University of London Library*)

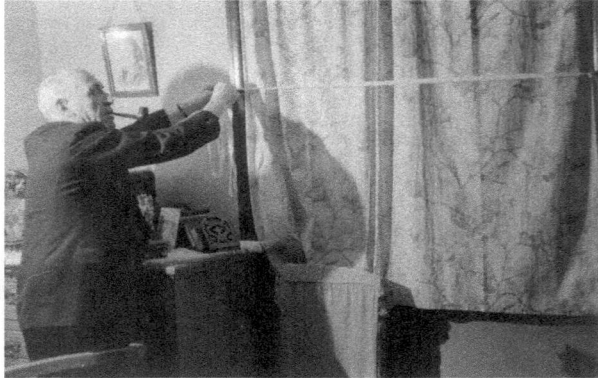

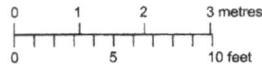

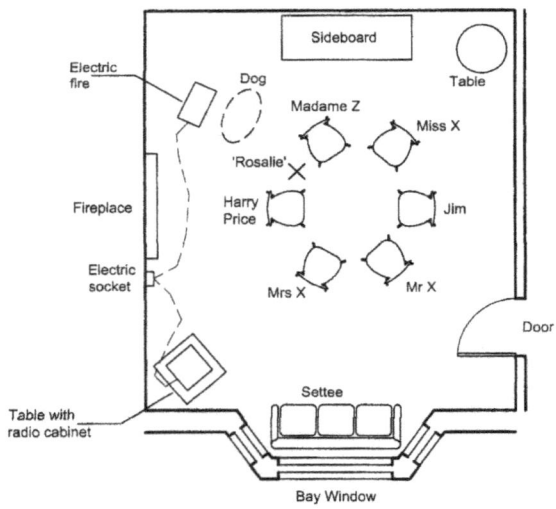

'Rosalie' Séance
Layout based on *Fifty Years*
Room size based on typical Victorian floor plan

The 'Rosalie' séance: A plan of the séance room based on the description and illustration in Price's *Fifty Years of Psychical Research* (*Paul Adams*)

146

The former Royal Societies Club building in St James's Street, Piccadilly, where Harry Price began writing his 'Rosalie' séance report in the early hours of 16 December 1937 (*Paul Adams*)

Kathleen ('Mollie') Goldney (1893-1992), photographed during a Ghost Club visit to Sherrington Manor, East Sussex, in the early 1960s. In the 1930s she assisted Harry Price with séances with Helen Duncan and visits to Borley Rectory (*Paul Adams*)

Fifty Years of Psychical Research, published in November 1939, the book in which the story of 'Rosalie' was presented to the general public (*Mark Davies and Laura Watson*)

The rare *Help Yourself* Christmas annual from 1946, in which Price described the final stages of his 'Rosalie' investigation (*Paul Adams*)

Eric J. Dingwall (1890-1986),
a former collaborator who
subsequently became one of
Harry Price's greatest critics
(*Mary Evans Picture Library*)

Trevor H. Hall (1910-1991), out
and about in the Borley district
during the SPR retrospective
investigation in the early 1950s.
(*Andrew Clarke*)

Peter Underwood (1923-2014),
former President of the Ghost
Club, photographed at Dent's the
publishers in the early 1960s, the time
that he assisted David Cohen with his
search for 'Rosalie' (*Paul Adams*)

Psychical researcher David
Cohen who researched the
'Rosalie' case in the 1960s. A
newspaper photograph taken
at the time of the Tully Street
investigation (*Paul Adams*)

The 'spirit' portrait produced through the mediumship of Richard Boursnell in 1908 and subsequently used by David Cohen as an illustration in his *Spirit Child* book in 1965 (*Paul Adams*)

21 Wickham Road, Brockley, South London, where the Medhurst and Barrington investigation culminated in 1965 (*Paul Adams*)

A modern view of Arun Bank, Price's former home at Pulborough, West Sussex, aspects of which were used to disguise the appearance of the séance house in the 'Rosalie' report (*Leighton Barrable*)

Richard Medhurst and Mary Rose Barrington during the time they were searching for the 'Rosalie' house in the mid-1960s (*Mary Rose Barrington*)

A page from the 'Rosalie letter' written to David Cohen in April 1966 (*Paul Adams*)

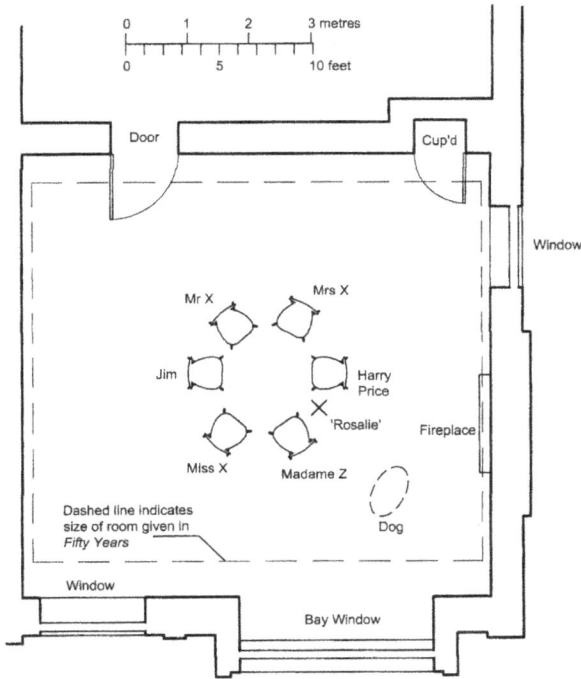

A layout plan of the First Floor room at 28 Cadogan Square, Kensington, showing its relationship to the proportions of the séance room from Price's Fifty Years (*Paul Adams*)

28 Cadogan Square, Kensington - First Floor Plan

28 Cadogan Square, Kensington, showing the corner location, entrance steps, bay windows and basement area retained by Price in his 'Rosalie' report (*Paul Adams*)

intention being to try to succeed where Dingwall and Hall had failed and track down the location of the 'Rosalie' circle. One can only admire the optimism that Cohen possessed with regard to the venture, which he described in the following terms:

> From the minute description of this house there was the possibility that I might trace the previous tenants Mr X and Mrs X or perhaps Miss X (if her parents were dead). Then there was the chance of finding out some information from, by chance, an old neighbour; at least to ascertain whether séances did take place at a similar house. Who knows by a stroke of luck I might find *somebody that claimed to have witnessed the "Rosalie" materialisation* [Cohen's italics].[213]

It was a tall order, but, even twenty-five years after the event, there was a slim chance of success and, unlike the researcher in the same predicament today, in 1962 several people who were connected in some way with 'Rosalie' were still around to provide information.

At this time, Cohen was understandably influenced by Paul Tabori's comments, together with the ruthless analysis of Dingwall and Hall, that the enigmatic séance '*must* [Cohen's italics] have taken place at Brockley'[214]. It was here that he made a concerted attempt to find a clue that would lead him to what is perhaps the most sought after residence in the history of psychical research. Despite enlisting the help of clerks from the Surveyor's department at the Town Hall to check local street maps, as well as making visits to several Spiritualist churches in the area, the researcher quickly drew a blank. At the Manor House Library in Lewisham it was suggested that two possible addresses, both in Brockley, might be potential candidates and Cohen set off to check them out. These were Breakspears Road and the nearby and now familiar Wickham Road, Harry Price's old mediumistic hunting ground and the end of the line for the Dingwall and Hall investigation of only a few years before. Walking the course Cohen passed by and noted what he took to be the double-fronted house with twelve steps up to the front door in Wickham Road where Trevor Hall had momentarily held his breath back in 1957; but this and several other journeys connected with the enquiry came to nothing. Disappointed, the researcher returned to Manchester and the mackintosh factory and it was not until the August Bank Holiday that he was able to devote a further week to paranormal study and return to the investigation again.

Looking at David Cohen's work on the 'Rosalie' case, it is clear that his optimistic and 'hands on' approach left no stone unturned and he was prepared to explore all avenues, no matter how unlikely, in the hope that they would lead to a solution of the mystery. On Monday 6 August 1962, he visited Pulborough in West Sussex in the hope that an interview with Price's widow, then still living in the house she and her husband had shared for forty years, might elucidate some vital clue: particularly 'as Mr. and Mrs. Price were childless, the amazing materialisation of a little girl might be the one thing that Price could have mentioned to his wife.'[215] He was to be disappointed as Constance Price, who died in 1976 at the age of ninety-four, was arguably the person who shared the ghost hunter's paranormal world the least. 'He was a clever man' she told Peter Underwood during a similar visit in 1967, but admitted that she had no interest in psychical research or her husband's energetic career in this field, and that, towards the end of his life, 'Harry had overworked himself.'[216] Despite finding his way to 'Arun Bank', a substantial two-storey building which still stands, Cohen soon realised that Price's widow would be of no help. An attempt to question the rector of St Mary's church, where Price had officiated as a sidesman for several years, proved similarly fruitless. After spending a short time discussing the Borley case with Mrs Royle, the rector's wife, Cohen admitted defeat but, still enthused about continuing with the case, returned to London.

The following day, Cohen spent the morning at the University of London where Alan Wesencraft (1912-2007) – who since the time that Dingwall and Hall were researching their *Four Modern Ghosts*, had taken over from John Pafford as the Goldsmiths' Librarian and Curator of the Harry Price Library – allowed relevant letters from Price's archive to be examined. Of particular interest was the letter from Clarice Richards, discussed above, which Dingwall and Hall had cited anonymously as being positive proof that Price had revealed the 'Rosalie' séance's having taken place at Brockley. This was part of correspondence in connection with Price's attempt to get his *Psychic Practioners (Regulation) Bill* through Parliament, a document which as we have seen was included with great prominence in the pages of *Fifty Years of Psychical Research* in 1939. Although, as he himself notes, this 'seemed a perfectly valid inference that Brockley was the locality in which the séance could have taken place'[217], the lack of any specific 'Rosalie' reference made him suspect its actual validity. By the time he wrote to Paul Tabori in November 1962, this suspicion had hardened into a crusade to rescue the reputation of Harry Price from the mud and the 'Brockley Letter', as he subsequently termed it, was a particularly vital document. '[I]n my defence of Price it is important that I should discredit the claim of Messrs Dingwall and Hall – namely that they regard the letter Mrs Richards wrote as *positive proof* [Cohen's italics] that the "Rosalie" séance did indeed take place in Brockley,' he wrote. 'As serious investigators and members of the S.P.R. they know that the standards of evidence must be almost irrefutable.'[218] In the hope that it might be possible to interview Mrs Richards herself in connection with the letter, Cohen subsequently spent the afternoon tracking down her address in Regents Park but again met with an impasse – Clarice Richards, a veteran of Price's Rudi Schneider and Borley investigations, had died on 7 April the previous year. The visit to the University of London was not entirely wasted as, apart from the Richards' letter, Wesencraft also provided access to other critical correspondence, from Richard Lambert and Frank Whitaker, already discussed in the present work.

Continuing with his psychic holiday, Wednesday 8 August saw Cohen travel to Twickenham to keep an appointment with Peter Underwood, then the relatively newly elected (1960) President and Chairman of the venerable Ghost Club. This club had been revived in 1954 following a lengthy hiatus created by the death of Harry Price. Although, as has been noted above, he was somewhat reserved about accepting some of Cohen's paranormal theories and interpretations, Underwood was a good ally and was able to provide introductions to persons likely to be of help. He was also interested in Cohen's work enough to offer to preserve his records and tape recordings in the Ghost Club archives when it became clear, at a later date, that Cohen was too ill to continue with his psychical work. During their meeting, Underwood telephoned 'Mollie' Goldney and she and Cohen subsequently arranged to meet later on in the week. The two men also spent time examining a collection of historic 'spirit' and séance room photographs published by F.W. Warwick in 1939[219], and, at this point, it is important to set down some facts about their time together as it had long lasting ramifications on later aspects of the 'Rosalie' case.

In his biography of Price, Richard Morris closes his dismissive account of the 'Rosalie' episode by saying that '[t]he single most important piece of evidence about the Rosalie ghost is the absurd picture Price produced to support the fact that she appeared during the sitting,' adding 'It shows a one-dimensional drawing of a small girl taken through a fish-eye lens, muffled against the cold, which was obviously clipped from a Christmas card or seasonal number of a long-forgotten maga-zine.'[220] This 'Rosalie' photograph, used by Cohen as the front dust-jack-et illustration of his *Price and his Spirit Child "Rosalie"*, has become closely connected with the story, but Harry Price never promoted it in any of his published writings on the case. Its association can be traced back specifically to the meeting between Peter Underwood and Da-vid Cohen in August 1962. Writing about the photograph in his book, Cohen states (p.131) 'It is a photograph of a child in a crystal. That is ALL [Cohen's emphasis] the information I had. Strange, long before I thought of "Rosalie" during my slide lectures, it was my favourite slide, usually kept to the last. Until, Mr. P. Underwood, rippling the pages of F.W. Warwick's book, stopped at page 277 and there was a picture of a child ... it was not "Rosalie" but looked like her.'

The photograph in question originates from James Coates' 1922 book *Photographing the Invisible*[221]. It is described by Lt-Colonel E.R. Johnson[222] as having been obtained in 1908 by the photographer, Hen-ry Blackwell, working with a medium, Robert Boursnell, and is no dif-ferent from the numerous 'spirit extra' portraits of the era created by the likes of William Hope and Mrs Ada Deane. As with the flat cut-out faces immersed in the ectoplasm of later mediums such as Eva C, its unconvincing nature is explained away by believers (both Spiritualists and convinced psychical researchers alike) who consider that, rather than the image of a real person, the 'extra' is in fact a memory picture (Schrenck-Notzing used the term 'ideoplasm'). This is projected by a discarnate spirit onto a photographic plate, or materialised in solid form, in an attempt to recreate its former appearance in life. Wheth-er one believes in this explanation or not, the fact is that Cohen's use of this particular portrait, both as front cover and frontispiece illus-trations in his book, has resulted in its being erroneously connected with Price's publicising of his 'Rosalie' experience. But although Price would have been familiar with Boursnell's mediumship, (he included slides of his 'spirit' pictures as part of illustrated lectures on Spiritual-ism and possessed a copy of Coates' book in his library), he never is-sued any photograph or illustration claiming it represented a part of his investigation[223].

In order to clarify Cohen's statement about his discovery of the pho-tograph (particularly as he gives the impression that he had a personal copy of it beforehand), I asked Peter Underwood what his recollections were of their meeting. The relevant parts of his response are as follows: 'My understanding is that Cohen got things a bit muddled,' he wrote on

11 July 2009. 'During the course of a visit to my home we talked about "spirit photography" and I asked him whether he had seen Warwick's book, *Experiments in Psychics*. He hadn't and, as we thumbed through it, we came across p.277 and "the" photograph. Immediately he said: "That is just how I imagine 'Rosalie' to have been. Can I borrow this and take a copy?" He did so, returned the book to me, and published the photo. To the best of my knowledge it had nothing whatsoever to do with Harry Price and I feel certain Cohen had never seen it before. That is certainly how he acted and why would he borrow the book if he had a slide of it?'

The following day (9 August), Cohen visited the offices of Longmans in the hope that the archives of Price's former publisher might contain some vital clue overlooked by previous researchers. By this time Ken Potter, who had commissioned Price's *Fifty Years* and had overseen it through to publication, was dead but one of the company directors who knew Price, and had visited Borley Rectory during the time of the 1937-38 tenancy, agreed to meet for lunch. Although Cohen only refers to him as Mr K, it seems likely that this person was Allen Drinkwater who enrolled as one of Price's observers and paid two visits to the rectory, the first with a group of friends on the night of 13-14 November 1937, and again on the 14th December. Unfortunately for Cohen, as with his earlier efforts, it was a trail that led nowhere, as the death of Ken Potter and the fact that Longmans' Paternoster Row offices had been destroyed in the Blitz meant that the records of Price's book, including all of the correspondence in connection with the 'Rosalie' chapter, had been obliterated.

Despite the lack of progress, Cohen was keen to put what was left of his psychic vacation to good use. His fifth and final day was spent at Hurlingham on the Thames where 'Mollie' Goldney, 'perhaps the best known woman psychical investigator in the world'[224], listened patiently as the Manchester ghost hunter played her his poltergeist tapes and plied her with questions about Price and his spirit child. Despite being dismissive of Cohen's recordings, she was able to confirm the truth of the events of the morning of 16 December 1937 as set down by Paul Tabori in his biography when, during her impromptu visit to his office Price, 'looking more haggard and perturbed than she had ever noticed him before, stuttered out the full account of this amazing alleged materialisation.'[225] Then in her mid-seventies, Goldney had long passed the point reached by many psychical investigators where the initial and all consuming drive to unlock the secrets of the paranormal has become tempered by both the passage of time and an inevitable lack of progress. Where the investigation of the séance room is concerned, the frauds and fakery of bogus psychics and mediums are a major factor. However, there is also an impasse unique to the field of psychical enquiry that the late Colin Wilson has called 'James' Law' (after the American psychologist William James), which suggests that, no matter how impressive, no paranormal phenomenon can ever be one hundred percent convincing. Cohen found her to be 'rather blasé, ultra-critical,' and, as he notes, 'only willing to accept evidence that has to be of such a high standard, that I doubt whether anybody would be able to satisfy her that any part of an investigation is supernormal.'[226] In reality, Goldney had already experienced what she herself later described as being the peak of her personal experience of the paranormal: the mediumship of Rudi Schneider, something that thirty years after the fact and at the time of her meeting with David Cohen she would have been well aware of[227].

As well as the initial aftermath of the 'Rosalie' séance itself, Mrs Goldney was also of interest to an area of Cohen's enquiry that assumed significant importance once permission had been granted by Paul Tabori for the copying of Price's correspondence, viewed earlier in the week at the University of London. This concerned the letter from Clarice Richards to Price, cited by Eric Dingwall and Trevor Hall in their *Four Modern Ghosts*. Due to their involvement with Price's series of sittings with Rudi Schneider in 1932, as well as the administration and running of his later revival of the Ghost Club, 'Mollie' Goldney and Mrs Richards knew each other well. Both kept in touch and were on friendly terms with Price right up until his death. 'When I interviewed Mrs Goldney, who was as you know a very close friend of Clarice Richards (and in fact met almost daily), she told me that this letter could not refer to the "Rosalie" case whatever,' Cohen wrote to Tabori on 11 November 1962. 'Her friendship with Mrs Richards, at the time until her death, was so close and, of course, they must have discussed the Rosalie case many times; if the "Brockley" locality was known by Mrs Richards' he reasoned, 'she would almost certainly have informed Mrs Goldney.' The missive became a particular touchstone that Cohen made numerous references to in his correspondence with Tabori, and later in his published book, as his campaign to clear Price of the *Four Modern Ghosts* accusations gathered pace. 'That letter by Mrs Richards, Messrs Dingwall and Hall [used] WITHOUT [Cohen's emphasis] any attempt of confirmation,' he grumbled to Tabori on 26 May 1963, ' ... is only another example of their incompetence and prejudice.'

Cohen was not in fact the first person who had made this particular discovery. In 1958, shortly after the publication of *Four Modern Ghosts*, Robert Hastings had visited the Goldsmiths' Library at the University of London and, with the permission of John Pafford, had examined the letter for himself. Today Hastings is mostly known for his lengthy critique of the SPR's 'Borley Report', published in the Society's *Proceedings* (Vol.55, Pt 201) in March 1969. His other main contribution to the psychical literature is a reappraisal of the famous Dieppe Raid case, which appeared in the SPR *Journal* the same year[228]. Like Cohen, Hastings felt that much of the post-war criticism of Harry Price had got out of hand and was particularly vocal in his attempts to force the SPR to publish an alternative viewpoint. In 1958, he wrote to George Fisk, then Editor of the Society's *Journal*, calling attention to the fact that he had been 'astonished to see' that the letter copied for Dingwall and Hall 'did not specifically mention the "Rosalie" case', and that the reference 'to "people at Brockley" might mean anything at all.'[229] Fisk declined to publish Hasting's letter but suggested along with Professor Broad (see also Chapter 13), the current SPR President, that it should be sent to Eric Dingwall privately for his comments – Trevor Hall having previously refused to enter into correspondence on the matter. Dingwall did not respond, but, on the occasion of the Society's AGM on 24 March 1962, around the same time that David Cohen began taking an active interest in Price and 'Rosalie', he admitted to a number of people present that the letter referred to in *Four Modern Ghosts* did not prove Price had visited Brockley in December 1937, and was quoted by Hastings subsequently as saying at the time, "I told Trevor he was claiming too much, but it is too late to do anything about it now."[230] At Hastings' request, Mrs Goldney had telephoned Clarice Richards on 25 September 1958 and asked her whether she could recall writing to Price about 'Rosalie' and also whether he had discussed the case with her. Not surprisingly, given the passage of time and the fact that by then she was partly bed-ridden and very unwell, Mrs Richards could not remember any specific correspondence and could only reiterate what Price had published: that the sitting took place somewhere in the South London area. 'What she DOES [original emphasis] remember,' Mrs Goldney reported to Robert Hastings later the same day (in a typed note now in the SPR archive) 'is meeting Harry Price next day or very soon after, and that he was almost trembling with excitement as he told her about it.' She also claimed she had spoken with Ethel Beenham at the same time and that his secretary 'said she had never known HP so queer over a case before.'

Sadly for David Cohen he was unable to hear this first-hand testimony for himself. At the end of the week the ghost hunter packed up his tape recorder and notebook and headed back to Manchester. His psychical vacation was over but it had planted seeds, which were ultimately to take nearly two years before coming to fruition. The result, published at his own expense in the autumn of 1965, was *Price and his Spirit Child "Rosalie"*, now a rare and little known volume of some 150 pages, copies of which can today command a price of over £100 to collectors. It is a book very much of its time as shown by the wording of the dedication given by the author. 'To those pioneers of Psychical Science,' Cohen proudly stated, ' – Sir William Crookes, Von Schrenck Notzing, F.W.H. Myers, and Harry Price to name a few who have given their ALL [Cohen's emphasis] for the CAUSE [Cohen's emphasis] they so fervently believed in and have now ALL [Cohen's emphasis] been denigrated for their contributions to the supernormal by their lesser fellow-researchers.' Although the last to be mentioned, the first scalp claimed in this modern witch-hunt had been that of Harry Price himself, nailed to the totem pole by the publication of *The Haunting of Borley Rectory* in early 1956, and in the heady atmosphere of this post-'Borley Report' era, one of its principal authors, the redoubtable Trevor Hall, was able almost singlehandedly to instigate a campaign to which other sceptical authors also felt obliged in varying degrees to lend their support.

In May 1960, medium Eileen Garrett, the President of the Parapsychology Foundation in New York, invited Hall to undertake a funded examination of the work of the late Sir William Crookes (1832-1919). This was specifically in connection with his famous series of séances with the young Florence Cook (1856-1904) whose mediumship has been described (by Hall) as 'one of the cornerstones of the [Spiritualist] faith.'[231] Hall's subsequent report, published as *The Spiritualists* by Gerald Duckworth in the summer of 1962, delivered a powerful blow to both Spiritualists and psychical researchers alike. It concluded that Florrie Cook and the distinguished chemist Crookes, President of the SPR from 1896 to 1899, were lovers and had used Crookes' séance experiments as a cover for their affair. Not content to rest on his laurels, Hall followed this up two years later with *The Strange Case of Edmund Gurney* (1964), described in a review by Alan Gauld as 'a platform for what is probably the fiercest attack ever launched upon the competence, and even the honesty, of the early leaders of the S.P.R.'[232] Hall's principal argument was that Gurney (1847-1888), co-author with F.W.H.

Myers and Frank Podmore of the highly regarded *Phantasms of the Living* from 1886, had committed suicide on discovering that he had been tricked by two bogus psychics after publishing seemingly positive results of telepathy experiments in the pages of the SPR *Proceedings*. Gurney had been found dead of chloroform poisoning in somewhat mysterious circumstances in a hotel room in Brighton, leading Hall to speculate at some length that Frederick Myers, together with his brother Arthur, had conspired together to cover up the scandal. One of the founders of the SPR in 1882, Myers was also the subject of another alleged scandal, again involving suicide when, in the same year that Hall published his accusations, Archie Jarman, an author and humorist with a passing interest in psychical matters, reviewed Myer's autobiography, *Fragments of Inner Life* for the *Tomorrow* journal[233]. The work had lain unpublished for many years before being issued posthumously by the SPR in 1961. Here Jarman suggested that Myers drove the wife of his cousin, Walter James Marshall, to take her own life after deserting her once she had become pregnant by him following an affair.

Appalled by what he described as 'this most disgusting form of denigration'[234] being heaped upon the reputations of such highly regarded and influential figures now unable to counter the accusations, David Cohen was one of several contemporary psychical researchers who took it upon themselves to challenge in print this onslaught of scepticism and ridicule. Mention has already been made of Robert Hastings, whose rebuttals of the criticisms against Harry Price were to encounter much political intrigue and setbacks within the echelons of the SPR before eventually being published by the Society in 1969. As has been noted above, in March 1964, 'Mollie' Goldney and Richard Medhurst issued a lengthy paper in the SPR *Proceedings*, "William Crookes and the Physical Phenomena of Mediumship", now regarded as one of the most important historical studies of Victorian Spiritualism. The authors challenged many of the accusations levelled by Hall in *The Spiritualists*[235]; while Alan Gauld followed up his critical review of Hall's *Edmund Gurney* with a full-length study of the discipline's early heroes in his *The Founders of Psychical Research*, published by Routledge & Kegan Paul in 1968. Another high profile contemporary researcher, Nandor Fodor, had already castigated the authors of the 'Borley Report' in the pages of *Tomorrow*, much earlier in 1956, for their attack on Price and his posthumous reputation. Now in the year before his own sudden death (from a heart attack on 17 May 1964), he returned to the fold in the pages of *Fate* magazine (Vol.9, No.3, March 1963), likening

Hall to 'a ghoul preying on the exhumed cadaver of Crookes, resuscitating gutter evidence based on gossip and hearsay'[236]. Fodor ultimately made substantial contributions to the psychical literature, but Cohen speculated that his posthumous reputation would also suffer. However, his descent into relative obscurity in the years following his death, was, as Colin Wilson has noted (*Poltergeist!*, 1981, p.296), due to his modest personality and conscious lack of self-promotion, rather than any deficiencies in his writings or investigations.

The writing of *Spirit Child* occupied Cohen for much of the year following his visits to London, but, on Christmas Day 1963, he was able to draft the acknowledgements on his completed manuscript and mention several of the people who had contributed and assisted with the difficult task he had now completed. One of those persons was Richard Lambert whose first-hand experiences of the case were of vital importance. Lambert had left the BBC and the country for a solo career in Canadian broadcasting on 31 March 1939, picking up a generous £1000 gratuity from his former employer and a lunch with Harry Price on the same day. As well as his collaboration with Price on Gef the Mongoose, Lambert had written a number of books of biography and true crime in the 1930s. In the ensuing years he followed these up with other titles including *Exploring the Supernatural*, an account of Canada's native ghost-lore issued by Arthur Barker in 1955. Once contacted, Lambert had supported, wholeheartedly, Cohen's efforts. In a lengthy foreword he described the book as serving 'a warning to the public not to accept uncritically the "debunking" studies' issued in recent years concerning Price and his work, as well as helping 'to speed the process of cleansing psychical research from muck-raking and personal vendettas.'[237]

The reformed Ghost Club had also played a part in Cohen's *Spirit Child* project. On Monday 7 October 1963, at the invitation of Peter Underwood, Cohen had addressed the Club at one of their regular London meetings at The Mayfaria Rooms in Bryanston Street, W1. There he presented his views and recent work under the title "New Light on the 'Rosalie' Case". To Cohen's delight, in the Chair that evening was Paul Tabori with whom he had carried out a lengthy correspondence over the preceding months but, until this point, had not met in person. Also present in the audience was 'Mollie' Goldney who, as reported by Anne Dooley for the *Psychic News* in the edition of 19 October 1963 ("Materialised Rosalie leads to row among researchers", p.5), at one point stood up and confirmed both her meeting with Price on the morning after the 'Rosalie' séance and his agitated demeanour at the time.

Two years were to pass, following the Ghost Club address, before the eventual publication of Cohen's book. During this time Cohen had moved onto other projects, including another psychic vacation, this time to Germany to carry out his reappraisal of Theresa Neumann. Although clearly a gallant effort to turn the tide of derision against Price and his work, the raw passion of Cohen's defence was to prove ultimately his own undoing. By devoting large sections to other areas, primarily a critique on the motives behind Trevor Hall's *The Spiritualists*, the focus on the case at hand was lost to the detriment of the investigation. This emotional approach was not lost on Mostyn Gilbert who reviewed *Spirit Child* for *Psychic News* ("What price Harry Price?: New book comes to defence of famous researcher) on 9 October 1965. 'David Cohen, in his book on Price, has done his duty as he sees it,' he noted, 'But he has weakened his case by injecting extraneous matter in a highly emotional manner,..'. Despite starting well, the author's 'attempts at a careful presentation of his inquiries are lost with the boiling of his blood.' Gilbert himself could come to no firm personal conclusion regarding the 'Rosalie' case itself, other than the fact that he felt Price was wrong to publish what was in effect an incomplete enquiry, The 'near-hysteria' of Cohen's defence was however unwarranted. 'I don't think Price needs such an emotional plea,' he concluded, preferring the objective and level tone of Richard Lambert's opening contribution.

For Cohen the prime mover behind the wholesale attacks on Price, not only with regard to 'Rosalie' but also Borley Rectory and beyond, was Eric Dingwall. It also seems likely that Trevor Hall's lack of support, at the time of Tully Street and its (for Cohen at least) painful aftermath, made the desire to cut the co-author of *Four Modern Ghosts* down to size all that more stronger. 'Dr Dingwall was certainly Price's most determined opponent and therefore would be prejudiced against him,' he wrote in a letter to Paul Tabori on 2 March 1963, following this up after much work on 26 May with the comment that, '[t]he results of my findings will furnish (impartial researchers at least) revelations of the machinations primarily by Dr Dingwall against the integrity of Price.' Due no doubt to the threat of a possible libel action, Cohen was unable to put into print views he was happy to circulate in private. But the passion that he clearly felt about wishing to clear Price's name is evident in his appeal and generous offer of a reward of £25 (over £400 today) to anyone passing on new information that would lead to the identification of Mr and Mrs X, or any other participants, who may have witnessed the materialisation of 'Rosalie' during the time of Price's investigation.

In fact, when stripped of all its extraneous material – Cohen's views on the reality of ectoplasm and materialisation, Hall's *The Spiritualists*, 'spirit' photography, psychological aspects of psychical research, together with his own personal investigations – *Spirit Child* only improves on the account in Tabori's earlier biography by including the views and recollections of Richard Lambert together with the reproduction *in extenso* of several of the letters from the Goldsmiths' Library. This comprises correspondence from Lambert himself, Price, Frank Whitaker and Clarice Richards. Crucially, Cohen did not locate, during his visit to the University of London, the 'Mortimer letter' described previously, the discovery and publication of which (as will be noted in the following chapter) would have added considerable weight and importance to his investigation.

Despite its deficiencies, the efforts of David Cohen, in the cold winter months of 1963, together with *Spirit Child's* eventual publication, were ultimately to prove of tremendous importance to the case as a whole. They were quite simply the catalyst for greater things to come.

THIRTEEN

CRUISING THE STREETS – MEDHURST AND BARRINGTON

※

In 1971, the world of organised psychical research in Britain suffered the loss of two important figures. On 11 March of that year, the distinguished philosopher Charlie Dunbar Broad died peacefully at the age of eighty-three at Trinity College, Cambridge, in rooms which had once been occupied by Isaac Newton. A former Knightbridge Professor of Moral Philosophy, Broad had been interested in paranormal research since 1906, and his distinguished career as an international writer, thinker and lecturer had given the discipline of psychical enquiry – as the American parapsychologists Arthur and Joyce Berger have suggested (*The Encyclopedia of Parapsychology & Psychical Research*, 1991, p.49) – a certain weight and respectability. Broad held the SPR Presidency twice during his lifetime, published papers on the mediums Gladys Osborne Leonard and Winifred Coombe-Tenant (Mrs Willet), and established what he termed 'Basic Limiting Principles' against which events that are ostensibly paranormal can be compared.

Although Broad was in full possession of his faculties right up until the end, his contributions to psychical enquiry as a whole were essentially known and complete. The death, therefore, just over a month before, of Richard George Medhurst on 26 January 1971 at the age of fifty was a particular tragedy as Medhurst was a researcher, then at the height of his powers, who had already contributed enormously to the post-war psychical scene and still had much to give to the subject. Benson Herbert (1912-1991), a fellow researcher who knew Medhurst well, described his demise (following a protracted struggle against a malignant brain tumour) as having deprived psychical research 'of one of its ablest and most brilliant protagonists'[238], a sentiment that was echoed by many other colleagues at the time. A gifted mathematician, Medhurst graduated from Queen Mary College, London, in 1942 and subsequently worked for nearly thirty years at the GEC Hirst Research Centre in North Wembley. There he was twice awarded the Heaviside Premium of the Institute of Electrical Engineers for the best mathematical paper of the year. Achieving international distinction for his contributions to aerials theory and distortion problems in communications, a Doctorate in recognition of his work was awarded by the University of London in December 1970 only a month before his death.

Medhurst's interest in psychical matters was stimulated by assisting with telepathy experiments organised by fellow mathematician Samuel Soal (1889-1975)[239], whose lectures he attended during the Queen Mary College's wartime residency at Cambridge. There was also a personal curiosity with mediumship and the phenomena of the Spiritualist movement. These two factors – the experimental and the Spiritualistic – were to shape the course of his involvement in psychical research during the 1950s and 1960s when he was able, despite his demanding full-time career, to devote enormous amounts of time and energy to the subject. Like David Cohen, Medhurst felt the need to explore the phenomena of the séance room, attending weekly home circles over the course of many years. These began shortly after the end of World War II in a basement flat in Chelsea, and extended right up until the onset of his illness in 1969. Like his contemporary Kenneth Batcheldor (1921-1988), who began a lengthy series of séance experiments in the mid-1960s, Medhurst eschewed the use of professional mediums and, with a small circle of friends, appeared to experience much remarkable and, at times, startling phenomena. These included raps and other noises, the movement of objects, as well as table levitations and trance communications. Medhurst himself described some brief aspects of these sittings in a posthumously published interview with Paul Tabori in 1971[240]. A more detailed account was included by Benson Herbert (who attended many of these post-war séances) in an obituary issued in the *Parapsychology Review* the following year.

As well as physical mediumship, Medhurst carried out hypnosis and ESP experiments for the SPR (for whom he undertook much Committee work), and also acted as a consultant for several television programmes including BBC's *Horizon* in 1967 and the ITV series *Margins of the Mind* in 1968. Both of these were involved with the subject of telepathy. He was also (along with several others including Peter Underwood, Brigadier F.C. Spedding and Arthur Ellison) a panel member of an ultimately unrealised prize of £25,000, offered by *Penthouse* magazine and endorsed by the Ghost Club, to be awarded for the demonstration of a paranormal phenomenon under reasonable test conditions. Medhurst's personal admiration for the work of Sir William Crookes led to the noted collaboration with 'Mollie' Goldney, already described, while a long held project to issue a collected edition of Crookes' psychical writings was only interrupted by his death. The posthumously published *Crookes and the Spirit World* (Souvenir Press, London, 1972) is dedicated to his memory. Described by a colleague as *a man who never did things by half measures and was not content with near accuracy,* it is perhaps not surprising that, when confronted with such a tantalising puzzle as that of the 'Rosalie' case, Richard Medhurst would tackle the task in hand with all his customary energy and exactness.

Although his close association with 'Mollie' Goldney, (who, as we have seen, attended David Cohen's Ghost Club talk during the writing of their Crookes/Cook paper in 1963), may well have aroused some interest in Price and his spirit child mystery, it seems likely that his active involvement with the case began towards the end of the following year, when a flurry of 'Rosalie'-related correspondence appeared in the December issue of the SPR *Journal.* Instigated by Robert Hastings' criticisms in the previous issue of the handling of evidence by Dingwall and Hall in *Four Modern Ghosts*, Richard Sheargold, Peter Underwood and James Robertson Justice wrote giving their own mostly supportive views on the matter. Also included was a lengthy letter from David Cohen who disclosed that his book on 'Rosalie' was now complete and ready for publication. Cohen also confessed that the process had forced him to alter his own previously critical views on Harry Price. 'I was indoctrinated by the allegations made posthumously against Price, accusing him of charlatanism. I believed them to be true,' he stated. 'Since then, like Mr Hastings, after personal investigation, I have found little or no substance in these accusations.'[241] There the matter appeared to rest but, while the ghost hunter from Manchester continued valiantly to get his magnum opus into print, a small group of SPR members led by Richard Medhurst began to make their own private enquiry. The results of their endeavours were included in the *Journal's* December 1965 issue two months after the publication of Cohen's book.

Like Cohen, Medhurst felt it was imperative to go back as much as possible to original sources as the basis for his examination of the 'Rosalie' case. Following in the Manchester researcher's footsteps, he made arrangements with Alan Wesencraft to view Price's papers at the Goldsmiths' Library in London. Almost immediately he made an important discovery, namely the carbon copy of the 'Mortimer letter' written by Price to Mrs X on 13 December 1937, which had been over-looked by David Cohen over two years before, as well as by Dingwall, Hall and Mrs Goldney much earlier in the mid-1950s[242]. As has been mentioned, the somewhat chaotic state of Price's archive at this time no doubt hindered the efforts of previous investigators, at least where Cohen and 'Mollie' Goldney are concerned, the latter it will be remembered having searched the archive on Dingwall and Hall's behalf. Its late discovery, bearing in mind that Price's material had by then been held at the Senate House for over fifteen years, shows that neither Wesencraft nor his predecessor John Pafford were aware of its existence. By the end of the 1950s, a strained relationship existed between the Goldsmiths' Library and Trevor Hall, brought about by Hall's controversial possession of the famous 'Locked Book' of Borley Rectory[243]. With this being the case it seems likely that, had he known about the 'Mortimer letter', John Pafford (who eventually retired from the University Library in August 1967) would, after the publication of *Four Modern Ghosts*, have made its existence known, contradicting as it does (along with the testimony of Richard Lambert) the entire Dingwall and Hall case against Price and 'Rosalie'. As Alan Wesencraft had only recently taken up the position his ignorance is understandable bearing in mind the enormous amount of material that he had so recently inherited.

'With such a clue,' Medhurst later wrote, '[discovering] the location of the "Rosalie" sitters seemed only a matter of time.'[244] There was clearly some justification for his optimism. Now at last researchers had a name for the mysterious Mrs X. As there had been a telephone in the house it would be possible (as long as the household was not ex-directory) to examine the public phone books for the period involved, and compare the addresses of all people with that surname against the detailed de-scription that Price had given in *Fifty Years* in the hope that one would prove a match. As Robert Hastings had now publicly cast doubt on the certainty that Price had visited Brockley on that cold winter's night nearly thirty years before, for safety Medhurst decided to include not only the whole of South London, but addresses north of the river as well. 'As a first step,' he recorded, 'Mrs K.M. Goldney undertook the tedious task of copying out the names and addresses of all the Mortimers in the Greater London area who were listed as being on the telephone in 1937 ... In the directory issued at the beginning of that year we found 108 Mortimer entries and, in a second directory issued in November, there were eight more. The Post Office Guide was also scrutinized for Mortimers living in the London and suburban areas who had resided in the same houses for some nine years, the period during which the "Rosalie" sittings were said by Price to have taken place.'[245]

Armed with this information, Richard Medhurst took to the streets of the capital and, over the course of the first half of 1965, he began visiting each of the addresses on the list and examining the houses from the outside. In this somewhat onerous and time-consuming task he was assisted by an SPR colleague, Mary Rose Barrington, who like Medhurst also successfully juggled psychical research with a full-time professional career (in this instance as a barrister). At the time she was also a sitter with him in a home circle experiment at her home in Richmond in West London. In the mid-1940s, Barrington had met Harry Price on the occasion of his visit to deliver a lecture on Borley Rectory to the Oxford University Society for Psychical Research of which, at the time, she held the Presidency. At Price's invitation she joined the Ghost Club for a year and was one of the 446 people who attended its 500th Meeting and Dinner at The Savoy Hotel on 9 April 1947.

Despite their concerted efforts, as the weeks progressed, Richard Medhurst's initial confidence and optimism began to slip away. Certain types of building – office premises, shops and public houses – could quickly be discarded, and it was discovered that several on the list had either been destroyed by wartime bombing or were now demolished and their sites redeveloped. A small number of houses remained uninspected as there was only a name and not a numbered street address. As Price suggests less than an hour elapsed between leaving the séance house and starting to write the report at his Club, houses in outlying and therefore unlikely districts were ignored. Between them, both Medhurst and Barrington felt confident that none of these houses were likely candidates and it was safe to cross them off the list. However, as the months passed and the investigation continued, it soon became clear than none of the addresses on the gradually dwindling list matched the target house set down in *Fifty Years* in 1939. 'To our disappointment,' Medhurst later wrote, ' ... none of the houses fitted Price's description at all closely, and hardly any even turned out to be substantial detached Victorian houses. Such as there were could almost all be eliminated for various reasons.'[246]

Curiously, out of the total of 116 addresses drawn from the 1937 telephone directories, only one seemed remotely relevant. This was to bring the search back full circle, not only to the Brockley of Harry Price's youth, but specifically to Wickham Road where Price had had his adventure with the drunken medium and David Cohen and Eric Dingwall had pounded the pavements looking for clues only a few years before. No.21 now as then *is* a substantial detached double-fronted Victorian house but, as Medhurst and Barrington examined it from the street outside, they realised that it falls short of many of the details specified by Price in *Fifty Years*. Most glaring of the differences is that it is not situated on a corner plot and there are no dormer windows to the second floor. To this can be added the eight steps up to the entrance rather than twelve, while the front door has a bay on one side only and this does not extend to the first floor above. The total number of windows on the front elevation is also wrong. These inconsistencies would have been enough to warrant no further investigation had it not been for the efforts of the editor of the SPR's *Journal* and *Proceedings*, Dr Alan Gauld, a psychology lecturer at the University of Nottingham, who, with the 'Rosalie' case in mind, also spent time at the Goldsmiths' Library looking through Price's papers.

As has been shown, Harry Price's BBC broadcast and subsequent article in *The Listener* in the early winter of 1937 were the catalysts that brought the entire 'Rosalie' mystery into being. As well as dealing with Peter Pooley, an Empire Service Talks assistant in connection with his haunted house broadcast, Price was again in touch with Seymour de Lotbiniere for whom he had carried out the live relay from Meopham Manor the previous year. De Lotbiniere was keen to organise a similar broadcast if a suitable location could be found and, with Borley Rectory currently being actively investigated by Price and his observers, made arrangements to visit the house in order to assess its suitability for himself. On 7 December 1937, the day before the telephone call from Mrs X, Price wrote to de Lotbiniere enclosing a letter of introduction for presentation to Lionel Arbon, then living in the adjacent Rectory Cottage and, as a key holder and nominal caretaker, allowed access into the building on his behalf[247]. Looking through de Lotbiniere's reply of 9 December, Gauld was the first to spot the significance of the writer's final line before signing off: 'I look forward to hearing how the *Brockley séance* [my italics] goes.' Was it possible that, during his period of levity before conceding with Richard Lambert and deciding to take up Mrs X's offer, Price had, in an unguarded moment, gone against the requirements of the circle and revealed its location?

With 21 Wickham Road being the only address that was in any way 'semi-plausible' out of all the houses examined, Medhurst and Barrington decided that it warranted closer inspection. By 1965, the Mortimer family that lived there during the latter half of the 1930s had moved, but the investigators obtained a forwarding address and were able to get in touch with one of the married daughters of the household. However, like the house itself, the former Mortimers of Wickham Road only partially fitted the criteria set down by Price in 1939. Medhurst wrote:

> We found a similar, tantalizing situation as regards the family living in the house in 1937. Mr Mortimer, who now lives in a seaside town, could indeed have been described as a "City businessman". There was a Miss Mortimer, but in December 1937 she was only just fifteen, whereas the daughter of the family was said by Price to have been nearly 17. This Miss Mortimer, moreover, also has a sister two years younger. She says that if anything in the nature of a séance had taken place she and her sister would have been sent to bed and would not have known anything about it. Furthermore, while Mrs Mortimer has a long-standing interest in psychical matters, Mr Mortimer does not share this interest at all.[248]

There seemed no reason to doubt what the Mortimer family said. The impasse was made complete when, in response to an enquiry, Seymour de Lotbiniere, then close to retirement but still involved in British broadcasting, confessed that due to the passage of time he was no longer able to shed any light on the séance reference contained in his letter.

Looking at the conclusions of Medhurst's paper subsequently published in the SPR *Journal*, it seems clear that, on the face of the evidence revealed by their enquiry, Medhurst felt that Brockley was the locality in which the 'Rosalie' episode took place, despite the coincidence of its association with Price's early life, and his own and Mary Rose Barrington's failure to locate the house. 'It may well be that Price, in fulfilment of his promise to conceal the identity of the sitters, omitted some vital step in his narrative,' he surmised, 'It is not inconceivable, for example, that he was met, and taken to a house other than the one he had anticipated.' Clear proof existed in Price's own files that he arranged a sitting at that time, following which, as Medhurst himself notes, 'it then becomes plausible to postulate that the events related in his book took place more or less as he describes, since otherwise he would surely be running the appalling risk of the sitters coming forward to contradict his story.' As to the genuineness of the materialisation itself, it was obviously not possible to comment. 'Evidently Price envisaged [from the caveats contained in the "Rosalie" section of his autobiography – p.293] the possibility that the manifestation reported by him was a clever fraud, and this conclusion may be considered to receive strong support from the continued silence of the sitters, which seems otherwise inexplicable.'[249]

David Cohen was not so certain that 'Rosalie' could be explained away as a fake. Several pages and illustrations in his *Spirit Child* had been used to support the existence of ectoplasmic materialisation. In a letter responding to Medhurst's paper[250] he set down his belief (as well as a number of responses to general criticisms of his book), that the reluctance of Mr X to reveal his and the other sitters' true identities was due to his high standing in the world of business being affected by a perceived stigmatism associated with Spiritualism and paranormal phenomena.

By the beginning of 1966, it seemed that all that could be done to solve the 'Rosalie' case had been carried out. Some major new piece of information was required in order to move the enquiry forward. Neither Richard Medhurst nor David Cohen realised that this was soon to take place, and the provider of that information would be none other than 'Rosalie' herself.

FOURTEEN

'YOURS SINCERLEY, ROSALIE'

———————>❧◆❧———————

The document known as the 'Rosalie letter' is an anonymously authored handwritten script, running to approximately 5000 words, written on lined paper and dated April 1966. The only indication of an address is the single word 'London' which was also the postmark on the envelope that, after being forwarded by his publisher, David Cohen opened just over six months following the publication of his *Spirit Child* book. With his characteristically optimistic appeal he had hoped to obtain some insight and explanation for the events that Price had set down over thirty years before. It is hard to believe that he would have been able to anticipate the response he was ultimately to receive.

At this point before proceeding any further, I suggest turning to Appendix B and reading the text of the letter in its entirety. It is, in the words of Paul Tabori, 'an extraordinary document'[251] and its contents can briefly be summarised as follows: The writer claimed to be Miss X, the daughter of the household that Price had visited on 15 December 1937, and had taken part in the séance as described in his *Fifty Years of Psychical Research*. The sitting, together with others held previously at the house, was bogus and the materialisation witnessed and described by Price was fraudulent. The writer herself, then between eleven and twelve years of age, played the role of the spirit child by undressing (and redressing herself) during the blackout phases of the sitting.

She was also made up with a padded bust-bodice, a suitable dress and high-heeled shoes etc. to play the teenage version of herself who was seen by Price at the beginning and end of the evening. The family were hoaxing a wealthy French widow (Madame Z) whom the writer's father had previously persuaded to invest a large amount of money in a non-existent business deal. This had been in order to bail himself out of his own heavy financial losses on the Stock Market. Some years before, Madame had lost a child to whose memory she was absolutely devoted and the séances (with the writer's mother as the 'medium') were a ploy, acted out on a regular basis, to gain the writer's father time to pay back the money he had embezzled and avoid a serious court action. The reason for calling in Harry Price was to prevent a potential exposure after Madame had become suspicious of the proceedings, and had demanded that the séances be investigated by a suitably qualified psychical researcher: Price being the obvious man of choice. Having successfully fooled the great ghost hunter, and with Madame's suspicions allayed, the fraudulent sittings continued on a reasonably regular basis for several more months until the time was reached when Mr X was able to pay back the money he had 'invested'. At this point the writer's mother conveniently lost her mediumistic abilities and the home circle was quickly brought to an end. Now, nearly three decades after the event and prompted by the publication of Cohen's book, the writer wished to set the record straight once and for all, but, in order to prevent any dishonour to the family name, and in respect of the memory of her parents who were by then both dead, all involved were to remain anonymous. The letter was simply signed 'Rosalie'.

Had the truth behind Harry Price and his spirit child adventure been revealed at last? Although the location of the séance and the identities of the people involved were still a mystery, the reason and motives behind it taking place, something that as he made clear in his essay for the *Help Yourself* journal even Price could not work out, were now clear. And, most importantly, Harry Price himself had been vindicated – yes, the veteran investigator and exposer of numerous fraudulent séances and mediums had been hoodwinked, but his reporting of the incident was correct. It was now his accusers, in the personages of Eric Dingwall and Trevor Hall, who were shown in a bad light to have both selectively used and ignored evidence in order to continue their crusade against him.

For David Cohen this was of the highest importance even though the letter itself was very much a double-edged sword. Price, his hero, had been cleared of any wrong-doing and had acted with the highest intentions in order to keep to his word that the 'Rosalie' circle would never been publicly identified. Yet gone was the hope at last of a genuine spirit materialisation under excellent conditions of control in the presence of a highly experienced and sceptical investigator. 'The "Rosalie"/Price séance was no doubt a fake,' he subsequently told Paul Tabori just over four months after receiving the letter, '- in any type of materialisation (genuine or spurious) *the entities do not manifest naked* [Cohen's italics]. It is strange I did not think of this before. But then even experienced séance room attendees (like Barbanell) did not account for this discrepancy.'[252] For the Manchester researcher, his own personal experiences and belief in the reality of spirit materialisation were enough to make the advantages of clearing Price's name outweigh the loss that had been suffered. 'I shall need ALL [Cohen's emphasis] the help to fight the anti-supernormalists,'[253] he had written to Peter Underwood in the Spring of 1965 during the time that his *Spirit Child* was in the final stages of publication. Now here was just the kind of evidence he needed and it was vital to make its existence known as quickly as possible, both within the paranormal community and beyond. As well as the duty to psychical research, there was also another pressing reason: Cohen was now fighting a battle with cancer and time was of the essence in order to continue his aims to rehabilitate the former pioneers of paranormal enquiry and their posthumous reputations.

As well as the basic reasons for both holding the séance and revealing the ways and means that the spirit child materialisation was achieved, the 'Rosalie' of the letter also gives various other details, which can be compared with Price's account. The Brockley locality, although not confirmed, can be inferred by reference to 'a fashionable suburb of S.E. London', the location of the family home during the 1930s, while the writer's father is described as having 'a position of trust, in a City firm'. This corresponds to Price's 'City businessman' reference in *Fifty Years*. However, the 'Rosalie letter' claims that Price was fed bogus information about the length of time the circle had met, in order to make it appear that the séances had begun well before the point that Mr X created his phoney business deal with Madame Z. Rather than the nine years described by Price, the sittings appear to have been held over a period of some sixteen months, starting at the beginning of December 1936 (the first sitting is said to have taken place 'about two days after the Crystal Palace fire', i.e. 30 November 1936) and ending around the time of Hitler's invasion of Czechoslovakia, which took place on 15 March 1939. The point that the teenage Miss X was first introduced to Madame Z can be placed to mid-May 1937 by reference to the Coronation of George VI and Queen Elizabeth, which was held on 12 May that year. The letter writer also claims that the séances were held less frequently than the weekly sittings reported by Price, averaging around one or two a month. An explanation is also given for the unusual presence of the Airedale dog reported by Price, while the family's Continental motor tour and the loss of Madame Z due to the outbreak of war are also confirmed.

A close reading of the 'Rosalie letter' does in fact reveal a number of contradictions in the writer's narrative. Hitler's annexing of Austria is also used in the context of dating the final séances, which would bring the sittings to a close a year earlier, i.e. shortly after 12 March 1938. However, the writer uses the phrase, 'But I must return to a time about two years before this happy ending' in a subsequent paragraph, which would mean the fake séances started in the spring of 1936, contradicting the start date given by reference to the Crystal Palace fire. The length of time between the beginning of the sittings and the introduction of the teenage Miss X would also increase to well over the time suggested in other parts of the letter, making March 1939 more likely as the period that the séances came to an end. Having said this, in a later paragraph it is stated that the sittings finished the year *after* the 'test' séance with Price and that Mr X and his family took Madame Z to Paris in the summer of 1939 'about a year later', which adds confusion by pointing to March 1938 being the time that the final sittings were held.

Although David Cohen was certain that the 'Rosalie letter' had indeed come from a member of the household that had fooled Harry Price in 1937, other interested parties, both at the time it was received and in subsequent years, have expressed doubt as to its genuineness. Prominent among these critics was Paul Tabori. He first became aware of its existence in the summer of 1966 during the course of the Parapsychology Foundation's annual conference which that year was held at Le Piol, near Saint-Paul-de-Vence, in the south of France. For this meeting, David Cohen had prepared a typescript of the letter and had sent copies to a number of the attending delegates. In the congenial surroundings of the French Riviera, Tabori was able to study the document at some length and later, back in England, view the original itself.

As Literary Executor to the Price estate, Tabori had a vested interest in clearing Harry Price's name of fraud and misconduct. In his biography, he had made it clear that he felt it 'a duty to psychical research and to Harry Price's memory'[254] that the 'Rosalie' case be solved once and for all. Yet despite what seemed a clear solution to the mystery, Tabori was unhappy. 'I, personally am inclined to think that it is true in the main outlines,' he later wrote[255], i.e. that the reasons and motivation for holding the fake séance and bringing it to the attention of a researcher of Price's calibre were highly likely, but the devil in the detail made him suspicious and here it came down to the problem of age. 'Was it possible for a girl to play two parts within the space of half-an-hour, which entailed an age difference of eleven years?' he later asked, 'Rosalie was supposed to be six; Miss X. – seventeen. In reality, by the time the Price séance was held, she must have been twelve. At one end or the other there was a gap very hard if not impossible to bridge,' and he went on:

> She might have been accepted for seventeen with suitable padding and make-up. But when she undressed, how could her eleven-year-old body become that of a six year old? Biologically, anatomically, these five years represent a considerable difference. There was no indication in Rosalie's account that she was underdeveloped, retarded physically. She might have been a small girl – but she was on the threshold of puberty and "Rosalie" would still carry her puppy-fat. Perhaps Price did not have the opportunity of examining many naked six-year-olds at such close quarters – but he must have been a singularly obtuse man not to notice such differences.[256]

One would sincerely hope that Price did not associate himself in such a way, but obviously it is clear what Tabori means and here it is possible to cut him [Price] some slack. As we have seen in his original account in *Fifty Years* (p.142) he states, 'Her features were classical and she *looked older than her alleged years* [my italics]', which goes some way to supporting the ruse that an older child played the role of the ghost girl, at least on this one occasion. But would it have been possible to effect the change from teenager to spirit child and back to teenager again in total darkness without giving away some indication of what was going on? Could Miss X have kept her exact appearance after removing her clothes, putting down her hair etc., and then reversing the process, while all the time a few feet away and ever on the alert for trickery was one of the most experienced investigators of séance room phenomena in the world?

Tabori was not convinced and added to his doubts were others connected with the free rein that Price had been given in controlling the sitting in any way he desired. The positioning of the people in the room and the decision to test that they were still in their respective seats while the 'materialisation' was present were all spontaneous actions and controlled by Price. It seemed too fortuitous that these events could have been anticipated by the circle members and they had practised a routine that would cover for them. All these factors made it seem that what Cohen had received was in fact a carefully contrived and thought out hoax itself. At Le Piol, a number of delegates who examined the typescript came to the same conclusion. It was felt the writer had gone through Price's account in *Fifty Years* and produced a solution 'in which each step, each fact, each circumstance seem perfectly enmeshed'[257]. Cohen however stood firm. 'I am not surprised that you believe that the "Rosalie Confession" is a hoax – this is only what I expected,' he wrote to Tabori on 17 August 1966, 'Yet there is very little doubt in my mind that it is a genuine document ... I realise that the idea that a young girl of 11 posing as a 6 years old and a 16 year old teen-ager is a very difficult task. Yet in the extremely dark conditions of that séance it was quite possible. Miss X could change without betraying herself (after careful practice) during the music part of the séance, or perhaps during conversation. Price believed the account of the "Rosalie" séance's history by Mr X. He had no cause to doubt the integrity of this very cultured family. It is true that he became rather emotional and excited during the alleged materialisation of "Rosalie". But then Price did become emotional at times during some of his psychic experiments.'

By the summer of 1966, however, David Cohen, the enthusiastic ghost hunter from Manchester, was fast running out of options. Now seriously ill, he continued to work simultaneously from his bedside on several new psychical projects, but 'Rosalie' and the continued need to publicise her anonymous 'confession', was never far from his mind. 'How to make Miss X reveal herself and confess everything with all the correct names and house?' he mused to Paul Tabori on 17 August 1966, 'This would need a national appeal from some newspaper – I would need a lot of publicity. I have had a lot of promises,' he added somewhat sadly, 'but now I found [*sic*] myself a sick man alone as usual.' To the end Cohen was always hopeful of some progress. 'To deposit it in Harry Price's Library, I am afraid that it will only remain there, no doubt, for many years,' he decided in what was to be his last letter to Tabori on 2 September 1966. '*Action on this document is needed as soon as possible* [Cohen's italics].' It was to be a final but characteristically passionate outburst. David Cohen died at the Alexion Brothers Nursing Home in Moston, Manchester, on 13 November 1966 aged fifty-one. Despite an attempt by Peter Underwood to preserve for posterity his psychical records in their entirety within the archives of the Ghost Club, together with an appeal in *Psychic News* (30 April 1966), today less than a dozen of his letters, all connected with the 'Rosalie' case, are all that appear to survive. His numerous tape recordings, together with his unpublished reports on Rudi Schneider and Theresa Neumann, were discarded by his surviving family, uninterested in his obsession with ghosts and the spirit world. The result is that today he is all but forgotten.

Along with David Cohen also went the impetus and the driving force to persevere with a solution to the spirit child mystery. Despite his interest in the case, his busy career both in Britain and in America meant that it would be five years before Paul Tabori was able to pick up the reins afresh. In 1970, the Souvenir Press established a line of paranormal-related books under the general title "Frontiers of the Unknown", and his continued association with the world of psychical research and the occult made Tabori the ideal general editor for the series. As well as commissioning other authors, Tabori himself contributed a title, *Beyond the Senses*, in collaboration with the young American writer Phyllis Raphael, which examined the progress that psychical research had made during the course of the previous decade. Published in early 1971, the book was the ideal platform to bring readers up to date with recent work on the 'Rosalie' case, and Tabori made the decision to publish the text of the 'Rosalie letter' in its entirety in the hope that it would act as a stimulus for further research.

Richard Medhurst, like Paul Tabori, was another interested party who doubted the letter's genuineness. Shortly before his death he was asked for his views and raised several relevant points, which were posthumously included in Tabori's book. Before using the luminous plaques, Price had estimated the height of the materialised figure by touch as being around three feet seven inches tall. 'If the height were substantially greater, Price's statement would be clearly wrong,' he noted, 'If, however, it is about right it would be quite absurd for a girl of such a height to pretend to be nearly seventeen. Even with "some inches" (due to high heels and hair arrangement) extra she would look like a dwarf.'[258] Medhurst also pointed out that if the sittings had in fact been going on for only a short period of time and not the nine years that Price was told, it was likely that he would have found this out while talking with Madame Z during the refreshments afterwards and become suspicious of the differing accounts. A third point was that Richard Lambert had been refused entry as it would have meant two strangers being present, something that Madame Z was unhappy about in case it prevented her beloved daughter from materialising. But according to the 'Rosalie letter', there were in fact *three* new people there that evening – Price, the teenage Miss X, plus her uncle playing the part of her boyfriend. Granted Madame had been introduced to Miss X in person on an earlier occasion, but this was the first time she had attended a séance. This went against what Price reported in *Fifty Years* and, as a result, made Medhurst suspicious of the letter as a whole.

Similarly, author and researcher Andrew MacKenzie was likewise nonplussed as to the anonymous letter's value and devoted a large part of his review of *Beyond the Senses* in the SPR *Journal* to the 'Rosalie' chapter. 'When we recall that the address of the house where the séance was held was never published, nor were the names of the sitters, and an explanation of the "materialisation" is now advanced by a person who gives no name or address (the "Rosalie" is hardly sufficient),' he wrote, 'it will be seen that there is not enough evidence here on which to form a firm opinion about the case.'[259]

It seemed that the 'Rosalie' enquiry had stalled again, but the following year the Ghost Club attempted to renew interest by devoting one of its regular lecture meetings (titled 'The Mystery of "Rosalie"') to the case. Members, assembled at the Constitutional Club in St James's Street on the evening of Monday 2 October 1972, listened as Paul Tabori himself led the discussion, with its intention of suggesting possible lines of new research that might be undertaken. Despite the potential, very little was to come out of the meeting: the most enthusiastic response being from a Canadian member, Stan Farnsworth, who, despite being based in Nova Scotia, devoted time during visits to England to work on the case. Farnsworth was keen to explore the psychic angle in his enquiry and, as such, and with the permission of Alan Wesencraft and Peter Underwood respectively, took the originals of both the carbon-copy 'Mortimer letter' and the handwritten 'Rosalie confession' to the Spiritualist Association of Great Britain in Belgrave Square. There on 27 December 1974, medium Irene Taylor carried out a psychometric examination.

Despite Farnsworth's enthusiasm, nothing of importance was achieved and by then the 'Rosalie' case (and the paranormal community as a whole) had suffered another heavy blow. On 9 November 1974, within a quarter of an hour of returning from the Annual Ghost Club Dinner in London, Paul Tabori collapsed and died of a heart attack at his home in Stafford Terrace. He was sixty-six. His death left Peter Underwood, who acted briefly as his successor to Harry Price's literary estate before the role was taken over by the University of London, as one of the last original connections with the 'Rosalie' investigation of the previous decade. For Underwood the loss was a deep and personal one. The two men had been friends for several years and, as editor of "Frontiers of the Unknown", Tabori had commissioned Underwood's first published book, *A Gazetteer of British Ghosts*, which also appeared in 1971.

As Price's Literary Executor, Peter Underwood held, as it were, the keys to the kingdom and, in August 1976, he granted Bristol-based television producer Anne Owen and her team access to the archive. Owen was interested in presenting the 'Rosalie' story objectively as an episode of the BBC's supernatural documentary series *Leap in the Dark* and, with subsequent national exposure, it was hoped (particularly by Underwood) that some progress would finally be made with the case. However, earlier the same year the BBC had commissioned and put into production a series of original plays, also with a supernatural theme, under the collective title *The Mind Beyond*. One of the scripts that had been given the green light by producer Irene Shubik was written by David Halliwell (1936-2006), a former actor turned playwright, today best remembered for his 1965 stage play, *Little Malcolm and His Struggle Against the Eunuchs*. For his "Meriel the Ghost Girl", Halliwell took the lengthy account included by Tabori in *Beyond the Senses* and presented the 'Rosalie' case as a series of dramatised monologues whose fictional characters each represent a particular phase of the real-life investigation. As such, Harry Price becomes George Livingston, played for the small screen in a suitably clipped and brusque manner by horror veteran, Donald Pleasance; the *Four Modern Ghosts* period of Dingwall and Hall is represented by John Bluthal's American gumshoe, Sam Nicholls; while David Cohen changes sex and becomes Janet Street-Porter's hoydenish amateur psychical researcher, Robina Oliver. For good measure, Halliwell introduces an original character, Dr Delane, played by Charles Keating, a psychologist who ultimately explains the entire episode away as a collective hallucination created by the individual emotional and psychological needs of the 'Meriel' circle.

Helmed by *Armchair Theatre* director, Philip Saville, "Meriel the Ghost Girl" was broadcast on 29 September 1976 and has never been repeated nor issued on DVD, due most likely to the high level of nudity included in the séance episode. The play proved something of a surprise and a disappointment to a number of people, not least Anne Owen who was unaware of how much Halliwell's drama overlapped with her own project. Amongst the paranormal community, veteran Spiritualist Maurice Barbanell was also unimpressed. 'The mystery about "Meriel, the Ghost Girl", the first of six psychic plays screened by BBC2 TV last week, is that no mention was made of the famous case on which it was based,' he wrote in *Psychic News* (9 October 1976) and went on to complain, 'It was, alas, the usual mish-mash we see when TV "psychic" plays are portrayed on our screens ... What a pity these dramatists fail to do their homework properly. Livingston was told the child's materialisation would be "guaranteed". *No medium could make such a claim* [my italics].' Barbanell had locked horns with Harry Price on many occasions over the years and his frustration with Price over the spirit child episode went back, as we have seen, right to its public debut in 1939. In giving his views on 'Rosalie's' dramatisation, it seems likely that he was also giving some measure of his own views on the case as a whole. To Peter Underwood's dismay, the similarities between the 'Meriel' of *The Mind Beyond* and the 'Rosalie' as proposed for *Leap in the Dark* proved prohibitive, with the result that further work on the episode was postponed and the programme ultimately abandoned. 'Following David Halliwell's mischievous use of the facts,' he grumbled to the editor of *The Sunday Times'* "Opinion" column on 10 October 1976, '... instead of having a serious reconstruction of this remarkable case we have an ill-conceived and crummy fictional presentation – without credits of any kind as to the origin of the material.'[260] An accompanying book, *The Mind Beyond*, containing a short story version by David Halliwell of his "Meriel" script, was simultaneously issued by Penguin during the series' transmission. The story was briefly resurrected just over five years later when, in 1982, a stage adaptation took place at the Old Red Lion Theatre in Islington.

Although his annoyance is understandable, the dramatic potential of the story is clear. Given the notoriety of the case it had, not surprisingly, been attempted before, although Underwood may have been unaware that the person behind a previous attempt to put 'Rosalie' onto the small screen was none other than Paul Tabori. In the 1950s and 1960s he had written outlines and completed several scripts for *The*

Locked Book, an ultimately unproduced television series based on a number of Harry Price's well-known cases including Gef the Talking Mongoose, the R101 séance, the Carshalton fire-walks, medium Helen Duncan, and the opening of prophetess Joanna Southcott's mysterious box. Each episode featured a personal introduction by Price himself followed by a full dramatisation and, in collaboration with fellow screenwriter Lee Backman, Tabori had completed, "The Case of Rosalie", which gave the spirit child story a suitably dramatic ending full of pathos. Together with several other refugees fleeing the German advance through wartime France, Madame Z is killed by an attacking enemy plane. As she lies dying by the roadside, the ghost of 'Rosalie' appears to her mother and the two embrace once again ...

Unfortunately I never established what Peter Underwood's true views were as to the genuineness of the 'Rosalie letter', although he clearly believed the circumstances of the séance as described by Price in *Fifty Years.* Like David Cohen, he felt the writer still had a duty, as the years passed by, to come forward. Nearly two decades after David Cohen's death, in his 1985 book *The Ghost Hunters* and as part of a lengthy chapter on the career of Harry Price, he included a photograph of one page from the original letter along with a passionate plea for more information. 'I undertake to respect in every way the privacy and total anonymity of the writer or person who contacts me,' he wrote, 'but for the sake of posterity, for the sake of the reputation of Harry Price and for psychical research in general, it is imperative that the writer or someone concerned and I meet and talk in complete confidence.'[261] Despite his high profile in the world of psychical research, both in this country and abroad, no response was received and, in reality, the curtain had effectively come down on the 'Rosalie' investigation nearly ten years before with the ending of "Meriel the Ghost Girl".

Although as a pioneering figure, Harry Price has remained strong within the paranormal community of the past four decades since that time, the popularity of his other investigations, most notably that of Borley Rectory, has had the effect of pushing 'Rosalie' onto the sidelines, with the result that no new research has been carried out on the case since the mid-1970s. When actor Tom Baker hosted *Ghost Hunter,* an hour-long retrospective, broadcast on the Sky One channel on 9 January 2005 with contributions from such interested parties as psychologist Professor Richard Wiseman and conjurors Derren Brown, Marc Paul and Ali Cook, 'Rosalie' was nowhere to be seen, marginalised by discussions and re-enactments of paranormal heavyweights Helen Duncan, Rudi Schneider, Gef the Mongoose, and Borley.

Yet of all of his many cases, that of the spirit child appeared to have had the most effect on Harry Price himself. Borley Rectory may have brought him financial success and worldwide fame, but his encounter with 'Rosalie' was, I believe, the one, out of all his dozens of psychical adventures, that brought him closest to the essence of his life's work as a psychical researcher. On that cold winter's night in 1937 he had a remarkable experience, one that, for all his bluster and ego and heavy-handedness, makes him appear the most human. Therefore to let the case of 'Rosalie' continue to hang in limbo without a resolution seems unfair, not only to the memory of Harry Price, but also to those who, as we have seen, have over the years expended time, passion and energy in searching for the truth.

FIFTEEN

SEARCHING FOR MRS MORTIMER

I n the preceding chapters I have set down as comprehensive a history of the 'Rosalie' case as I have been able to establish using material from a number of diverse sources. These include published accounts, correspondence and interviews with interested parties, as well as research in both public and private archives and collections. My intention to produce a book on Price and his spirit child encounter began in the latter part of 2008 following completion of my first Price-driven project *The Borley Rectory Companion*. As has been mentioned in the Introduction, it was given added stimulus by personal experience of physical mediumship séances around the same time. In the ensuing years since then I have worked on it intermittently, when personal commitments and other writing projects have allowed.

Of all Harry Price's adventures it has been the one that I have found most compelling, second only to the Borley story itself. I encountered it unknowingly before I had even heard of either Price or Borley, as a ten year-old with my parents, through the "Meriel" dramatisation on a Wednesday evening during the long hot summer of 1976. Not long after, popular books by Daniel Farson[262] introduced me to both the paranormal as a subject outside of fiction and drama, and to the work of Price himself. Sometime in late 1979 or early 1980, I read the Sphere Books reprint of the Tabori biography[263] and realised where this strange séance room story, that had made such an impression, had actually originated. Encouraged and in no small way assisted by my partner Leah Mistry, who has followed my work on 'Rosalie' since its very beginning, in March 2016 I picked up the project again.

Like all the researchers that have been encountered in the preceding pages, the hope of achieving a solution to the 'Rosalie' mystery, of discovering just what happened to Harry Price all those years ago, of finding out where he went and whom he met, has never been far from our thoughts. With the development of online resources, particularly historical and genealogical records, now providing access to information that was either unobtainable or difficult to locate by previous 'Rosalie' researchers, it seemed that we were in a position to make the historical account of the case as complete as possible. At the same time we were hopeful of achieving, in some way, an advance into the mystery itself, always bearing in mind the various caveats and associated problems that will be described later in this chapter.

At the outset it was important to distil and set down various key points that could reasonably be relied on as the basis for a further investigation. For the patient reader who has waded through all the 'Rosalie' material presented above, it also, hopefully, acts as a staging post to gather the thoughts before pressing on. These points and the material/evidence justifying them are as follows:

1. The carbon-copy of the 'Mortimer letter' together with the written statements of Richard Lambert, show that Price did attend a séance on the evening of 15 December 1937 which corresponds with his claims in *Fifty Years*.
2. By default, the 'Mortimer letter' also appears to give the surname of the organisers of the 'Rosalie' circle, or at least the name that was given to Price over the telephone by Mrs X.
3. The written statements of Richard Lambert and 'Mollie' Goldney, the latter's being supported by oral testimony in front of witnesses at the Ghost Club meeting in 1963, show that on 16 December 1937, Price was working on an initial version of a report on his experiences of the previous evening. This was finished by the end of the same day and carbon-copies of Price's own correspondence also support this.

4. Carbon-copies of correspondence from Price and original letters from Frank Whitaker, show that Price's statement that he published (what I have termed an initial version) of this report 'verbatim and uncorrected' in *Fifty Years* is untrue.

5. Leading on from 4 above, clear evidence that Price had changed part of the description of the front of the séance house (i.e. the description of the steps leading to the front door) prior to publication, makes it unsafe to rely on the description in *Fifty Years* as being a completely accurate one. However, it was felt that aspects of the description *could* be true. It may have been located on a corner site and/or was in some respect a large detached Victorian property with bay windows to the front elevation, and that Price had made various alterations to further protect the people involved.

6. Although offering a plausible scenario for the séance taking place, issues in connection with the age of the Miss X of the 'Rosalie letter' received by David Cohen in 1966 suggested that this document was most likely a carefully crafted hoax.

7. Evidence supporting the notion that the 'Rosalie' séance took place in the South London suburb of Brockley is based, in the first instance, on correspondence from Seymour de Lotbiniere shortly before the sitting took place (in which the locality is named specifically), and secondly in undated correspondence from Clarice Richards (in which it can be derived by implication). Mrs Richards also subsequently stated to 'Mollie' Goldney, when interviewed at the request of Robert Hastings, that Price had told her the séance house was 'on the outskirts of Brockley'.

8. The surviving typescript of *Fifty Years* describes Mr X's profession as that of a 'hop merchant'. This was subsequently revised prior to publication as 'in business in the City'. As the former is very specific it suggests it *might* be what Price was told, but was later changed in order to give a greater degree of anonymity. The reference to the City of London is also somewhat specific: 'in business in London' would have made a safer description.

9. There is nothing in Price's account to suggest that 'Rosalie' is the real name of Madame Z's dead child and not a pseudonym invented by Price.

These various points are mostly self explanatory but, in order to use them as the foundations for further investigation, it was necessary to examine some in greater detail. Our reasoning and research is presented next under the following headings.

The 'Mortimer Letter'

When compared with other carbon-copies of the period (i.e. the mid-1930s), the format, typeface, paragraph spacing and indenting all point to the 'Mortimer letter' having originated at that time from Price's office in the usual manner. The only thing of importance missing is the correspondent's address, which was normally placed above the salutation and justified to the left-hand margin. Here the only wording is 'Mrs. Mortimer' followed by a gap and then the letter begins 'Dear Madam'.

Is this carbon-copy letter, first noticed by Richard Medhurst in the Harry Price archive at the University of London in early 1965, a genuine document or is there a possibility that, as he himself suggested in his subsequent SPR paper, it may be a fabrication? Did the sarcastic comments by Eric Dingwall, following the revelations at the Ghost Club in January 1939, make Price feel that a little subterfuge was needed, in order to ensure that his posthumous reputation remained intact should his case files be examined at some future date? 'Dr Dingwall and Mr Hall will perhaps suggest,' Medhurst noted, 'that Price himself made a carbon copy of a spurious letter and placed it in his files to deceive either his secretary, Miss Beenham ... or the investigator [i.e. Medhurst himself] who found it twenty-seven years later.'[264] As the 'Mortimer letter' is of primary importance in the 'Rosalie' case, it was essential to examine it to see if it was anything other than what it appears to be.

Interestingly, after looking through the whole of Price's correspondence for the year 1937, I found I couldn't agree with a point raised by Richard Medhurst, namely that the omission of the addressee's details was a commonality on many surviving examples of Price's outgoing correspondence of the period. During the winter of 1937/38, and specifically in the months of November and December 1937 around the time of the haunted house broadcast, the invitation to the séance, the séance itself and afterwards, Price wrote letters to a number of people both in this country and abroad. They included the widow of Dr Robin Tillyard (5 November), the BBC's Photographic Dept. (8 December), Major Huth of Breslau (15 December), Samuel Soal (16 December), the publishers Putnam & Co. (14 & 20 December), and James Leigh, the Editor of *Prediction* magazine (15 November & 29 December). The carbon-copies of all these letters include the name and address of the recipient, making the 'Mortimer letter' stand out from the pack. Another point which became apparent is that it seems likely that Price typed the letter himself rather than his secretary, Ethel Beenham. The carbon lacks the characteristic 'HP/EB.' initialling at the bottom that all the letters noted above contain. Do these two points give enough ground to dismiss the letter as a forgery?

A simple explanation for Price's typing the letter is that Ethel Beenham worked part-time and on 13 December she was absent. Up until the end of December 1937, she also did secretarial duties for J. Arthur Findlay's International Institute for Psychical Research, which then operated out of premises in Walton Street, Kensington[265]. At the end of the previous week (10 December 1937), Price had written to a local contractor concerning work at his house in Pulborough and, similarly, the HP/EB initials are missing. However, a letter written on 13 December to Sidney Glanville *does* contain them, proving she was present in the office at least for some time on that Monday when the 'Mortimer letter' was drafted.

Although for Medhurst the idea that the 'Mortimer letter' is a fake was a moot point, I don't believe for a minute that he felt it was true. His comment is clearly a dig at the authors of *Four Modern Ghosts* that, despite their published assurance, evidence does exist amongst Price's papers to support his attending a séance when he said he did in *Fifty Years*. For the purposes of my own investigation, I have taken the view that it is a genuine document. Although we will never know what was actually said over the telephone the previous week, Price may have felt obliged, due to issues of sensitivity, to type the response himself. After taking down the address, and in keeping with this need for confidentiality, he omitted it from his letter. It may well have been a stipulation that the address was not to be included on any correspondence involving the 'Rosalie' circle.

An alternative explanation for the lack of the usual HP/EB initials is that Miss Beenham may well have left Berkeley Street for the day by the time Price took the decision to take up Mrs X's offer. As we have seen, Mrs English felt that she *had* at some point typed correspondence in connection with the 'Rosalie' case, but was unable to quote specific examples. This is understandable given the volume of Price's outgoing correspondence and the length of time that had passed since she had worked for him. The question should also be asked that, if Price was at some later date going to fake correspondence to support a bogus story, why did he not write additional letters to show he had continued to press for a second sitting, as he claimed both in *Fifty Years* and *Help Yourself,* and, like the 'Mortimer letter', ensure they were amongst his papers ready to be discovered in the future?

The 'Rosalie Letter'

In *Beyond the Senses*, Paul Tabori describes the sceptical attitude shown by a proportion of the paranormal community towards the 'Rosalie letter', both at the time it was received and also on publication in the early 1970s. He also notes (but without giving specific details) that the letter was compared with the handwriting of a number of known hoaxers in the psychical field during this period (the mid-late 1960s), and that the results were entirely negative.

In discussing this aspect of the case with a long-standing member of the Spiritualist community, it was suggested to me (and subsequently supported by a well-known journalist involved with psychical matters at the time), that if the 'Rosalie letter' *was* a fake then one person who could quite well have carried out the hoax was the journalist and some-time researcher Archie Jarman (1909-1982). Jarman has already been briefly mentioned above in connection with his contemporary review of the posthumously issued Myers autobiography. A former lover of medium Eileen Garrett, Jarman was an at times troubled man, prone to periods of depression created by the uncertainty of being able to communicate with his sister, the poet Wrenne Jarman, through various mediums following her death in 1953. Of independent means, Jarman at times subjected the contemporary psychical and Spiritualist scene of the 1960s to his not inconsiderable wit with a raft of satirical writings. In 1963, and much to the later ire of editor Francis Clive-Ross, he carried on a spurious correspondence with himself in the pages of *Tomorrow* magazine (of which he was then an associate editor), arguing the case for and against survival with a fictional alter-ego, Charles Bottle of Geneva. Later in 1970, he wrote under his own name a full-length book, *High Jinks on a Low Level*, lampooning (under pseudonyms) well known mediums, journalists and psychical researchers of the time. Prudently he obtained beforehand their written agreements that they would not sue him for slander.

As well as satire, Jarman was particularly outspoken when confronted with criticism of his own opinions. In 1964, he issued a lengthy

SEARCHING FOR MRS MORTIMER

pamphlet, *Dr Gauld and Mr Myers*, which responded to criticisms published in the SPR *Journal* of his review of the Myers autobiography[266]. It was therefore of great interest to find that another person who had criticised Jarman over his accusations against Frederick Myers was none other than David Cohen. In *Spirit Child*, Cohen had drawn attention to what he believed to be the wholly negative attitude of the editors of *Tomorrow* towards the great researchers of the past. 'Lastly, I read a review by Anne Dooley in the *Psychic News* (February 22nd, 1964) on an article by Archie Jarman,' Cohen grumbled, ' ... denigrating F.W.H. Myers – by (reminiscent of Hall at Crookes) *dragging out his sex life* [Cohen's italics]. Perhaps Jarman would reveal his own sex life for the readers of *Tomorrow*? I would certainly not like to reveal my own ... '. Cohen finished by saying, 'What use are these sex-prone articles to Psychical Science?'[267]

Archie Jarman would have been well aware of *Spirit Child's* publication. If he had taken offence to Cohen's response, it is not too farfetched to suggest that the 'Rosalie letter' may well have been his response, a private joke on Cohen's 'sex-prone' attitude, containing as it does the notion of young ladies stripping off to play shenanigans in the dark. With this being a distinct possibility, my own attitude was to treat the 'Rosalie confession' at the outset with a high degree of caution.

The Brockley Locality

For Eric Dingwall, Trevor Hall, Richard Medhurst, Mary Rose Barrington and David Cohen, all roads in the search for 'Rosalie' led to Brockley. Leaping out of Price's own files, it permeates the psyche of all previous investigations, and therefore was one place out of necessity that I knew would form part of my own.

Of the two references discussed earlier, the one by Seymour de Lotbiniere is the most compelling. Despite all the precautions taken in drafting the 'Mortimer letter', was it possible that Price had let slip the location of the sitting at the very outset, before he had been persuaded by the enthusiastic Richard Lambert to take the offer seriously? Or had he actually kept to his word and covered the real location with one that he would have been highly familiar with, but which, at the time, very few people in his professional life in psychical research would have been aware of his connection to? In 1937, *Search for Truth* was still several years away, while the previous year in *Confessions of a*

Ghost-hunter, he had emphasised his family's Shropshire connections. Only members of his own family, and possibly close acquaintances, would have known of his youthful years spent in the South London suburb, making it safe to use if it became necessary to discuss the investigation in conversation.

An important question which needed addressing was whether 'the Brockley séance' *was* in fact the 'Rosalie' sitting that was being referred to, and not some other investigation that was taking place at the time. When considered at face value this is somewhat likely, particularly as de Lotbiniere himself, in his response to Richard Medhurst's enquiry in 1965, confessed that 'I was seeing quite a lot of Harry Price around that time and he was telling me of so many séances, past and present, that I cannot now distinguish between them.'[268] From my trawl through Price's 1937 files it was possible to shed some light on this issue.

In none of Price's correspondence, and in particular the period leading up to and immediately after the 'Rosalie' séance in December 1937, is there any mention of his organising or undertaking another séance investigation. The script for the haunted house broadcast had occupied him prior to its transmission on 4 November. On the day of the broadcast itself, he received a request by the publishers of the *Encyclopaedia Britannica* for a 400-word contribution to their forthcoming 1938 Yearbook. There was also administration work in connection with the forthcoming publication, under the auspices of the ULCPI, of a lengthy report by Samuel Soal[269] on the vaudeville telepathist "Marion" who later provided the entertainment on the occasion of the eventful Ghost Club Dinner in January 1939. He was also working privately on the *Fifty Years* project. The only séances that were taking place at the time were planchette sittings being carried out by the Glanville family, and a few other interested people, in connection with the ongoing Borley Rectory tenancy (both at the rectory at also at their home in Streatham). Price was not personally involved with these, although he was being informed of some of the alleged communications.

How Seymour de Lotbiniere became aware that Price was proposing to attend a séance around this time is unclear. In his reply of 9 December, de Lotbiniere refers to *two* letters from Price, one of which as has been mentioned, was written on the 7th enclosing the introduction to Mr Arbon for his Borley visit. The carbon-copy of the other letter mentioned by de Lotbiniere is missing from the Senate House archive, and the original is not among the correspondence between him and Price held at the BBC's Written Archive at Reading. The only previous correspondence between the two, amongst Price's papers, is a letter from Price much earlier on 4 November. It seems unlikely that this is the second letter to which the BBC man was referring, as he would no doubt have apologised for the lateness of his reply. It is possible that Price wrote a day or two before the 7th, or drafted a second letter on the 7th itself. If the second letter *was* written on 8 December, the day that Price received the telephone call from Mrs X, then it is almost certain that 'the Brockley séance' referred to is the 'Rosalie' sitting. Price either used his familiarity with the Brockley area as a suitable cover, or inadvertently gave the location away in a moment of indiscretion.

As well as the potential contained in the de Lotbiniere correspondence, there was another reason for returning to Brockley with a new investigation. One person who felt that it was highly likely that the 'Rosalie' séance took place there was the British biologist John L. Randall (1933-2011), a respected experimental psychical researcher and author of the 1975 book, *Parapsychology and the Nature of Life*. In July 2000, he published a lengthy paper defending the posthumous reputation of Harry Price ("Harry Price: The Case for the Defence", SPR *Journal*, Vol.64, No.860). In subsequently published correspondence, prompted by a request from Adrian Parker from the Department of Psychology at Gothenburg University, he gave his own views on the 'Rosalie' case. Randall believed the 'Rosalie letter' was genuine and that the writer had been prompted to break the silence, albeit anonymously, due to the recent attempts by various ghost hunters to solve the mystery. 'In view of her father's disreputable behaviour, it is understandable that Miss X would not want his name known, even after his death,' he reasoned. 'Various snippets of information point to Brockley as the location of the house, and it would not surprise me if the Mortimer family interviewed by the SPR investigators turned out to be the true participants after all. In the circumstances their denial and attempt to disguise the true facts would be expected. It may well have been the nearness of the SPR investigation which provoked "Miss X" into writing her letter, in an attempt to deter further probing.'[270] Clearly it was necessary to look further at the Mortimer family that lived in Wickham Road in 1937 to see if any of John Randall's views could be confirmed.

As mentioned previously, number 21 Wickham Road still stands and an enquiry to Lewisham Council's Planning Department showed it was converted from a single dwelling into self-contained flats in 1995. Through online resources we were able to view the 1937 telephone directory consulted by Medhurst and Barrington, as well as the Electoral

Roll for the Deptford Ward covering Wickham Road for the same period (dated 15 October 1937). From these, together with other online records, it was possible to identify the Mortimers who were living at 21 Wickham Road at the time of the 'Rosalie' séance. They were Frank Thomas Mortimer (b.1895), his wife Mildred (b.1895), together with their two daughters aged fifteen and thirteen. Mr Mortimer was a stone merchant and ran his own business at Samuda's Wharf on the Isle of Dogs. The couple appear to have left Brockley around 1960 and moved to Southend where they died in the early 1980s. These connections to a London business and a 'seaside town', together with the ages of their two daughters, confirm that they were the family contacted by the SPR investigators in 1965. Was it possible that this couple were Mr and Mrs X and that one of their children had played the ghost of 'Rosalie'?

The online Electoral Roll for 1937 and earlier years also confirmed an interesting coincidence revealed to Medhurst and Barrington during their interview with the former Miss Mortimer. Prior to residing in Wickham Road, Mr and Mrs Mortimer had lived for the latter half of the 1920s in a house (No.29) in the nearby Manor Road, where Harry Price had attended séance meetings in his youth. The Electoral Roll also quickly provided significant information about the household at 21 Wickham Road in 1937. Although it was listed as a single address, No.21 was in fact a house in multiple occupation. As well as the Mortimers, five other couples were living there which bears no relation to the domestic arrangement (single family with servants etc.) described by Price in *Fifty Years*. Clearly it would have been impossible for him to have had the free rein to visit and control the various rooms around the building that he claims took place. It is highly unlikely that, on that particular evening, *all* of these ten other people would have been out during the time that Price was there, and it would have soon become apparent that persons other than the family in question were living there. Also the dimensions given of the séance room, if reasonably accurate, indicate a much larger room than those that appear to exist on each side of the main front door at this property after the house was inspected by us from the outside. Unless Price significantly embellished his account, the 'Rosalie' séance could not have taken place at 21 Wickham Road.

Despite this, it was not possible at this stage to rule out entirely this Mortimer family as somehow being involved in the 'Rosalie' case. Further examination of the Deptford Ward Electoral Roll showed that there was a *second* Mortimer household in Wickham Road in 1937 that

Medhurst and Barrington make no mention of. This was No.45 and the person living there was Frank Mortimer's widowed mother, Cecilia. Had Price (as Medhurst himself suggested as a possibility) initially gone to No.21 and then subsequently been taken to No.45 Wickham Road where the séance actually took place? It seemed strange that Richard Medhurst, still revered by those who knew him as a meticulous and consistent researcher, had noted this as having potential, but, among the family details included in his paper, had failed to mention the existence of this second house. This gives rise to the suspicion that the information had been withheld by Miss Mortimer at the time, and that she knew more than she was willing to reveal. Although not complying with Price's published description (No.45 is a semi-detached house albeit a large Victorian one), there are some tantalising similarities. This second Mortimer house has seven windows to the front elevation, and a flight of twelve stone steps in total to the front door, making it conceivable that for the purposes of *Fifty Years* he created a hybrid house out of the two properties.

The existence of this second house together with the presence of Mr Mortimer's mother, then in her early seventies, gave more credence to a specific, but ultimately non-paranormal explanation, that I had considered might lie behind the whole 'Rosalie' episode. This was that Price had been specifically targeted by fraudsters and that the séance was a carefully organised scam. The whole back story of 'Rosalie's' life and death related that evening was fictional. There never was a real Madame Z, only a fake character played by an accomplice, in this case Cecilia Mortimer. If it was possible to fool the great ghost hunter, who then published an account championing the 'phenomenon' claiming that survival had been proved, he would lead himself open to ridicule and possibly even blackmail. However, Mr and Mrs X had underestimated Price's scepticism. He had loaded his published report with enough caveats that (for this and possibly other reasons), the couple had ultimately lost their nerve and 'Rosalie' was conveniently laid to rest, by both the hoaxers and Price himself. Although superficially fanciful, this scenario is, on the one hand, no more extraordinary than the concept of spirit materialisation itself, and, on the other, no less fanciful than claims advanced in other subjects, such as the many published theories offering a solution to the crimes and identity of Jack the Ripper. However, on closer inspection, the same situation concerning multiple occupancy was found to exist at No.45 as well. The house is listed as being divided into three flats in 1937 and Mrs Mortimer shared the building with four other people. Again, Price would not have been able to tour the entire building as he describes, and the domestic situation with servants etc. is also lacking.

It appears that there was nothing sinister in Miss Mortimer's failing to mention that her grandmother was living close by when questioned in 1965, and the most likely explanation is that she simply didn't realise it might be relevant. What this unassuming London family felt about ghost hunters turning up at their door and being drawn into a classic mystery of psychical research we will now never know. Looking at what we now do know of the Mortimers of Wickham Road, it is clear that they were not involved in the 'Rosalie' case and that their presence in the story is coincidental. Despite this, the possibility that Price *had* been set up on purpose by whoever organised the séance was, I still felt, a viable non-paranormal explanation.

Although the Wickham Road aspect of Brockley had been cleared up, the suburb as a whole still remained. As the online Electoral Roll for 1937 had picked up the previously undiscovered Mortimer connection with No.45, it was decided to check the whole of the Deptford Ward for all other Mortimers living in the area at the time. Dingwall and Hall claimed they had been unable to find a corner house matching Price's description by examining Ordnance Survey maps of the area, but their investigation was so biased against Price that it is difficult to accept they applied the maximum effort to the task. It is now also clear that a certain amount of ambiguity exists concerning the description of the house, published in *Fifty Years*, that they were following. This issue of the description was also a factor that went against Richard Medhurst and Mary Rose Barrington in 1965. In the present investigation, it was decided that what was of more importance was initially to see if a *household* matched the criteria stipulated by Price (by comparing the number of persons present, their surnames, ages and relationship to one another), and then check the house's location and other physical qualities. This latter factor was helped no end by the fact that historic Ordnance Survey maps are now available to view online, and buildings can also be checked visually using Google Streetview[271].

The Deptford Ward in 1937 covered an additional area around Wickham Road approximately one and a half miles north to the southern side of Greenland Dock, and around one mile to the west, taking in New Cross and New Cross Gate. Five Mortimer households were found, including one in St Donatts Road a few doors down from where Harry Price lived with his sister and their parents before World War I.

None of these families, or the houses themselves, fitted the profile we were looking for. In order to make the Brockley search as thorough as possible, the much larger 1937 Electoral Roll for Lewisham was also checked. As well as Lewisham itself, this picked up the adjacent suburbs of Catford, Honor Oak, Ladywell, Dulwich, Sydenham, and also parts of Bromley. Another thirteen addresses occupied by Mortimer families were located, but again both the households and the houses did not fit. In searching both Wards it became clear that the Mortimer name was not common, at least in that part of London in the mid-1930s. Out of a total of well over 110,000 individuals only 46 were named Mortimer. It also seemed certain that, to the best of our ability, unless he had (as Richard Medhurst had surmised), changed some part of his account in a substantial way, we had established that Harry Price did not visit the Brockley area of London on 15 December 1937. His use of the name, and the letter 'B' in correspondence at the time, had been done consciously to hide his real destination.

The 'Rosalie' Name

All previous commentators and researchers into the case have more or less assumed that Rosalie is the real name of the dead child whose materialisation Price claimed to have seen and touched. It is used without special emphasis on one occasion in *Fifty Years*, when the back story of the circle and Madame Z's history is being recounted. Elsewhere Price writes 'Rosalie' in the same way that he refers to 'Katie King' when discussing the mediumship of Florence Cook. In 1974, a Mr L.I. Macintyre from Hampstead, a correspondent of Stan Farnsworth, who also became interested in the mystery, spent some time searching all the 1921 death index records at Somerset House. Despite his efforts he was unable to find a record matching the information given by Price in his 'Rosalie' report.

Through online genealogy searches we also could find no record of a child with the Christian name of Rosalie having died, either in 1921 or two years either side of that date, who matched the family history that Price claims he was told by Madame Z and Mr and Mrs X. Of all the records examined, only two children seemed worthy of more detailed study, as their deaths do fall within the required parameters. In both cases I am withholding the surnames out of respect as they do not form part of the case in hand. Rosalie #1 from Shropshire is the closest date wise to the profile established in *Fifty Years*, being born in 1916 and dying in 1921, the date given by Price. However, the back story of Rosalie's father being killed in World War I does not fit as this Rosalie had siblings born after the end of the war. Her parents were also both alive and still together in 1937. Rosalie #2 from London was of more interest as her mother's maiden name, of Huguenot origins, suggested some kind of French or Belgian connection. This Rosalie died at the age of six in February 1920. However, the information gleaned from her death certificate proved to be something of a double-edged sword. Although the cause of death was given as heart failure following an attack of pharyngeal diphtheria, which tied in more or less with Price's account, a check on the father's name listed on the certificate showed that he was alive when the death occurred. Again the couple were together and, in this case, living in Wembley at the time of the séance in 1937. Diphtheria was in fact one of the leading causes of death in children up until a successful vaccination programme was launched in 1940[272], so to find it as a cause of death on this Rosalie's certificate is not surprising.

In the same way that the Brockley locality has no relationship to the case (other than Price's personal connection), the name 'Rosalie' also has no direct connection and appears to be a pseudonym created for the purposes of publication. If it was the name used by Mr and Mrs X and Madame Z, then it was either a false one, or, somewhat unusually, no official record of the child has survived. If Price did make up the name, then it entered the story from the very beginning, in his letter to Richard Lambert, written on 16 December the day after the séance.

The Senate House Archive

The possibility that some unguarded reference to the séance house location might exist amongst Price's papers at the University of London Library, was another line of enquiry that I felt needed to be followed up as far as possible. When researching for *The Borley Rectory Companion*, I found that a number of documents connected with the Borley case contained notes and other odd references and remarks, which had been written down on the backs of letters and other items. With this in mind and, as briefly discussed above, over the course of two full days, and with the patient cooperation of the University of London Library staff, I examined all the catalogued documents in their collection dating from 1937 to establish whether any direct and overlooked reference to the séance existed amongst Price's correspondence. This involved checking 127 separate folders containing in total several hundred individual items. Also, and more importantly, I wanted to see whether any notes, or possibly even an address, had been jotted down on the reverse of an unconnected, but contemporary letter or document, that might have conceivably been on Price's desk when he took the telephone call from Mrs X on the morning of 8 December 1937. Several letters were found to contain extraneous notes, all handwritten by Price. However, the name Mortimer was not among them. In addition, where an address was noted, it was either relevant to the letter it was written on, or was connected with some contemporary appointment, unrelated to the 'Rosalie' case, which could be established from other correspondence of the time.

Although it did not contain the smoking gun evidence I was looking for, one particular item (from a collection of miscellaneous papers dating from the 1930s in general), *was* of great interest. This was a lengthy list of Postal Orders received for the purchase of 'Telepatha' cards, that Price had handwritten for the benefit of Frank Whitaker at *John O'London's Weekly*. Dated 17 March 1939, it had actually been written on pages torn out of his office desk diary for January 1937. On this it was possible to see appointments for various meetings written in Ethel Beenham's hand. It is conceivable that other pages from the same diary, including those for December 1937, may have been similarly used for other notes or lists and could be present somewhere in Price's archive. However, the much higher probability is that the remaining portion of the desk diary has been destroyed. If other pages do exist, the remote possibility they would actually be from December and do contain reference to an appointment that Price went to great lengths to keep private, (including the likelihood that he wrote the 'Mortimer letter' himself and disguised the location in conversation), resulted in the decision not to proceed with an additional search through the archive.

The 1939 National Register

The results from the search through the 1937 Electoral Rolls showed that a desktop investigation of this sort was capable of yielding results. However, only a certain number of the 1937 London Electoral Rolls are currently available online. Personal circumstances also prevented either of us undertaking the extensive search through the London Metropolitan Archives at Clerkenwell that would be necessary in order to carry out a complete check of the records. One resource which has recently been made available online is the 1939 National Register, a snapshot census taken on the 29th of September of that year, as part of the wartime National Registration Act to issue the population with identity cards. Due to a number of factors we were aware that a certain percentage of London Mortimers would not be picked up. People out of the country at the time were not included, while records for persons who died after 1991 or who are younger than 100 and still living, are officially closed. Despite this, the archive is fully searchable and contains not only lists of households, but also professions and dates of birth. The fact that people tended not to move around then as much as they do today, made it seem likely that Mr and Mrs X would still have been living at the same address in September 1939 as they were in December 1937.

An initial search quickly established that there were no Mortimers listed as being 'hop merchants' in the entire register, a database of 41 million people. Eighteen people were listed as being hop merchants in London. However, none of the households matched the profile we were looking for, i.e. a married middle-class couple with a teenage daughter, living with servants in a reasonably large house that may or may not occupy a corner site. All these people were couples living either on their own, or in what were quite obviously boarding houses with several other persons.

The next step was to carry out a search for all London Mortimers living on both sides of the Thames, and at an address that could conceivably have been up to an hour's travelling distance from Price's club in St James' Street, Piccadilly. In this respect the search term 'London' generated a large catchment area that included representations from most of the suburbs north, south, east and west, which we felt Price could conceivably have visited in the time stated. This search initially created a list of 553 separate results from which, through careful examination, it was possible to identify 264 unique households involving a total of 486 people. These were arranged into a table that listed for each household all the individual occupants, their dates of birth, the address, and the occupation of the head of the family. Also included was the house type, i.e. whether it was terraced or end-of-terrace, semi-detached or detached, or located on a corner site. Another important point was to see whether Price's published description was matched in any way or, in the case of properties no longer in existence, if any features such as prominent bays or entrance steps could be determined from historic Ordnance Survey maps.

The search proved to be very much a poignant journey back into the past, revealing as it did a period of London's history fast fading from living memory. Many houses were located in small Victorian terraces: several of which, including the roads themselves, had been demolished and the areas completely remodelled. There were also newer inter-war houses, lodging houses and pubs, as well as affluent and well known streets and addresses. The occupations listed also covered the whole spectrum of society, from people of independent means through to school teachers, shopkeepers, factory workers, lorry drivers, porters, and, in one clear example of the Register's purpose, a gas mask inspector. All these people were linked, not only by their location and their surname, but also by the outbreak of the conflict that had taken place less than a month previously.

From the total of 264 houses it was not possible to locate 19 properties. However, from their occupants, (individuals, childless couples or groups of unrelated persons), it was clear they could be eliminated easily from the search. On inspection, one corner property in Balfour Road, Islington, was very close to Price's actual description in *Fifty Years*. Although attached to a terrace behind, it could easily be mistaken for a detached house during a single visit at night. However, the household again did not match. After a careful study, which took several weeks, we were able to shortlist only two properties whose households fell within the criteria we had established.

The first, Key House in Lambeth close to the Oval cricket ground, was occupied by a Mortimer family in their early forties who had two children, a son and a daughter. They would have been seventeen and sixteen respectively in December 1937. The household was a large one and, despite there being six other closed records, it was possible to establish that one occupant was employed as a kitchen maid. Although promising, there were other factors which went against these particular Mortimers. The property was clearly a large apartment in a block of flats, not an individual house, and the description of this Mr Mortimer as a builder's labourer did not seem to be the profession that Price was alluding to in his report. It seems likely they were lodging with another unrelated family whose records were amongst those unavailable to view. As a result, this property and its family were ruled out of the investigation. The second shortlisted property, in Kensington,

West London, together with its occupants, forms the basis for the remainder of this book.

The Mortimers of Cadogan Square

No.28 Cadogan Square is a large late Victorian end-of-terrace townhouse situated on the junction of a side road, Clabon Mews. As befitting its location, midway between Sloane Square and Knightsbridge on the edge of Belgravia, the Mortimers that lived there in 1939 were an affluent upper-middle-class family, and the household was a large one. The census taken on 29 September lists a total of nine people, which includes two closed records. The principals were a middle-aged couple, Haliburton Mortimer, a stockbroker, and his wife Dorothy, together with their daughter Joan who was in her early thirties. The remaining persons were live-in staff and it is possible to establish from the open records that they were a ladies maid, a housemaid, a cook, and a butler. From the online Electoral Rolls it was also possible to confirm that this family were at the same address in December 1937, and had in fact lived there since 1926. Of all the households generated from our search of the 1939 National Register, this one fitted the profile to a striking degree: a City businessman and his family, including a daughter, living with permanent staff in a large corner house for a continuous period of nine years (the period that Price stated the sittings had taken place). The location was also easily within the stipulated travelling time from the Royal Societies Club in Piccadilly. This was the closest we had come so far in locating a family that had the potential to be Mr and Mrs X and their daughter. Further investigation was to prove to be an intriguing exercise, which was to alter our established views on Harry Price, as well as the history of the 'Rosalie' case as a whole.

Haliburton Stanley Mortimer was born on 16 October 1879 in the village of Shortlands in Kent, now part of the London Borough of Bromley. His father, Stanley Mortimer, was a former Captain in the Kings Royal Rifle Corps. It was also the 60th Rifles in which his son enlisted in 1914 at the age of thirty-five, serving and surviving the Great War in the rank of Lieutenant. A distant relation of Sir Walter Scott, he had been named after the novelist's grandmother, Barbara Haliburton. At All Saints Church in Harrow on 11 October 1905, aged twenty and now engaged as a London stockbroker, he had married Dorothy Frances Blackwell, five years his junior, and an heiress of the famous

Cross and Blackwell company. Following their marriage, the couple initially set up home at 11 Cadogan Gardens in Kensington. Their first child, Joan, was born on 18 October 1907 and a son, Roger, followed on 22 November 1909. The 1911 Census shows an exceedingly affluent household with a total of eight live-in servants. The family moved to two other addresses, one near Berkeley Square and another in Chelsea, before finally returning to Kensington and 28 Cadogan Square, a house they would occupy for several years before finally retiring to a flat in nearby Sloane Square.

A debutante, Joan Mortimer was introduced to fashionable London high society by her mother at the Spring-Gardens Galleries in April 1926. A swimming instructor at the Francis Holland School, she remained single until late in life, eventually marrying a barrister, Reginald Cockburn, in 1948. Educated at Ludgrove School and Eton, Roger Mortimer entered Sandhurst and was eventually commissioned into the Coldstream Guards in 1930, obtaining the rank of Captain. Initially reported as killed in action[273], he was captured during the retreat at Dunkirk and spent the rest of World War II as a POW. Between 1947 and 1975, he enjoyed a successful career as racing correspondent to the *Sunday Times*, and published a number of books including, in the early 1960s, a highly regarded history of the Derby. Much later after his death in 1991, between 2012 and 2014, his children Jane, Charlie and Louise, published their father's letters in three widely reviewed anthologies[274]. Haliburton Mortimer died in 1957; his wife Dorothy in 1968. Joan Cockburn, the last of the Mortimer family to know the household at 28 Cadogan Square in the 1930s, died in London in 1998 aged ninety. Even from such a brief overview, this is a family history that seems to be as far removed from the world of séances, Spiritualism and psychical investigation as it is conceivable to get. Was it possible that these Mortimers were the family that Harry Price visited on that cold winter's evening in December 1937, and in whose house little 'Rosalie' had made her appearance?

Up until our research effectively ruled the location out, I was always convinced that the Mortimer house was located in Brockley. The subject of coincidence, of events somehow overlapping and linking up in time, is a long-held personal interest, initiated in the early 1980s by reading an account of the oboe player Léon Goossens. In 1952, Goossens lost a diary during the course of a country walk. A year later he found the now deteriorated diary in a field and discovered that the leather cover had been packed with squares of old newspaper, one of which was a gossip column item about his own marriage nineteen years before. Unlike Dingwall and Hall, I felt it was quite within the realms of possibility that Price had gone to Brockley. Perhaps he had even been inspired to accept the appointment as it meant a return to the byways of his youth. Now the enquiry had moved to Kensington, I was immediately reminded of two connections to the same area that have already been mentioned in this book. These are the references to the area contained in Clifford Bax's review of *Fifty Years* in *John O'London's Weekly*, in which he talks of 'The Kensington Ghost Girl', and David Cohen's opinion, in *Spirit Child* and based on the same article, that the séance may well have taken place there.

We had in fact looked briefly at the Kensington area early on in our investigation, during the time of searching through the Brockley and Lewisham Electoral Rolls as Leah, on reading the Bax review, was surprised that I had not given it more consideration. The reasons for dismissing it I felt were straightforward. Bax was a member of the Society for Psychical Research and would have known that Price operated his psychical laboratories out of two addresses in South Kensington for several years. The location also went against published statements by Price that the séance had taken place in a suburb south of the Thames. Add to this the fact that Bax refers to 'Rosalie' having died around three years prior to the sitting, rather than the sixteen years clearly stated by Price in his book, made it seem somewhat obvious that he had made a mistake. Despite this, a check through the 1937 Electoral Roll for Kensington was made, and 24 individual addresses were found where at least one person with the Mortimer surname was registered. Just over half of these were single people. The rest were either childless couples or couples who may have had children below voting age that were not shown. As at this stage we considered the 'Rosalie letter' to be a hoax; the fact that children were not included was not an issue. No.28 Cadogan Square was amongst the addresses examined but, like all the rest, the house did not comply completely with Price's description. As I was not convinced by the area overall it was dismissed, bringing this brief sojourn in Kensington to a close. Now that the same household had appeared again, by a completely different route, I was forced to concede that I may have been too quick to dismiss it before, and it now deserved serious consideration.

Comparisons With *Fifty Years* – The House

We already knew that the description of the house given in *Fifty Years* needed to be treated with a certain amount of caution. If 28 Cadogan Square was indeed the address that Price visited on 15 December 1937, then he specifically made alterations for the purposes of his book. However, it is clear he kept certain aspects the same. The house is on a corner of a main road and a smaller side road, it has a basement area, there is a flight of stone steps up to the front door, and there are rooms with bay windows, one on top of the other, to one side of the entrance. Where it differs is in being an end-of-terrace rather than a double-fronted detached house, and having a total of six floors rather than four. With hindsight it is possible to see why he would do this.

By giving what appears to be a highly detailed description, Price the journalist and writer is connecting with his readers, inviting them to share in his mysterious adventure. We can all picture the house in our mind's eye and imagine the dynamic ghost hunter arriving and climbing the steps to the entrance. Ever on the alert, nothing gets past his scrutiny – who else but Harry Price, on a cold dark night, would recall there being *twelve* steps up to the front door? At the same time, Price the professional investigator, who had given an assurance that discretion and anonymity would be observed at all times, was conscious that, by describing a grand West London townhouse, he would be making the location somewhat conspicuous. There was the possibility that an enthusiastic reader might attempt to track the location down. It would be necessary, therefore, to make changes and also relocate the house to another part of London. From the outset he had used Brockley, when discussing the séance with Seymour de Lotbiniere, and it is logical that this would be carried through later by issuing published references to the South London area.

Surely it would have been far easier simply to state that the séance took place in London, at an address that was being withheld, in order to protect the privacy of those persons involved? But here, as well as other cases, for Price the writer this was not good enough. The result is that a certain amount of embellishment was always needed. Although not deliberately dishonest, it shows that 'Mollie' Goldney was more or less on the right track in her unpublished pen-portrait for Paul Tabori. Here she suggests that Price, despite his passionate commitment to psychical investigation, ultimately lacked the dispassionate exactness of a scientist in presenting the results of his work.

Personally I have never been happy with the description of the séance house given in *Fifty Years*. Its appearance always seemed somehow contrived. I believe that, in his description, Price was in fact including aspects of his own house in Pulborough, a large double-fronted detached house with bay windows, which would have come readily to mind as he drafted out his report. There is also another aspect connected with the house which is of specific interest. This is the size of the séance room itself. During the 1980s, I spent a large amount of time in both North and South London, producing floor plans of Victorian houses, mostly for conversion into flats for various local housing associations. The rooms in these buildings were laid out in certain proportions, and, from experience, I can say that the dimensions that Price gives are much larger than those normally encountered in the average house from this period. Even at 21 Wickham Road, a good example of a large detached house, the *Fifty Years* séance room is much bigger than what is present, or what would be expected from a building of this type.

Although 28 Cadogan Square is private property, it was still possible to find a large amount of information about it. By the mid-1940s, the Mortimer family had moved out, and the building subsequently underwent a large amount of alteration. In the early 1950s, the Ground and First Floors were being used as offices for the Cadogan Estate, and the remaining parts had been converted into self-contained flats. It became a Grade II Listed Building in 1977 and in 2000 the entire building was converted back to a single family house. From the Planning Department website of the Royal Borough of Kensington & Chelsea, I obtained PDF copies of the survey drawings which were prepared for the conversion in 2000. By omitting the partitioning that had clearly been added as part of the later conversion work and scaling the plans, it was possible to work out the layout and sizes of the rooms during the time the Mortimers lived there. As mentioned previously, Price states that the séance took place in a room with a bay window located on one side of the front door. This room was 'nearly square' and measured 24' x 21' x 9'6" high. At 28 Cadogan Square, the room in this location on the Ground Floor does have a bay window and would have measured 24'6" in one direction, but this is the long dimension rather than the shorter one as the room is narrowed by the adjacent entrance corridor. However, the room directly above on the First Floor *is* very close to the size and proportions of the séance room given in *Fifty Years*. This room is nearly square, has a bay window and measures 25'5" x 24'6" x 12'9" high. If this was the room, then how can the difference in figures be explained?

I don't believe that Harry Price actually got out a tape measure and measured the séance room during his visit. He did what any other visiting investigator would have done in the time available, and that would be to estimate the room's size and its proportions as he carried out his inspection. His figures are easily within what would be expected as a margin of error in mentally measuring a large room. Heights can be difficult to establish especially in large spaces, which would explain the measurement in Price's book being around 3 feet lower. The illustration included in this book shows more effectively the comparison between the room from *Fifty Years* and the actual First Floor room at 28 Cadogan Square. In conclusion, the exercise shows that it is not beyond the bounds of possibility that Price did visit this house in December 1937, and that the sitting took place there.

Comparisons With *Fifty Years* – The People

Like the description of the séance house, the details of the X family, together with those of Madame Z and the history of the 'Rosalie' sittings, needed, we felt, to be treated with a certain amount of caution. This is again not to imply blatant dishonesty on Price's part. He himself was reliant on what his hosts revealed to him and, whether it was true or not, would have duly reported what he was told. However, he may have felt that it was necessary, in order to comply with his agreement to anonymity, that some aspects of the household or those involved, needed some artistic licence in the presentation in order for a report to be published. Anyone examining the 'Rosalie' case is therefore presented with an account that may be a composite of varying degrees of fact and fiction. This requires an interpretive, rather than a literal investigation, in order to establish the truth.

An obvious similarity between the Mr X of *Fifty Years* and Mr Mortimer of Cadogan Square is their business in the City of London. In 1937, Haliburton Mortimer was working in a family stock broking business, Roger Mortimer & Co., which operated out of serviced offices at 20 Copthall Avenue, EC2. The building still stands in a road south of London Wall, not far from Moorgate Underground station. The firm appears to have been named in readiness for his son to take over following his military career. At the time, Captain Roger Mortimer was aged twenty-six and stationed in North Africa, making it impossible for him to have played the part of 'Jim' in the séance with

Price. There are indirect references to the Xs being an affluent London family in *Fifty Years*. As well as employing servants, the account describes expensive items such as 'four large Persian rugs' on the floor in the séance room, a Pye radio set and a gramophone. These Mortimers easily fit that profile. Price also mentions the household including two staff, the cook and the 'trim' parlour-maid. In 1937 at Cadogan Square, the Electoral Roll lists four staff members, one man and three women, who, we have established, were a butler, a ladies maid, a house maid, and a cook. Another clear difference is the age of Miss X. Price states that she was nearly seventeen while Joan Mortimer had not long turned thirty. These did not seem strong enough grounds to necessarily dismiss the household out of hand. The butler and the house maid might well have been given the night off, while Miss X's age could be a detail added by Price himself.

Clearly more was needed to establish whether these were the Mortimers we were looking for. Here we were helped considerably by the recently published letters of Roger Mortimer to his children. These give many interesting insights into the household at Cadogan Square, a real life *Upstairs, Downstairs* if ever there was one, both before and after World War II. From the books compiled by Jane Torday, and Louise and Charlie Mortimer, it was possible to draw up profiles of their grandparents, aunt and father, that could then be compared with Price's narrative. Reading and note-taking from all three books took some time, at the end of which we were confronted with a situation that we never thought would exist. Where a non-paranormal explanation for the 'Rosalie' phenomenon was concerned, several aspects of the household at 28 Cadogan Square tied in, not so much with the account published in *Fifty Years*, but more with the scenario as set down in the 'Rosalie letter' of April 1966. This was a document that we had, up until this point, considered more or less to be a hoax.

It stands to reason that, if it is difficult to accept a twelve-year-old's being able successfully to masquerade as a six-year-old ghost, then a thirty-year-old woman would appear to stand no chance. Although the actual mechanics of creating the spirit child were clearly impossible, the suggestion that the letter was in fact an attempt to disguise a real happening, one in which the Cadogan Square Mortimers were involved had, we felt, a serious amount of credibility. Haliburton Mortimer is described (Louise Mortimer, p.xi) as being 'a charming man but by all accounts not a great stockbroker', suggesting that some financial mishap of his own doing could have created the need to borrow money from someone that he knew. His ability to perform magic tricks with coins (Torday, p.306), also suggests proficiency with the sleight of hand needed successfully to conceal and employ a device to wedge open the séance room door without detection. Dorothy Mortimer is described (Louise Mortimer, p.10) as having little interest in church going, so the idea that Madame Z was a wealthy individual known to the family, rather than a widowed stranger initially encountered at a church bazaar, appeared more credible. Roger Mortimer also states (Charlie Mortimer, p.144) that his father at one time had a mistress whom he saw on visits to the South of France, a place that his wife disliked. Was it possible that this woman, named as Mrs O'Malley Keyes, could have been the wealthy French widow of the 'Rosalie letter' whom he knew he could exploit for money?

Outside of Roger Mortimer's letters, further research into the life of Haliburton Mortimer soon turned up some interesting information. As mentioned previously, the 'Rosalie letter' gives one date of the ending of the bogus séances as being the time that Nazi Germany invaded Czechoslovakia. This would mean that Mr X came into suitable funds, paid back Madame Z, and ended the deception by the middle of March 1939. Through newspaper searches we were able to establish, from notices in the *Derby Evening Telegraph* and the *Nottingham Evening Post*, that, at the end of February 1939, Haliburton Mortimer inherited a considerable amount of money. This was from the estate of a relative, Francis Haliburton Scott of Derbyshire, whose funeral he had attended on 28 November 1938. As executor of Scott's will, Mortimer had undertaken the sale of the former's property, a substantial estate called Draycott House. As the major beneficiary he received a similarly substantial legacy, in the region of just over £30,000. If the 'Rosalie letter' was true and Haliburton Mortimer was Mr X, then he would have been able to pay back any outstanding debts, including money that had been 'invested' previously on behalf of Madame Z. The involvement of Price also makes sense if we realise that, as the letter states, Madame had become suspicious and wanted confirmation that the proceedings were real and not spurious. The overall vibe one gets from reading his accounts, particularly the later piece in *Help Yourself*, is that he could not fully understand what was going on and why he was there.

Some aspects of the anonymous letter clearly do not fit in with the Cadogan Square household, and its writer being Joan Mortimer/Cockburn. The 'Rosalie' of the letter claimed to be the only surviving member from those times, yet in 1966, if she was indeed Mrs X, Dorothy

Mortimer was still very much alive. The writer also emphases the South London location of the sitting. Haliburton Mortimer himself only had a sister, not a younger brother, so the idea of a sibling playing the part of the youthful bank clerk 'Jim' cannot be true. Most importantly, the elaborate deception that comprises much of the letter to David Cohen, a deception which managed to fool the most experienced séance room investigator of the day, clearly could not have taken place the way it is described. Unless both Price and Madame Z experienced a collective hallucination, the thirty-year-old Joan Mortimer could not have passed for the naked child, at least in the way that is described as appearing and being examined in *Fifty Years*.

Although we had reached something of an impasse, there was one option available that could tip the balance either way. Although the original 'Rosalie letter' is now missing, a photograph of one single page, prepared by Peter Underwood as an illustration for his book *The Ghost Hunters*, was amongst the papers passed to me by his family in 2014. A handwriting analysis of the letter had been undertaken before, in the 1960s by Paul Tabori, but with nothing to compare it with, this had been limited to a character profile that has never been published. From the Government's online probate service I was able to download a PDF copy of the Last Will and Testament of Joan Cockburn. This comprises a ten-page Will drawn up in 1985, plus a later single-page Codicil from 1997. Although the lengthy wording of the Will was in typescript, Joan Cockburn had handwritten the date '18 September' and signed her name. Her signature was also present on the Codicil. On 26 May 2016, I sent a scanned copy of the page from the 'Rosalie letter', together with a copy of Joan Cockburn's Will and Codicil, to Margaret White MBIG[dip]IGS, a professional graphologist, highly experienced in comparing signatures and handwriting for legal cases. The request was that she examine all the documents to establish whether the writer was one and the same person. In such instances, for legal purposes, results from such analyses would be graded by her in four ways: In all probability, Probable, Inconclusive, and No or little resemblance.

On 27 June 2016, I received Margaret White's completed analysis comprising character profiles of Joan Cockburn and the writer of the 'Rosalie letter', plus a statement on the authorship of the material. The text of this latter document is reproduced complete below:

Conclusion with regard to the authorship of the three documents:

After carefully examining and considering the characteristics in the handwriting of all three examples of handwriting it is probable that they are those of one and the same individual.

Whilst on initial examination they appear to be very different – there are various identifying features:

- the careful consideration and reproduction of the copybook taught in childhood
- the letter 'J' with its positive upward and rightward movement matches the 't' strokes with the earlier handwritten page [the 'Rosalie letter'] in its ambition and determination to move forward and aspire to 'better things'
- the letter 'k' that is virtually identical in its shape and form on all documents examined
- the letter 'p' with its extended starting stroke within the handwritten script [the 'Rosalie letter'] and on the Will dated 18th September 1985
- the pressure exerted on the writing instrument, whilst diminished on the Codicil dated 18th May 1997 is still evident in the name 'Joan'
- the 'tremor' in the handwriting that appears on the Will dated 18th September 1985 is again replicated in the lettering of the Codicil date 18th May 1997 but in greater detail particularly in the upper zone of the 'C' – 'k' and 'b'. But the loss of neuro-muscular control is evident throughout both signatures.

All examples of the handwriting were examined using a digital microscope and therefore the detail and texture of the script could be clearly discerned.

[Signed]
Margaret D White MBIG[dip]IGS
Consultant Graphologist
26th June 2016

Due to the time lapse between the execution of the three documents, and the fact that they were copies and not originals, it was not possible to use the 'in all probability' statement. However, in subsequent correspondence, Margaret confirmed that even if original handwriting *was* involved, it is very rare that it is sufficiently 'unique' to warrant the term 'in all probability', and in Court it is taken that 'probably' is sufficiently positive that, together with other evidence, a decision can be made. If the results of the handwriting analysis had been inconclusive or No or little resemblance, then some element of mystery would still remain. The Probable result together with other evidence, including aspects of the house contained in Price's description and the size of the séance room, makes it certain that a major part of the 'Rosalie' case has been solved. On 15 December 1937, Harry Price went to 28 Cadogan Square, Kensington, and Haliburton Stanley Mortimer, his wife Dorothy and daughter Joan were Mr and Mrs X and Miss X. It must now be accepted that nothing paranormal took place there, and that what Price experienced that evening was a clever deception by a group of desperate people.

In April 1966, Joan Cockburn, then living with her husband in an apartment building in Seymour Place, Marylebone, sat down and wrote the 'Rosalie letter' to David Cohen. I believe at some point she had bought or seen a copy of his book *Price and His Spirit Child "Rosalie"*. She knew that an attempt was being made to track down the location of the séance in which she and her parents had taken part, and identify those persons involved. She may or may not have known of the existence of the earlier *Four Modern Ghosts*. If she did then she would have realised that important figures in the world of psychical research at that time believed 'Rosalie' to be a colourful story and, as a result, the family secret was safe. No.28 Cadogan Square would have been picked up in Mrs Goldney's sweep of the 1937 Telephone Directory. However, the restricted circulation of such a specialised publication as the SPR *Journal* meant that she had been unaware that her parents' former house had already been considered, but quickly dismissed at the time, as part of another investigation by Medhurst and Barrington. Now Cohen's book championing Harry Price, together with his comment on p.127 that he believed the séance took place in South Kensington, made it seem likely that a further investigation might very well prove successful. With her mother still alive this could cause extreme embarrassment to the family. She therefore took the decision to tackle the problem head on and write anonymously to Cohen giving details of the background of the séance. At the same time she hoped to draw a line underneath and stop any continued enquiry by pretending to be the only person now alive who was involved. Her brother's own military career in North Africa provided a suitable scenario for the demise of the youthful bank clerk 'Jim'. In order to conceal the existence of an accomplice who had played the part of the materialised 'Rosalie', she made up the elaborate story of undressing and redressing in the dark. I believe that Price may have been asked to change certain details by the Mortimers in order to provide additional protection to the family, should an account of the sitting be published, one of which was the age of Miss X who was made to be a teenager.

The solution to the identity of the X family, together with the location of the 'Rosalie' séance, was effected by an interpretive examination of the evidence rather than a literal one. Previous investigations had failed because first Price, and later on 'Rosalie' herself, for their own individual as well as combined reasons, each only told part of the story. The current investigation was clearly not over, though, as several fundamental questions still remained to be answered: How did Clifford Bax seemingly know that the séance had taken place in Kensington when Price had gone to great lengths to conceal its location? How did this upper-middle-class family, with no real interest in psychical research and Spiritualism, manage to fool, at least initially, the great Harry Price? And was it possible to establish identities for 'Jim', and, in particular, Madame Z and little 'Rosalie' herself?

'The Kensington Ghost Girl'

As with the presence of Wickham Road in the 'Rosalie' story, the most likely explanation that Clifford Bax talks about the case in the way he does in his review for *John O'London's Weekly*, is that of coincidence, brought about by the reasons already discussed. If he did know the real location, then I don't believe he would have been told by Harry Price but by the magazine's editor. Frank Whitaker is the only conceivable person I feel may, at some point, have been let into the secret. Whitaker, who later went on to become the Editor of *Country Life*, was an experienced newsman who knew how the public's appetite for ghostly stories was of great value in terms of circulation and sales. His relationship with Harry Price, as with the latter's association with Richard Lambert, was one of mutual benefit and, following Lambert's departure to Canada, he was determined to get new material from Price's pen into his own publication.

Whitaker's association with Price began towards the end of 1938. The two men met socially on at least two occasions and in December he was invited to join the Ghost Club. His first meeting was on 24 January 1939 when, with his wife Hilda, he attended the 'Marion' demonstration and heard at first hand Price's first public account of his 'Rosalie' experience. The letter from Price already quoted shows that the day after the Dinner, he and Whitaker discussed the case, and Price sent the MS of *Fifty Years*, which was subsequently revised at Whitaker's suggestion. Although he was keen to include psychical material in forthcoming issues, such an encounter that Price had related in his after dinner conversation might well have proved too much to take in. When pressed for some assurance that what he had revealed was the truth and not a tall tale, it is at this point that Price, in order to keep Whitaker on his side, *may* have entrusted the location to him. If this situation did or did not take place the outcome of their association at this point proved to be the same. Whitaker clearly sets out his stall in a letter to Price dated 29 March 1939. 'For my part, however, I don't intend to leave the subject alone,' he wrote, 'and now that Lambert is leaving the country I hope you will allow me to step into his shoes when you wish to write anything about current experiments, such as the fire-walking and the haunted rectory.'

Several months later, and knowing of his connection with the SPR and psychical matters, Whitaker entrusted Clifford Bax, a previous contributor to *John O'London's Weekly*, to write a review of Price's newly published *Fifty Years of Psychical Research*. If he did know of the location of the 'Rosalie' sitting, a case that by prior knowledge he realised would be included in the book, Whitaker could have let this slip when discussing the assignment beforehand, and 'The Kensington Ghost Girl' was the result. There is no mention of 'Rosalie' in a letter from Whitaker to Price arranging a luncheon appointment on 8 December 1939 after the review had appeared. The only reference to Bax's piece is an apology for a misprint. If Price went on to berate the newsman for his error then he did it in private and in person. He may have simply kept his mouth shut as to make a fuss over the review could, quite easily, have had the effect of drawing more unwanted attention. The other alternative is that again coincidence has simply played another significant part in the strange history of this extraordinary case.

Creating 'Rosalie'

If Harry Price had only experienced a partial materialisation of the type witnessed and described by Tony Cornell in the 1980s, then I doubt very much whether anyone would have ever heard of 'Rosalie', other than perhaps Richard Lambert. Undoubtedly, Price was convinced that he saw and felt a complete human figure in order for the experience to have had the effect that it did, not only in the days immediately following the séance, but also for some time afterwards. As it would have been impossible for Joan Mortimer to have created the effect in the way she claims in the 'Rosalie letter', the Mortimers must have used an accomplice, at least for this sitting and possibly others. The letter to Cohen was a masterstroke. The entire 'Rosalie' séance as set down in *Fifty Years* is a locked room mystery with a paranormal twist. Unless someone else was involved, 'Rosalie' *had* to be inside all the time but, in order to make the scenario work, Joan Mortimer had to take several years off her age. Even then the mechanics are difficult to believe, which is why people like Paul Tabori and Richard Medhurst at the time simply could not believe it.

How much the family knew of Price and his reputation as a critical debunker of phoney mediums is unclear. Price states that their knowledge of his activities came mostly from articles in *The Listener*, yet Mrs Mortimer's comment that she could 'guarantee a ghost' to someone of Price's calibre displays a confidence that borders on arrogance, as does the free rein that was given with regard to the control of the séance itself. Either the family had a foolproof method for creating a convincing materialisation, or they were astonishingly ignorant of just who they were letting into their house. The fact that by the end of the evening both Price and Madame Z were convinced they had experienced something extraordinary shows that, however the trick was done, it was effective and it worked.

Although she had become suspicious of the proceedings, to the extent that she required the involvement of a professional researcher, for Madame Z, the somewhat comforting presence of Price in the séance room that evening would have perhaps calmed some of her previous fears. The result being that the will to believe (a human trait mercilessly exploited by all fraudulent mediums and psychics), made the fakery convincing again. Where Harry Price was concerned, I feel that the circumstances of the sitting may well have put him somewhat off guard. His initially light-hearted attitude shows he clearly expected to walk into a typical Spiritualist meeting of the kind he had so often derided and ridiculed in his writings. For certain he would have expected it to be a 'cabinet' séance, with the medium entranced behind a curtain, and the proceedings involving gramophone music and possibly singing as well. Instead, in one of the most exclusive areas of London, in an expensive house in cultured and well-to-do company, the sitting took place in the most untypical of circumstances, 'in the round' as it were, without any of the usual Spiritualist trappings. The séance chamber was not in a Spiritualist church, a cramped front room, or medium's parlour; rather a large, elegant drawing room. The Mortimers themselves were in the class of educated and titled people that Price actively courted over many years for his organisations and investigations. He was also on his own with no companion or secretary to assist him. That he was somewhat pressurised by the situation is clear from his temporary indecision on how to control the fireplace area, as well as the randomness displayed in removing some objects from the room and leaving others inside.

When questioned by George Lethem, the Editor of *Light*, at the Ghost Club Dinner in 1939 as to the possibility of there being some kind of secret opening or moving wall into the séance room, Price was adamant that it was impossible. I know Harry Price was no fool, but I believe there was one aspect of the séance room that he overlooked that evening, and this was revealed by looking at the floor plans of the building. In one corner of the First Floor room, where I am convinced the séance took place, is a small cupboard built into an inner dividing wall. Its configuration shows it is original to the house and not part of the later conversion work for the Cadogan Estate. Although it was present at the time of the Mortimers, there is now no way of ascertaining what it looked like externally, or whether that part of the room was possibly panelled in some way to conceal it. Price states that the walls were distempered so it is difficult to explain why he does not describe it in his report. I have tried contacting the architects who supervised the later refurbishment back into a private house in the hope that record photographs exist showing what it was like, at least at that time, but with no success. The proposed drawings show that this area has now been completely changed. However, it is of a suitable size that someone could have been concealed inside. At a specific point, most likely after the radio was switched off (which seems suspiciously like a pre-arranged signal),the confederate then emerged and impersonated the 'Rosalie' child.

I cannot say for certain who the accomplice was who was given the astonishingly challenging and difficult role of becoming the materialisation of 'Rosalie'. It was a role fraught with danger. Whoever did it was someone the Mortimers knew they could trust, both not to make a mistake but also to keep the whole thing a secret. I don't believe an actual six-year-old child was used but someone older – we remember Price noted that 'Rosalie' appeared older than her alleged years – and it could be that the age given by Joan Mortimer to Cohen for herself, i.e. around eleven-twelve, was the actual age of the person involved. Price's account shows that Mrs Mortimer was clearly guiding the proceedings as to when the accomplice was in the correct position, the amount of time allowed for the 'materialisation' to be examined, and when it was time to bring the deception to a close. 'Rosalie' would have been told to say and do nothing, and to ignore anything that Price may have said or asked. That she did crack and speak when asked finally if she loved her mother is a very natural and human response, from a young person in extraordinary circumstances and in the presence of strangers. It was at this point that Mrs Mortimer immediately intervened and brought the sitting to an end. Price only states he had the impression that Madame Z was fondling the child, and in fact this may not have taken place. Under the cover of the emotional responses of Madame Z and Mrs Mortimer, the latter's being prompted by the incredible tension of the trickery being undertaken, 'Rosalie' quietly returned to her cupboard. One of the most astonishing events in the life of Harry Price had come to a close.

If it *was* a young girl who played 'Rosalie' that evening in 1937, then it is likely that she was still alive in 1966. As well as the presence of her mother, this would be another reason that Joan Mortimer went to such lengths to stress to Cohen in her letter that she was the only survivor. For the Mortimers, the obvious choice for the accomplice would be a family member of a suitable age, as this would have avoided bringing other people who were outsiders into the deception. Roger Mortimer's children were not born until much later. As he was away in the Coldstream Guards and did not return to England until after the end of the war, he may not have known anything about 'Rosalie' at all. A year younger than her brother Haliburton, Mamie Mortimer his only sibling, did have children – two girls and a boy – but they would have been too old to have played 'Rosalie' in 1937. Mamie herself had died of breast cancer in 1917, twenty years before. Having looked at the genealogy of the Mortimers in some detail, I can find no suitable candidate for 'Rosalie' amongst any of the family members. I am, therefore, inclined to believe that the young girl who played the part of the ghost was the daughter, of either a family friend or a business colleague, who was sympathetic enough to the Mortimers' predicament to allow their child to be used in such a way. This person may well have been the 'Jim' sitter, whose presence in the circle was to provide reassurance to 'Rosalie' in order for the proceedings to run smoothly.

With what we now know of the 'Rosalie' circle as a whole, the presence of 'Jim' as Price calls him is somewhat problematic. As with 'Rosalie' herself, there is nothing to say that this was the man's real name and not another pseudonym invented for the purposes of publication. He is described as being a 'gentlemanly bank clerk' (*Fifty Years*, p.136) in his early twenties, and a potential suitor of Miss X. As Joan Mortimer was still a single woman at the time 'Jim' may well have been courting her, but as Price deliberately adjusted her age then he may well have been somewhat older himself. He could conceivably have been a genuine outsider to the deception and was admitted on the understanding that the proceedings remained confidential. In this instance his genuine reactions would have added considerably to the performance as a whole. Also, the 'Jim' of the séance does not have to be the same person who Joan Mortimer claims pretended to be her mother's spirit guide in earlier sittings. A friend or associate could have created these deceptions regularly over time as the Price sitting did not feature this kind of communication. In Price's presence it was only necessary to materialise 'Rosalie' herself, in which case it is possible the family used a completely different person, perhaps even someone in their own employ.

There is another scenario, also involving a hidden accomplice, that I feel needs to be seriously considered, too. Although this draws the 'Rosalie' case nearer to something akin to Nicholas Roeg's famous 1973 film *Don't Look Now*, it is based on information contained in the published letters of Roger Mortimer. It would mean that the Mortimers used members of their own staff to assist in the deception, and paid them off once the need to create the ghost child had passed. In a letter written to his son Charlie in 1983 (Mortimer, 2012, p.145), Mortimer mentions the presence of a *dwarf maid* who was employed at some point in the household at Cadogan Square. He gives no indication of her age, only mentioning that, as well as her household duties, she was able to play jazz on the piano to a reasonable standard. This talent unfortunately was the apparent reason for her eventual dismissal from the Mortimer household. 'She was given the sack,' he notes, 'because her playing made the butler over-excited.'

In his correspondence, Mortimer also makes brief mentions of a number of employees. Based on his recollections, together with information drawn from various Electoral Rolls and the 1939 National Register, the family appear to have had a somewhat high turnover of staff. The somewhat droll antics of some of these characters can be found by reading the various books issued by his children. The cook, Mrs Tanner, was something of a family retainer and it would have been her that Price saw on his tour of the house in 1937. As has been previously noted, there were three other live-in staff at that time, a ladies maid, a housemaid and a male employee, most likely a butler named James Simmonds. Price was let in by a maid and describes meeting the cook during the course of his inspection. This leaves two employees unaccounted for. It is conceivable that James Simmonds played the role of the male sitter that Price calls 'Jim', and if one of the two female servants was the dwarf that Mortimer only calls by the nickname 'Minnie', then she took on the role of 'Rosalie', emerging from the cupboard naked to play the ghost. In the dim glow from the luminous plaques her small stature would have created the effect of a childlike height, and, after the initial shock of her appearance, the will to believe created the effect of the spirit child in the minds of both Price and Madame Z. Again it should be recalled that Price states that the materialisation appeared older than her alleged years. As employers in that period, the Mortimers would have had a high degree of control over their staff, and both could have been sworn to secrecy and then let go at some later date.

If the idea of a jazz-playing dwarf impersonating the materialisation of a dead child stretches credulity to beyond breaking point, it should be remembered that, where the adventures of Harry Price are concerned, the element of farce was in fact never too far away. Elements of the bigamous antics of Marianne Foyster at Borley Rectory at times make a soap opera script look tame, and the idea of a talking mongoose driving around the Isle of Man on a bus speaks for itself. Price was quite happy to be photographed jumping into a haunted bed with Cyril Joad, while the image of the Wagnerian-sized Mrs Duncan clinging screaming to the railings in a London street and keeping ghost hunters armed with X-Ray apparatus at bay, is something that I am sure Joe Orton would have been happy to have included as a set piece. It could be added that the sight of the maid in the nude, rather than her abilities on the piano, was the real reason behind the excitement that led to her eventual dismissal, if indeed these two members of the Cadogan Square staff were involved in the 'Rosalie' deception.

At the time of writing, we have been unable to find any further information about the female employee who could conceivably have been the dwarf maid described in Roger Mortimer's correspondence. Mortimer's absence from Cadogan Square for long periods suggests that the reason for her dismissal was an anecdotal story, and he was not privy to the real reasons behind her leaving. One of the two female servants in the Mortimers' employ in 1937 was then in her mid-forties and unlikely to have been mistaken as a child in a convincing way. She died in her late eighties in 1979. The other female employee from 1937 has an extremely common surname. She may be a woman of the same name employed by a family in Paddington in 1939, but this would also make her aged over forty at the time of the 'Rosalie' sitting. A woman in her mid-thirties with what appears to be the same Christian name is present on the 1939 National Register entry for the Mortimer household, but the actual person may be one of the two closed records in the listing for 28 Cadogan Square. If so her details will be out of public view for some time.

In conclusion, although the matter of identity remains problematic, I feel certain that the Mortimers used a confederate to fake the 'Rosalie' spirit child. The effect was created by hiding this accomplice within the room, who crucially went undetected by Harry Price for the duration of the séance.

The Identities of Madame Z and 'Rosalie'

Despite the advances made during the summer of 2016 in identifying both the location and organisers of the 'Rosalie' circle, to our disappointment (and no doubt that of the reader as well) we have not been able – despite much continued work and study – to solve the mystery outright. The identities of the case's most tragic figures, Madame Z and little 'Rosalie', are still at present unknown to us. For this part of the investigation we considered and followed two quite different scenarios. The first was that the real Madame Z may have been known by, or was connected with, the Mortimers of Cadogan Square in some way, and that by continuing to examine them it might be possible to identify 'Rosalie's' mother and 'Rosalie' herself. Here we felt that the biography provided in *Fifty Years*, augmented by material contained in the 'Rosalie letter', might essentially be correct, but that elements may have been changed. Alternatively Price could genuinely be reporting a back story purposely camouflaged by the Mortimers themselves. The second and more radical line of thinking was that if Clifford Bax *did* know the real protocols of the sitting then, as well as the Kensington location, the rest of his brief account was also true. In this case, instead of a child who was born around 1915 and died in 1921, we needed to consider a six-year-old girl who had died much later, around three years before the sitting took place.

Based on the back story from *Fifty Years*, we are looking for a widowed French nurse in her late forties whose husband was an officer in the British Army. From the account given in the 'Rosalie letter', this person must also be wealthy enough to possess money that she was happy to have 'invested' on her behalf. Almost immediately Price's account looks somewhat suspect. Nurses working in the 1930s would not have been the most affluent of people, and the impression is that the amount of money Mr X needed to prop up his financial dealings was a considerable one. Price may have been told and believed that Madame Z was a Frenchwoman, and reported it as such. Alternatively, as with other aspects of his account, he set down out of necessity a synthesis of the truth in order to provide greater anonymity to the people involved.

The person who, for some time, was our front runner for the role of Madame Z was Jane Byrnes Malley, born in New Haven, Connecticut, on 25 February 1888. She was the daughter of Edward Malley (1827-1909), a successful businessman and owner of a famous department store, The Edw. Malley Co., from which he earned his not inconsiderable wealth. There is some confusion and inconsistency as to the actual year of Jane Malley's birth, which changes on various documents that I have examined. For example, on the death certificate issued by the American Consulate in July 1965, it is given as 25 February 1890, making her forty-seven in 1937, but this incorrectly states she was born in New York. On various passenger lists for ships sailing between Europe and America, the year changes regularly between 1888 and 1890. However, further study confirmed her birth year as 1888 ('on the right side of fifty' as Price puts it in *Fifty Years*, p.135) as her mother, Mary 'Mamie' Carey, died in childbirth on 15 March 1889; the child also did not survive.

In December 1937, Jane Byrnes O'Malley-Keyes, as she was then known, fills the profile of Madame Z extremely well. A wealthy socialite who counted Edward VIII and Mrs Simpson as close friends, her son Hamilton's marriage (later in 1941) took place in the presence of Queen Elizabeth, The Queen Mother. She had a long association with the South of France and was known by society gossip columnists as the 'Queen of Biarritz'. There she owned a villa and also rented a flat at the prestigious Bellvue Casino. She also had a large house in Anglet to which she later retired after the war. A widow, her husband Lieutenant-Colonel Middleton Joseph O'Malley-Keyes from Ross, County Mayo, formerly of the Royal Field Artillery, had died of heart failure in Trinidad while on a cruise in February 1933. During World War I, she had worked as a voluntary nurse at Brighton, where she also entertained injured soldiers with song recitals. It is easy to see how these details could, with a modest amount of retouching, either by the Mortimers or Harry Price, form the basis of the profile of the mother of ghostly 'Rosalie'.

We also found strong connections between Jane O'Malley-Keyes and the Mortimers of Cadogan Square. Her brother-in-law was married to Dorothy Mortimer's sister, and there was also another marriage between Jane O'Malley-Keyes' sister-in-law and a cousin of Mrs Mortimer. We also have Roger Mortimer's (albeit anecdotal) assertion that she and his father Haliburton were at one time lovers, or at least that their relationship was more than simply platonic. Roger also states that, as a young boy, he took part in a charity concert organised for the troops by Mrs O'Malley-Keyes at the Wigmore Hall in London in which she also performed. Both families moved in the same high social circles and attended the same society functions and parties. For example, *The Times* for 2 July 1931 shows one of Jane O'Malley-Keyes' daughters attending a cabaret dance, given by a Mrs Converse for her daughters, at a house in Mansfield Street, Marylebone, at which Joan Mortimer was also present. In 1938, Mrs O'Malley-Keyes' eldest son Hamilton was briefly engaged to an Angela Tod, the daughter of Colonel A.A. Tod of the Prince Consort's Own Rifle Brigade, who lived close by the Mortimers at 19 Cadogan Square. If, as Roger Mortimer claims, his father and the 'Queen of Biarritz' were at one time lovers, then this wealthy woman would be an ideal choice to approach when large amounts of money were needed to support his failed business dealings. He would also have learned, at the pillow it could be guessed as well as through family talk, details of her private life that could later be used to his advantage. Mr Mortimer would also clearly want no detail of such an important person to be made public at a later date by Harry Price in his books or articles. Price may or may not have known who she really was, but it would have been made clear to him that everything about her needed to remain completely confidential.

The essential problem with Jane O'Malley-Keyes is that, although she did have five children, three of whom were girls, all survived infancy, grew to adulthood and later married. Her first son Hamilton was born in 1910, the year after his parents' marriage. The daughters Eugenie, Rosemary (also known as Rose Marie) and June were born in 1913 and 1914, while her second son Nial was born in November 1915. Although by the time Joan Mortimer sat down to write the 'Rosalie letter' their mother had died – at the age of seventy-six at her villa "Castel Meretmont" in Anglet on 28 August 1964 – all of her children were still alive. There are no documents that we have been able to examine that show Jane O'Mally-Keyes had another child who died around the age of six, whom she would want to contact through séances with the Mortimers. The next logical progression, that 'Rosalie' may have been not her own child but one of her children's, also does not equate as all of Mrs O'Mally-Keyes various grandchildren were born after the 1937 séance. If Jane O'Malley-Keyes was Madame Z, then how to explain her meeting with Harry Price? Why was the 'Queen of Biarritz' grieving so bitterly for what, for all intents and purposes, was her own dead child, but for which no records appear to exist?

An unsatisfactory solution is that 'Rosalie' may have been born prior to her marriage in 1909 but is unacknowledged in the official family history. This child was given up for adoption, but Jane Malley knew that she had subsequently died at a young age. In these circumstances, the guilt generated by her death could well have created the need to be reunited with a child she never knew much later in life. Although in no way does it set a precedent, it must be said that the Malleys of New Haven were in fact no strangers to mystery and potential scandal. In 1882, Jane Bynes Malley's half-brother Walter, by her father's first marriage was, together with his cousin Jimmy Malley, accused and put on trial for the murder of Jennie Cramer, a local beauty who was found raped and poisoned to death on a sand bar in the sea off West Haven on 6 August the previous year. The case became known as 'The Elm City Tragedy' and, despite the widespread local feeling that the two men were guilty as charged, they were eventually acquitted. This verdict gave rise to further speculation that rich and influential Edward Malley had in fact paid off the jury. It could be argued that, if Mr Malley had been able to save his son from an appointment with the hangman, then the covering up of a potentially embarrassing teenage pregnancy would have been a relatively straightforward undertaking for such a suitably affluent and, it must be said, unscrupulous person.

Where the needs of the Mortimers was concerned, once Price had served his purpose in allaying the fears of Madame Z, the family clearly kept him at arm's length until the outbreak of the war conveniently brought their association to an end. There may be some truth in the account of the family taking a motoring trip abroad, one that was cut short by the invasion of France, but it is unlikely that Jane O'Malley-Keyes was with them in the way that Price describes in *Help Yourself.* Passenger lists for liners crossing the Atlantic show she made two trips to New York in January and March 1939, and it seems likely that she spent the war years in America, returning to Biarritz much later after hostilities had ceased. If she was Madame Z, then by this time Jane O'Malley-Keyes had also served her purpose, and Joan Mortimer could truthfully state that 'Rosalie's' mother was dead when she wrote her letter to David Cohen in the Spring of 1966.

With our second line of enquiry, the 'believing in Bax' route, we are able to suggest a solution to the identities of both Madame Z and 'Rosalie', albeit a controversial one. For this scenario, although our reasoning is presented, the names of those persons involved are withheld. If through Frank Whittaker, Clifford Bax was given details of the séance location and the history of the real life 'Rosalie', then we felt that there may have been some truth in Price's account of Mrs X's meeting Madame Z at a local church function, or at least socially in the Kensington area. Guided by Bax's closing remark that the materialisation was of a girl 'who had been dead for, I think, three years', we restricted our search to children who were born and died in the Kensington area between 1927 and 1935. This produced a list of fourteen female children aged five and over. Of these, one child stood out from all the rest as, due to her background and history, there seemed the possibility that, as with other aspects of his reporting, Price's commitment to anonymity had resulted in another synthesis of the truth. This child died from appendicitis aged eight in a private hospital in early 1935. The mother's family background was in brewing (cf. the 'hop merchant' aspect of Price's original typescript) and, although from Scotland, the family was of French Huguenot descent. They also lived in the Kensington/Chelsea area close to Cadogan Square. Everything seemed to fit except for one salient point: this 'Rosalie's' natural mother had in fact died in 1927. Therefore, we suggest that instead of meeting 'Rosalie's' mother on that dark winter's night, Price could have actually met her grieving father and for the purpose of publication made the crucial decision to alter his identity completely. This 'Rosalie's' father also worked as a broker in the City of London, so could have known Haliburton Mortimer socially. In that way, he was chosen as a financial backstop when the Mortimers ran into trouble in the period that culminated in Price's visit in December 1937. Once Mr Mortimer returned to funds, there was no longer any need to continue the subterfuge and Mrs Mortimer again lost her 'mediumship'. In her letter to David Cohen, Joan Cockburn, like Price before her, continued the pretence, as to reveal more details could have resulted in further investigation, which was the opposite of the letter's intention.

Whatever the real truth, the story of 'Rosalie' continues to retain some of its mystery. This is something about which I have mixed feelings. To close the case file is the ultimate aim of the researcher, but perhaps it is fitting that, even today, decades after the event and years after his own death, Harry Price the maverick 'psychist' can still hold some of the cards close to his chest. Whether they will finally be revealed is something that only time will tell.

SIXTEEN

'ROSALIE' – SUMMING UP AN EXTRAORDINARY CASE

Ad of the information, facts and conclusions established by the present author have now been presented to the reader. Much of the mystery of previous decades has been explained although some secrets still remain. Eighty years after the event we now have a much clearer perspective on what, without any exaggeration, is an extraordinary chapter in the history of twentieth century psychical research. It is somewhat apt that the catalyst which brought such a case into existence was no less an extraordinary personality in his own right. Harry Price emerges vindicated of many accusations levelled at him by previous investigators, accusations that were believed by a generation of previous readers. It is clear that Price acted honourably in his dealings with the Mortimer family, and went to great and successful lengths to keep his promise to protect their identity. However, the actions of the Mortimers, in cruelly tricking a vulnerable person for their own means are no less than those of the many heartless charlatans who have battened onto the bereaved down through the years and, as a result, speak for themselves.

227

I have stressed throughout this book that Harry Price was one of the most experienced séance room investigators of his day, but he was not infallible. Despite his shrewd outlook on life he had no clear idea of the real reasons behind the need for the Mortimers to hold their séances, and was as exasperated by his experience as many subsequent commentators. Although Madame Z, the mother of 'Rosalie', was tricked and upset by Mr and Mrs X and their family, Price was in many ways their greatest victim, harangued and ridiculed as he was both while alive and later posthumously, by both psychical researchers and Spiritualists alike. 'Rosalie' became a painful memory from which, in later years, he clearly attempted to distance himself. His later contribution to *Help Yourself* was very much a ghost story for Christmas that provided a convenient opportunity to draw the line under it once and for all. Eventually, in private, he adopted a similar stance, such as telling the wife of Professor John Flugel, a ULCPI Council Member, that the séance house had been destroyed by bombing in the Blitz[275].

Price's situation in 1939, after first revealing his experience to the public, is not unique where paranormal investigation is concerned. There are a number of instances where investigators of some standing, who have experienced what they believe to have been genuine psychical phenomena, have found themselves distanced and criticised by colleagues and members of their own organisations, over and above the usual sceptical response levelled by hard-line critics and non-believers. Two well known examples from recent years, with similar histories and backlashes, are the Scole Experiment from the 1990s, mentioned in the Introduction, and the earlier and more well known Enfield Poltergeist from 1977-78. In both instances the researchers found themselves at odds with colleagues unable to accept their findings and conclusions. By his own sharp practice, Price also mired his own investigation into the mediumship of Rudi Schneider years before.

Although at the end of my 'Rosalie' journey I now concede that no genuine mediumistic phenomena took place, I do still believe that materialisation of some sort can occur, and is likely to have been demonstrated at some point in the past. Physical mediumship therefore remains a particularly close interest. What also continues is the subject's enduring controversy as demonstrated, in the summer of 2016 when this book was nearing completion, by the exposure of a prominent physical medium and healer from England who was caught, faking phenomena, by an infra-red camera at a blackout séance in Ashford, Kent[276].

Harry Price was one psychical researcher who did believe that genuine materialisation phenomena can take place. He was adamant that he experienced it in sittings with both Rudi Schneider and Stella Cranshaw. It is perhaps fitting then to close this book with a quotation from his final letter to 'Mollie' Goldney, written on 27 March 1948. As Anita Gregory has suggested, this may be the very last letter he ever wrote[277], set down less than forty-eight hours before his death. The main talking point was the man who not only became one of his fiercest critics, but who eventually lost his own belief and interest, both in the paranormal and its investigators[278]. 'Talk about thrashing a dead horse!' he grumbled, 'It would have been impossible *by any means* [Price's italics] to have secreted an "accomplice" at the Rudi sittings. The lights were on half the time, the door locked or sealed, and similar séances have been held all over the Continent.' 'And how can Dingwall apply that theory to the séances we had with Willy [Schneider] at Munich?' he continued, '...I wonder if D. has forgotten that signed statement he gave me after a Stella sitting (when he was lying on the floor!) to the effect that he saw a bulbous materialisation, attached to an ectoplasmic cord, writhing about near Stella's feet,' adding somewhat whimsically, 'D is a strange chap ... '. Whether in fact thoughts of a cold wintry evening in London several years before, and a little girl named 'Rosalie', passed through his mind in the days and hours before he wrote these final words is something that we will never know.

PRICE'S 'ROSALIE' INTRODUCTION IN *FIFTY YEARS OF PSYCHICAL RESEARCH*

T his is the page length Introduction to the original 'Rosalie' report, which headed Chapter VIII of Harry Price's *Fifty Years of Psychical Research*. It was drafted initially at some point during 1938, and was revised by Price in March 1939 at the suggestion of the editor at Longmans, Ken Potter, prior to publication:

Before we leave the subject of physical phenomena, I must describe the most remarkable case of materialization, or rather alleged materialization, I have ever witnessed. It is with considerable hesitation that I publish this account, as I have had only one sitting, and have been unable, as yet, to obtain independent corroboration of the extraordinary 'phenomenon' which I witnessed. Though I am satisfied that I took every precaution against deception which my long experience in these matters suggested, it is still possible that I *was* [Price's italics] deceived, and I do not, as yet, accept the materialization at its face value. But if I *was* [Price's italics] deceived, how was it done and what possible motive could there have been? The séance was held fifteen months before these introductory remarks were written, and the publishers of this volume saw the report soon after I wrote it, within a few hours of the termination of the séance. After careful consideration, they think that, with the above reservations, the protocol of the séance should be printed. Striking as my experience was, it is not comparable with the classic experiments of Sir William Crookes with the medium Florrie Cook, more than sixty years ago (*Researches in the Phenomena of Spiritualism*, London, 1874). He not only saw, felt and embraced the "spirit", "Katie King," but actually photographed it forty times. Sometimes Florrie and "Katie" appear in the same photograph. To the end of his days, nothing could shake Sir William's conviction that he had contacted with the spirit world. To conclude, although I am publishing a record of this most interesting séance, which much impressed me at the time, I am suspending judgment as to whether the "materialization" was what it purported to be.

THE 'ROSALIE' LETTER

The following is the complete text of the 'Rosalie' letter sent to David Cohen in April 1966. It was first published in its entirety in Paul Tabori's *Beyond the Senses* in 1971 and here, as then, is reproduced with its original spelling and punctuation. The letter was passed by Paul Tabori to Peter Underwood who kept the original in his possession for many years. Its whereabouts today are unclear as it was not amongst the papers and books passed to the present author by Chris Underwood following his father's death in November 2014, and may now be lost.

London

April 1966

Dear Mr. Cohen,

I have read your book about Harry Price and his spirit child with interest and; forgive me; with some amusement for I am always amused at the various guesses which are constantly being hazarded about the Rosalie ghost. But then I am in a rather privileged position being now the only living person who knows the whole truth about the séances held in our house thirty years ago. As this long-kept secret concerns the honour of my father, it is a matter of some doubt whether I am justified in divulging it now, particularly as I promised my parents never to do so, but as my parents are dead, and as I have no intention of disclosing their identity, perhaps I may be forgiven for this breach of trust.

I suppose that anyone who did not know my father would think his actions shameful but he was the kindest and most lovable man and the trouble he got himself into was more the result of weakness than of any real defect in his character. Of course, I was only a small girl at the time of my father's trouble and knew nothing of the cause of his distress, but many years later, after his death, my mother told me that it was a case of one deceit leading inevitably to another – one deceit being used to cover a preceding deceit. However, if it had not been for my father's trouble, there would never have been a Rosalie.

My father had a good position; a position of trust, in a City firm and we were living, in the nineteen-thirties, in a fashionable suburb of S.E. London. My mother did not know when or why my father started to speculate on the stock market. She told me that he lost money in what I think she called "staggering" and "borrowed" money from his firm in order to cover his losses. Naturally the time arrived when this money had to be returned and, about this time, my father became acquainted with a wealthy French widow who lived in our neighbourhood. When, some time later, I met Madame I took an instant dislike to her. She was a grasping, suspicious woman and something of a miser. The only soft spot in her hard nature appeared to be a love of her dead child; if such a morbid fixation can be called love. According to my mother, my father suggested to Madame that he could invest some money for her at a high rate of interest and this appeal to her cupidity proved too great a temptation for Madame to resist. But poor father, although he was now able to return the money he had "borrowed" from his firm, was completely in Madame's power. He was able to pay the interest on the money he had pretended to invest, but Madame had to be prevented from asking for the return of her capital, or from making any enquiries about some worthless "securities" my father had given her. My mother told me that she was convinced that had Madame discovered she had been tricked, there was absolutely no doubt that she would immediately have started legal proceedings. However, my mother assured me, that this deceit was merely a matter of time, because my father had cause to believe that he would, within a year or two, be in a position to pay Madame the money she had given him. In fact this is actually what did happen and sometime before the last war, my father persuaded Madame to sell her shares in the pretext that they were likely to depreciate in value. My mother thought this was when Hitler invaded Czechoslovakia, or Austria, because she remembered that my father used the international situation as a reason for the likelihood of depreciation. Of course, some twenty years had passed when my mother told me about my father's financial difficulties, and she was then a little vague about details, but I remember my father returning from the City one evening and saying to my mother with some excitement, "XXXX [word crossed out that Tabori states (p.167) could be deciphered as the name 'Edith' from the original letter], we can now exorcise the ghost." This, I now believe, must have been a reference to the ending of a period of great anxiety suffered by my parents.

But I must return to a time about two years before this happy ending, when it was deperately [*sic*] necessary to retain Madame's faith in my father and to prevent her from asking embarrassing questions about her "investments". Unfortunately, for my father, Madame started to show some suspicious interest in her capital and her inquisitiveness had, in some way, to be diverted. As Madame was contantly [*sic*] talking to my father about her dead child, Rosalie, he came to the conclusion that this was the only weak link in her armour: the only interest stronger than her interest in money, and therefore the only interest that could be used to save him, and his family, from disgrace. So my father turned towards spiritualism, purchased some books on the subject and informed Madame that my mother was an amateur medium and that séances were sometimes held at our home.

It was at this time that I was first brought into the deception. My parents asked me to take part in, what they called, "a ghost game" to be played as a harmless joke on a French lady. At first my part in this business was childishly simple. I was to slip noiselessly into the darkened room soon after the others had settled down, take up a position in the corner of the room and answer some questions in a hushed, childish lisp. I was then, at a pre-arranged signal from my mother, to slip silently out of the room before the lights were switched on. But when we started to rehearse the procedure we came up against our first snag. Although my father oiled the hinges and handle mechanism of the door, the latter could not be persuaded to act noiselessly. My father overcame the difficulty by making a small wedge which he stealthily inserted into the door catch when finally closing the door before the séance commenced. A wedge which he removed when opening the door after the séance had ended. Thus I did not have to touch the rather loose handle when entering and leaving the room.

When my parents were satisfied with these rehearsals, my father told Madame that a child voice had asked for her at a séance held at our house. Madame showed great interest and asked to be allowed to visit our home, meet my mother and attend a séance.

I have to admit to experiencing a feeling of excitement and pleasure of the anticipation of this game of ghosts. Perhaps this was reprehensible of me but, it must be remembered, that I was a mere child of ten years at this time and the idea of playing a trick on a grown-up seemed to be an intriguing adventure. This feeling, I have no doubt, came from the child-desire to be important and to be clever enough to put one over an adult world which, the child feels, is constantly exerting its grown-up superiority.

The second snag which my father had to contend with was Jack, our Airedale dog, who was greatly attached to us, as we were to him. Whenever any of the family were in the house, Jack was completely miserable if he could not be with us, whining and scratching at doors until he found us. My father said he could not trust the servants to keep him in the kitchen during the séances, because Jack was an adept at slipping out of any door which had to be opened, even for a second. The danger had to be overcome of his flinging open the unlatched séance door and so father decided to have him in the room during the séances where, as long as mother and father were there, he could be relied upon to remain quiet. Much later my father realized that the presence of Jack at the séances could have been a clue to an intelligent investigator, but here we were lucky for the clue was never discovered, not even, I believe, by any of the many authors who have written about Rosalie.

My mother was, at first, rather apprehensive about these séances and my father had to give up the idea of asking her to simulate a trance condition. She was to play as passive a part as possible and merely to ask certain questions of the spirit, commencing with, "I feel the child is in the room – are you there – are you there Rosalie?" After she had repeated this three or four times, I was to whisper, in as childish a voice as I could answer, "Yes – Rosalie is here."

If I remember correctly, Madame first visited our home for a sitting about two days after the Crystal Palace fire, an event which caused a great stir in our part of London. The séance went without a hitch. I waited in the hall after Madame and my parents had entered the room and I listened for the wireless to be switched-off, which was my signal to slip into the room. I was very nervous and excited at this first séance and nearly forgot to switch-off the hall light before opening the séance door, an omission which could have been fatal to our purpose. The door opened noiselessly at a slight pressure and I crept into the room and waited. I answered about five or six questions, giving the answers which had been suggested by my father: "I am very, very happy" – "I walk in meadows filled with beautiful flowers" – "I play with the other children – they are very kind to me" – "A beautiful lady in shining white looks after us" etc. After Madame had departed, my parents told me that they were very pleased with my performance – I gathered that Madame was suitably impressed.

Many such séances followed, although I do not think they were as frequent as one a week, as Mr. Price suggested. My impression is that we held one or two a month, usually, if not always, on a Wednesday evening. As the sittings progressed my father became more adventurous, and when Madame asked whether she would ever see her child at a séance, father told her that this might be possible. Thus we began to practise with an electric-torch whose bulb had been covered by one or two layers of blue tissue paper. This I held at chest level, pointing it away from the sitters and towards my face. The very dim, slightly blue light gave a suitable ghostly appearance to my face. Indeed I remember almost frightening the life out of myself when I tried this out in front of my bedroom mirror. I wore a black dress, black stockings and black gloves for this trick and my mother told me that the apeparance [*sic*] of a disembodied face, dimly underlighted in blue, was most eerie. Madame seemed to accept this face as that of her dead child, so I presume that I must have looked rather like Rosalie or, what is perhaps more probable, I looked like nothing on earth and therefore was accepted as not of this world.

After some months my father decided to ask his young brother, Uncle Jim, to help him in this ghost game. I think the reason for this was that Madame had asked whether Rosalie was the only spirit which appeared at our séances, and what had happened before the child had made an appearance. Father, who was always anxious to allay Madame's slightest suspicion, said that several other spirits had spoken, but that her presence attracted Rosalie more than the other spirits, who would, no doubt, return when Rosalie became less insistent. Uncle Jim was a very dear person and the family was terribly distressed when he was killed, in 1942, fighting in North Africa. He was divoted [*sic*] to my father, as we all were, and eager to help in what he thought was "rather a lark". So Uncle Jim, on occasions, waited in his stockinged feet in the hall with me, and we took it in turns to enter the dark room. He spoke in the voice of Big Chief Eagle of the Mohawk Tribe, or an ancient Chinese philosopher, or any other person who appealed to his imagination. I remember on one occasion he became General Gordon, I think he was reading a biography at the time, and on another, when I had a bad cold, he took the whole séance using one or two different voices. My uncle's sense of humour caused my parents some anxiety. Listening to him from the hall, I had great difficulty in suppressing a giggle.

Some time before my father had thought of producing the spirit of Rosalie, he had told Madame that he had a daughter, but had not mentioned my age. Soon after the séances had commenced, Madame asked my father how old was his daughter and father, always on his guard and thinking that there might be some suspicious connection in her mind between the spirit child and myself, said I was sixteen years old.

Unfortunately, a month or two later, Madame asked why she had never met this teenage daughter and father countered that by saying that I usually attended physical training classes on Wednesday evenings but, no doubt, she would meet me before very long. I believe there were gym classes for adults much publicised at this time and the claim that I attended these classes made it seem impossible that I could have been young enough to have impersonated Rosalie.

However it was now rather imperative to produce a teenage daughter so – what to do?

My parents considered the possibility of bringing a young person into the house to play the part of their daughter, but they soon abandoned the idea as impracticable, – whom could they ask to play this part? – would it not be dangerous to allow the Rosalie secret to go outside the family? It was finally decided that I must impersonate myself, or more correctly, my elder self. I had played the part of a child some years my junior and now I must play the part of a girl, some years my senior.

My mother went to work on me and with the aid of cosmetics, a teenage dress, a padded bust-bodice, a new hair-do and high heeled shoes, brought about a fairly convincing transformation. It is true I was a little short for a sixteen year old, but the high heeled shoes and the hair-do had added some inches to my height. For several evenings I was rehearsed in my new part until I became, more or less, accustomed to moving and behaving without awkwardness. Strangely enough I felt quite at home as a teenager and seemed to put on a new personality with my new clothes. My mother was rather frightened that Madame, having seen my face during some of the séances, would recognize me, the teenage daughter, as Rosalie, but my father said that even he could not have recognized me in the peculiar light of the séance room and did not think it possible that Madame would so. As the Rosalie séances continued my parents were forced to take greater and greater risks, but they had passed the point of no return and therefore could not retract.

Some two or three weeks later I was introduced to Madame who seemed to accept me without question. This was the first time I had seen her, although we had been in the same room many times. I cannot say I was exactly attracted to this severe, taciturn Frenchwoman. She seemed permanently disgruntled and I cannot remember ever seeing her smile. I remember that at this first meeting we spoke about a coronation which had taken place about a week previously – I suppose this must have been the coronation of George VI because I remember the now Duke of Windsor had abdicated at the end of the previous year.

After this introduction I was in the room for about a quarter of an hour before excusing myself by saying that I was going to my gym class. My mother had bought for me a white blouse and pair of black shorts, their being, I believe, the fashionable uniform for physical training classes at that time, and these had been placed on the sofa in the séance room in order to impress Madame. These I picked-up on leaving the room and, after waiting for a moment or two in the hall, opened and closed the front door before slipping upstairs to remove my teenage disguise. I passed Uncle Jim on the stairs who was coming down to impersonate the first spirit.

For some months after this all went well until one disasterous [*sic*] evening in, I think, late November. This mishap was entirely my fault. I had become, after so many successful séances, rather over-confident and ignored my father's instructions. He had told me that if Madame asked the spirit anything about Rosalie's life on earth, I was either to remain silent or to say I could not remember. I cannot recall the question that Madame asked me on that evening but I foolishly attempted to answer and, of course, it was the wrong answer. After the séance something like a quarrel broke out between my parents and Madame. She said she was far from satisfied that she had not been tricked and my father said that even spirits could forget instances in their earth life and that it was many years since Rosalie had been on earth. Naturally, I was not present during this altercation, but I learnt about it later, and the upshot of the dispute was, I was told, that father offered to have a séance investigated by a trained investigator and Madame suggested Harry Price.

For the first time since the séances had commenced my father was worried. During the past year he had been reading books on spiritualism and realized that a séance with controls would be the most difficult one we had yet given. So my parents, Uncle Jim and I went into a huddle and worked out a method of procedure. My mother was to telephone Mr. Price, invite him to a séance and extract from him an assurance of secrecy. Considering the danger of one investigation, my father did not want to risk further investigation and should Mr. Price publish our names and addresses it would be difficult, if not impossible, to avoid further investigation and enquiry. Apart from my parents, Madame and Mr. Price, I, as the teenage daughter, and Uncle Jim, as my boy-friend, were to be sitters at the séance. The importance of my being in the room if Mr. Price sealed the door, and father assured us that he would wish to do this, was obvious. There were two reasons for Uncle Jim being a sitter. One, my father thought it advisable to have an extra helper in the room to cover, if possible any minor, or unexpected mishap. Two, he would, as my boy-friend, add testimony to my assumed teenage. Although Madame had heard Uncle Jim speak in several different voices, she had never seen him and therefore he could be safely introduced to her as "young Jim". Uncle Jim was, I believe, in his late twenties at that time but looked very much younger.

My parents and Uncle Jim then discussed the question of what form the spirit should take. My father, after my faux pas, was against my speaking and the materialization of a spirit face seemed impossible because of the difficulty in concealing the torch. My father said that Mr. Price would possibly search the room and the male sitters, and he might ask Madame to search the ladies. Looking back on this séance, it is perhaps surprising that my father thought it possible that Mr. Price would ask Madame to do this but this was because we thought of our séance as being investigated by both Mr. Price and Madame, and did not see it from Mr. Price's point of view. To Mr. Price, Madame was someone to be investigated equally with everyone else in the séance room, and it would obviously be futile to ask one suspect to search another suspect – a point which evaded us at this time.

My father suggested that the spirit should be lighted by hand mirrors coated with luminous paint because these would not require to be concealed. Uncle Jim pointed out that, if Mr. Price wished to handle a mirror, it would be impossible to assure that he would direct its light only to the face and he might see, and recognize the dress of the girl he believed to be sitting opposite to him in the dark. My mother said that I could change into "spirit clothes" but my father very logically said that, should there be a search of the room, "spirit clothes" would be as impossible to conceal as a torch. It was finally suggested that the spirit should appear in the nude – a suggestion I didn't much like but to which I eventually agreed.

It was agreed that Mr. Price should be invited to arrive at our house some considerable time before Madame arrived in order that my father might have time to tell his own version of the Rosalie story before Price met Madame.

We had some days in which to practise our new routine; the most difficult part of which I found was to dress in complete darkness. My mother showed me how I could overcome this difficulty by the careful and methodical placing of my clothes as I undressed.

On the evening of the appointed day Mr. Price arrived. He was, I thought, a charming man although rather ugly and seemed pleased at being asked to attend our séance. I believe my father told him that séances had been held in our house for a longer period than they had, and this exaggeration was, I think, in order to put the beginning back to a time before he had any financial connections with Madame – in case Mr. Price subsequently discovered these financial dealings. He also told Mr. Price that Rosalie had first appeared to Madame when she was alone and at home, thus suggesting to Mr. Price that the spirit first appeared when there was no possibility of trickery on the part of our family.

The séance held on that December evening nearly 29 years ago has been described by Mr. Price in his book and, although I have not read this for many years, I think he described it fairly accurately. There are, however, one or two points which need to be explained and these I will attempt to remember.

It struck me as very amusing that Mr. Price should take so much trouble to seal the doors and windows when he was actually sealing Rosalie inside the room, and I could not suppress a smile which caused my father to give me a very severe look.

After he has [*sic*] searched my father and Uncle Jim, I had a moment of panic because I thought he might wish to search the ladies and would discover my padded form. In my agitation I lifted my skirt in the attempt to convince him I had nothing to hide and displayed my black shorts; these I was wearing because they were very easy to remove in the dark. My father very quickly commented on these shorts and told Mr. Price I had been attending an adult physical training class, and thus turned my impulsive gesture to some account. As it was necessary that I should not sit too near Mr. Price, my father suggested that, as Mr. Price could not search my mother or Madame, they should sit on either side of him and this was agreed to.

In the complete darkness, I was able to leave my place in the circle and undress in a corner of the room. As my mother had remarkably small hands, we had agreed on the following procedure. After Mr. Price had felt the spirit form, my father suggested that, while holding the spirit's hands, Mr. Price might like those not sitting next to him to speak, and thus assure himself that they were in their proper places. My mother, who had rolled up the sleeves and removed her rings in the dark, then placed her hands in front of Mr. Price, which he held while I returned to my seat in the circle and spoke a few words.

When it came to using the luminous mirrors, my father asked Mr. Price to commence from the feet and work upwards. This was because when he came to light the face, the mirror would be beneath the chin and therefore the face would be underlighted. We had discovered, when experimenting with the torch, that a face which is underlighted is completely unrecognizable as the same face when normally lighted, and it was obviously necessary that Mr. Price should not recognize my face. But although we were reasonably sure that Mr. Price would not recognize me, we were rather afraid that Mr. Price would think that my face was not that of a six year old. I was then eleven and therefore looked older than six, but he did not comment on this so I suppose my looking slightly older than Rosalie did not occur to him.

I was somewhat nonplussed when Mr. Price spoke to Rosalie because my father, after my unfortunate reply to Madame, had told me that I must not speak at this séance. But as Mr. Price persisted in asking questions, I eventually ventured a "yes", and this reply fortunately put a stop to his questions.

After the séance Mr. Price examined his seals and found them intact. He seemed very perplexed but absolutely satisfied that trickery had been impossible. Madame's suspicions had vanished and once more she appeared to be friendly towards the family, or, at least, as friendly as she was capable.

That night, after Mr. Price and Madame had left us, my father suddenly exclaimed: "Good heavens! The dog!" Jack had been sleeping in his accustomed place before the fireplace during the séance. When my mother asked him what he meant by this exclamation, he replied by quoting a scrap of conversation between Sherlock Holmes and Dr. Watson: "I would draw your attention, Watson, to the extraordinary behaviour of the dog in the night" "But the dog did nothing in the night, Holmes." "Exactly, my dear Watson, that was the extraordinary behaviour of the dog." As my mother was still perplexed, my father explained that, because it is generally believed that dogs show intense fear when confronted with the supernatural, Mr. Price might reasonably conclude that as Jack remained peacefully sleeping throughout the séance, no spirit form could possibly have been in the room; but Mr. Price was no Sherlock Holmes and apparently this point did not occur to him.

We continued to hold séances for the benefit of Madame, for some months after this test séance, but, in the following year, my father was able to repay the money to Madame and my mother lost her power as a medium. My father explained to Madame that my mother was tired and far from well – which was actually the case after so many months of worry – and must have a rest from séances. Madame was not pleased but as we were no longer an obligation to her, this did not concern us. I never saw Madame again, but, about a year later, my parents spent some days with her.

My father, in the summer of 1939, had arranged to take my mother for a holiday on the Continent and meeting Madame by accident one evening at xxxxxxx [erased word] the Station, he happened to mention the holiday to her. She asked him whether she could accompany them as far as, I think, Paris, and he could see no way of refusing this request. I was spending my summer holidays with my paternal grandmother and Uncle Jim and only heard of this when they hurriedly returned to England. No member of the family saw Madame again and, to tell the truth, we were not sorry to have done with this reminder of a very worrying time.

Indeed I sincerely wish people would cease to write about the Rosalie affair. I have no intention of giving any clues which might connect me, or my family, with this sorry, and rather reprehensible, business and this I think you will understand. There is now, I believe, no other living person who knows the whole story. The servants were never in our confidence although it is rather impossible to know how much servants guess or find out. However, the cook is dead and our housemaid, I have been told, married just after the war and left England to live abroad.

I think I should in fairness to the memory of Mr. Price, write to Dr. Dingwall and tell him he is mistaken in thinking that Mr. Price invented Rosalie, but I must, of course, remain forever anonymous.

Yours sincerely,
Rosalie

ENDNOTES

INTRODUCTION AND ACKNOWLEGEMENTS

1. Douglas Baker, *The Phenomena of Materialisation* (1981), p.7.

2. For an account of Foy's activities up to the creation of the Scole Experimental Group, see Robin Foy, *In Pursuit of Physical Mediumship: A Psychic Autobiography* (1996).

3. SPR *Proceedings*, Vol. 58, Pt. 220, November 1999.

4. John Beloff, "On Trying to Make Sense of the Paranormal", Presidential Address to the Society for Psychical Research, October 1975, SPR *Proceedings*, Vol. 56, Pt. 210, January 1976, p.186.

5. *Op. cit.* p.53.

6. *A Basic Guide to the Development of Physical Psychic Phenomena using Energy*, The New Spiritual Science Foundation, Educational Booklet No. 1 (1996).

7. The final official Scole sitting took place on 6 November 1998 – see *Witnessing the Impossible* (2009), p.545-547.

8. The International Scientific Association (for) Research (into) Transcendental Objective Phenomena.

9. www.physicalmediumship4u.ning.com – Retrieved 25 November 2014. The website eventually closed at the end of 2016.

10. Now disbanded and formerly known as the Zerdin Fellowship, this organisation operated in a similar way to the Noah's Ark Society in promoting the development and practice of physical mediumship and its phenomena. As well as producing a bi-monthly newsletter, which carried articles on materialisation mediums past and present, it also organised public séances and lectures. The NAS effectively stopped all its public activities in the early 2000s.

11. *Fifty Years of Psychical Research* (Longmans, Green & Co. Ltd., London, 1939), p.130.

12. Eric J. Dingwall, Kathleen M. Goldney and Trevor H. Hall, "The Haunting of Borley Rectory – A Critical Survey of the Evidence", SPR *Proceedings*, Vol.51, Pt.186, January 1956; also published simultaneously as *The Haunting of Borley Rectory* by Gerald Duckworth & Co. Ltd. A French translation by Robert Amadou was issued by Editions Denoël, Paris, in 1958.

Chapter 1 – Tales From the Séance Room

13. Renée Haynes, *The Society for Psychical Research 1882-1982 A History* (1982), p.146.

14. Colin Wilson, *Poltergeist!* (1981), pp.277-296; Peter Underwood, *The Ghost Hunters* (1985), pp.13-31; Paul Adams, Eddie Brazil & Peter Underwood, *The Borley Rectory Companion* (2009), pp.240-247. A short biography and descriptive bibliography of his works, "Harry Price Ghost-Hunter" by Peter Underwood, is included in the *Book and Magazine Collector*, No.211, Oct. 2001, pp.86-97.

15. *Op. cit.* pp.*v-vi.*

16. John L. Randall, "Harry Price: The Case for the Defence", SPR *Journal*, Vol.64, No.860, July 2000, p.160.

17. Letter from Hall to Richard Lee-Van den Daele, 6 November 1984.

18. *Op. cit.* p.213.

19. "A Plea for a Better Understanding", *British Journal of Psychical Research*, Vol. 2, Jan/Feb 1929, No. 17, pp. 129-140.

20. *Search for Truth* (1942), p.38.

21. *Ibid*, p.44.

22. E. Feilding, W.W. Baggally and H. Carrington, "Report on a series of sittings with Eusapia Palladino", SPR *Proceedings*, Pt.59, November 1909, pp.309-569. Although Eusapia admitted she would cheat if given the

chance, all three authors of the report claimed that the phenomena they witnessed during the course of eleven séances in a hotel room in Naples was genuine. See also Hereward Carrington, *Eusapia Palladino and Her Phenomena* (B.W. Dodge & Co. Ltd., New York, 1909).

23. Theodore Besterman, *Some Modern Mediums* (Methuen & Co., London, 1930), p. 71.

24. *Investigating the Paranormal* (Helix Press, New York, 2002), pp. 169-70.

25. *How to Go to a Medium: A Manual of Instruction* (Kegan Paul, Trench, Trubner & Co. Ltd., London, 1927).

26. An essay originally written but not used in Tabori's *Biography of a Ghost-Hunter*. It was eventually published in Trevor Hall's *Search for Harry Price* (1978), p.9.

27. Both quotes from "Was Harry Price a Fraud?", included in *Tomorrow*, Vol.4, No.2, Winter 1956, p.55.

28. "Brilliant Phenomena in the Home of the Schneiders", *British Journal of Psychical Research*, Vol.1, No.2, July-August 1926, p.52.

29. *Harry Price – The Psychic Detective* (2006), p.65.

30. *Op. cit.*,Vol.1, No.1, May-June 1926, pp.11-20.

31. *Stella C. – An Account of Some Original Experiments in Psychical Research* (Hurst & Blackett Ltd., London, 1925), p.88.

32. *Op. cit.*, p.85.

33. *Ibid*, p.87.

34. *The Phenomena of the Séance Room* (Rider & Co., London, 1936).

35. *Leaves From a Psychist's Case-Book* (Victor Gollancz Ltd., London, 1933), p.274.'

36. Later the same year at Portsmouth, Mrs Duncan is alleged to have materialised a dead sailor who confirmed the sinking of *HMS Barham* (on 25 November 1941), three months before the loss was officially announced. However, the date of the séance has not been established and the local community was aware of the loss. Letters were sent out to families of the ship's crew within days informing them of the sinking with a request that the news be kept private as the German fleet were unaware that the *Barham* had been destroyed. See also Simeon Edmunds, *Spiritualism: A Critical Survey* (Aquarian Press, London, 1966), pp.142-143, and Leslie Price, "We Shall Fight Them on the Websites?", *Psypioneer*, Vol.2, No.6, June 2006, pp.117-118 – Retrieved 28 November 2014 fromwww. woodlandway.org.

37. *Fifty Years of Psychical Research* (1939), p.2.

38. "A Report on the Telekinetic and Other Phenomena Witnessed Through Eleonore Zügun", *Proceedings* of the National Laboratory of Psychical Research, Vol.1, Pt.1, January 1927.

39. Harry Price, *Rudi Schneider: A Scientific Examination of his Mediumship* (Methuen & Co., Ltd., London, 1930), p.140.

40. "An Account of some Further Experiments with Rudi Schneider" (*Bulletin IV* of the National Laboratory of Psychical Research, London, 1933).

41. *Dictionary of the Supernatural* (Harrap Ltd., London, 1978), p.276.

42. *The Strange Case of Rudi Schneider* (The Scarecrow Press, London, 1985), p.329.

43. Harry Price Library, University of London.

44. Harry Price Library, University of London. Dingwall's suggestion is that the controlling sitters were misdirected, allowing Webber to free his hands and fake the dematerialising coat effect. Eusapia Palladino was caught using the same technique on a number of occasions.

45. Harry Price Library, University of London.

46. From a report dated 14 March 1940 by a Mr C.A. Powell, one of the sitters, sent to the Society for Psychical Research – SPR Archive, Cambridge University Library.

47. *Op. cit.* p.293.

48. *Op. cit.* p.200.

49. The SPR's PRISM (Psychical Research Involving Selected Mediums) project, set up in 1994, was a specific attempt to kindle a sympathetic working relationship with contemporary psychics and home circles. It was through PRISM that contact with the Scole Experimental Group was achieved. One of the most active investigator of physical mediumship in recent years has been Prof. Stephen Braude, Emeritus Professor of Philosophy at the University of Maryland Baltimore County. His work has included a protracted examination of medium Kai Mügge of Hanau, Germany, and his Felix Experimental Group – see "Investigations of the Felix Experimental Group: 2010-2013", *Journal of Scientific Exploration*, Vol.28, No.2 (2014), pp.285-343, and "Follow-Up Investigation of the Felix Circle", *Journal of Scientific Exploration*, Vol.30, No.1 (2016), pp.27-55.

50. *Fifty Years of Psychical Research* (1939), p.293.

Chapter 2 – Background to an Investigation

51. "A Report on Two Experimental Fire-Walks" (*Bulletin II* of the University of London Council for Psychical Investigation, London, 1936).

52. For a detailed analysis of the Price tenancy including evaluation and criticism, see *The Borley Rectory Companion* (2009), pp.247-253.

53. 21 September 1937 – Harry Price Library, University of London.

54. *Fifty Years of Psychical Research* (1939), p.v.

55. *Op. cit.* p.131, both quotes.

56. Grant & Jane Solomon, *The Scole Experiment: Scientific Evidence for Life After Death* (Piatkus, 2009), p.ix.

57. *Op. cit.* p.132.

58. Melvin Harris, "Lost for Words", *The Unexplained:Mysteries of Mind, Space & Time* (Orbis Publishing, London, 1980-1983), p.1948.

59. "Harry Price and 'Rosalie'", SPR *Journal*, Vol.43, No.726, December 1963, p.206.

60. Harry Price Library, University of London. The text of the letter to Lambert was reproduced by David Cohen in his *Price and His Spirit Child "Rosalie"* (Regency Press, London, 1965), p.121.

61. *Fifty Years of Psychical Research* (1939), p.133.

Chapter 3 – A Mystery House and Its People

62. *The Times* for 26 January 1939 stated that the séance had been held 'at a private house in South London' where the 'spirit of a child aged about seven years appeared in material form'. There are several South London references in the typescript copy of *Fifty Years of Psychical Research* held at the Senate House, University of London. Price describes the location as being in one of the 'better-class South London suburbs', while one of the sub-headings was originally titled 'A Visit to South London'. Price also writes ' ... I journeyed alone to South London – to the most amazing séance ... ' etc. All these passages were subsequently revised when the book was published.

63. *Op. cit.* p.293.

64. *Op. cit.* p.133.

65. When describing the 'Rosalie' case and the earlier R101 séance held with Eileen Garrett in 1930, Alson J. Smith in *Immortality – The Scientific Evidence* (Prentice-Hall, New York, 1954) refers to Price throughout as Dr Harry Price of the University of London.

Chapter 4 – Check and Double-Check

66. *Search for the Truth* (1942), p.92.

67. *Fifty Years of Psychical Research* (1939), pp.136-137.

68. *Op. cit.* pp.291-304.

69. See *Investigating the Paranormal* (2002), pp.327-338.

Chapter 5 – The 'Rosalie' Séance

70. *The Scole Report*, SPR *Proceedings*, Vol. 58, Part 220, November 1999, p.393.

71. *Fifty Years of Psychical Research* (1939), p.141.

72. *Investigating the Paranormal* (2002), p.352.

Chapter 6 – Aftermath

73. Paul Tabori, *Harry Price: The Biography of a Ghost-hunter* (1950), p.244 – both quotes.

74. Michael Roll, "A First-Hand Account of Materialisation Mediumship" (March 1983), included in Ronald Pearson, *Intelligence Behind the Universe II* (www.lulu.com, 2008), pp. 53-64. Also available on Roll's website, www.cfpf.org.uk – Retrieved 2 December 2014. Two versions of Roll's paper have been published in *Psychic News* in 1992 and 1997.

75. *Op. cit.* pp.302-303.

76. Letter from Price to Mrs Rickey dated 17 October 1938, Harry Price Library, University of London.

77. *Fifty Years of Psychical Research* (1939), p.144.

78. *Fifty Years of Psychical Research* (1939), p.144.

79. "Was Harry Price a Fraud?", *Tomorrow*, Vol.4, No.2, Winter 1956, p.56.

80. Donald West, Obituary, SPR *Journal*, Vol.58, No.827, April 1992, p.285.

81. *Harry Price – The Psychic Detective* (2006), p.91.

82. From an undated and ultimately unused typescript (*c.*1949-50) of personal recollections written at the request of Paul Tabori for his biography of Price (Author's collection).

83. *Op. cit.* p.32.

84. Recorded conversation made on 11-12 May 1958 at the Governor Clinton Hotel in New York. The interview was carried out by Robert Swanson, a private detective, at the behest of Trevor Hall who was researching the life of Marianne Foyster following his work on the SPR 'Borley Report'. A transcript was published by Marianne's adopted son, Vincent O'Neil, in his *Borley Rectory: The Ghosts That Will Not Die*, issued on CD-ROM (ISBN 09644938-4-5, 2001), Chapter 5, "Marianne Confesses".

85. SPR *Journal* Vol.39, No.697, September 1958, p.305.

86. Quoted by Dingwall and Hall in *Four Modern Ghosts* (1958), p.52.

87. *Op. cit.* p.137.

88. SPR *Journal* Vol.39, No.697, September 1958, p.305.

89. Donald West, Obituary, SPR *Journal*, Vol.58, No.827, April 1992, p.286.

90. *Price and his Spirit Child "Rosalie"* (1965), p.56.

91. Quoted by Dingwall and Hall in *Four Modern Ghosts* (1958), p.53.

92. "William Crookes and the Physical Phenomena of Mediumship", SPR *Proceedings*, Vol.54, Pt.195, March 1964, pp.25-157.

93. In the General Introduction to *Crookes and the Spirit World* (Souvenir Press, London, 1972), a collection of writings by Sir William Crookes compiled by Richard Medhurst, Mrs Goldney gives her own belief (p.5) that the great scientist 'was indeed deluded' over the materialised 'Katie King'. However, in the same piece, she admits that 'each surmise in turn has its formidable drawbacks'.

94. *Op. cit.* Vol.II, No.2, Spring 1960, p.110-113.

95. Quoted from invitation card prepared for David Cohen's talk on the 'Rosalie' case to the Ghost Club on Monday 7 October 1963 (Author's collection).

Chapter 7 – *Fifty Years of Psychical Research –* The Story of a Book

96. Typescript original, Harry Price Library, University of London.

97. Harry Price Library, University of London.

98. Letter from Price to Potter, 24 September 1937, Harry Price Library, University of London.

99. *Harry Price – The Biography of a Ghost-hunter* (1950), p.6.

100. *Op. cit.* p. vii.

101. *Op. cit.* p.290.

102. *The Widow of Borley*, Gerald Duckworth & Co., London, 1992.

103. *Op. cit.* p. vii.

104. Lambert states, in his letter published in the *International Journal of Parapsychology* in 1960, that he visited Borley 'in the summer of 1937', but Price makes no mention of this in either of his two Borley books. I suspect that he was a member of a party, which included Cyril Joad, who spent the night of 28 July 1937 at the house when Price was ill and unable to attend.

105. Letter from Price to Potter, 11 August 1938, Harry Price Library, University of London.

106. Although Richard Lambert was not officially involved in the writing of Price's first Borley book, there is evidence that he may have supplied some un-credited contributions. In a letter to Price dated 8 December 1937, the day that Price was contacted by Mrs X, he wrote offering to make an immediate start on drafts of several chapters using material already in Price's possession. This would be used without any acknowledgement as long as Price was willing to go shares in the £75 advance that had been offered by Longmans. Whether Price took up this offer and *'The Most Haunted House in England'* does contain material by Lambert is unclear.

107. Letter from Price to Potter, 28 October 1937, Harry Price Library, University of London.

108. Letter from Price to Potter, 13 July 1938, Harry Price Library, University of London.

109. *Op. cit.* p.294.

110. *Op. cit.* p.294.

111. In his biography of Price (p.251), Paul Tabori incorrectly states that this meeting took place in November 1939.

112. *Harry Price – Biography of a Ghost-hunter* (1950), p.251.

113. *Psychic News*, No. 350, 4 February 1939, p.1.

114. "A Remarkable Séance", *Light*, 2 February 1939, p.62.

115. Harry Price Library, University of London. Sturge-Whiting is referring to a famous passage in a letter by Sir William Crookes, published in *The Spiritualist* in April 1874, in which Crookes describes viewing the materialisation of 'Katie King' by the light from a phosphorous lamp.

116. Letter from Price to Sturge-Whiting, 6 February 1939, Harry Price Library, University of London.

117. Quoted in *Four Modern Ghosts* (1958), p.133.

118. Malcolm Gaskill, *Hellish Nell – The Last of Britain's Witches* (Fourth Estate, London, 2001), p.169.

119. Harry Price Library, University of London.

120. Harry Price Library, University of London.

121. Letter from Whitaker to Price dated 31 January 1939, Harry Price Library, University of London.

122. Harry Price Library, University of London.

123. Harry Price Library, University of London.

124. Quoted by David Cohen in his *Price and His Spirit Child "Rosalie"* (1965), p.126.

125. *Fifty Years of Psychical Research*, p.326.

126. Harry Price Library, University of London.

127. Harry Price Library, University of London.

128. Letter from Price to Eileen Kelly, 10 August 1939, Harry Price Library, University of London.

Chapter 8 – What The Papers Said

129. See *Price & His Spirit Child "Rosalie"* (1965), p.127. Cohen makes the comment, 'I would not be surprised if the séance took place in South Kensington', after making reference to Bax's article.

130. *Daily Telegraph*, 5 November 1990.

131. "David Icke – Destroyed on Television For the Second Time" by Michael Roll, May 2001 on the website www.cspr.org.uk. Retrieved 20 September 2009.

132. Letter from Longmans to Price, 31 December 1941. Harry Price Library, University of London.

133. Longman's warehouse suffered a direct hit and fire on the night of 29 December 1940. As well as *Fifty Years*, copies of Price's first Borley book were also lost.

134. *Op. cit.* p.293.

135. Harry Price Library, University of London.

136. *Op. cit.* p.76.

137. *Op. cit.* p.76.

138. *My Occult Diary* (Living Books Inc., New York, 1966).

139. *Op. cit.* p.252.

140. *Light*, Vol.69, No.3345, January 1949, pp.29-30.

141. *Beyond the Senses*, Souvenir Press (1971) , p.142.

Chapter 9 – Mr Hall and the 'Borley Report'

142. *New Light on Old Ghosts* (Gerald Duckworth & Co. Ltd., London, 1965), p.ix.

143. "A Note on Borley Rectory" included in *A Skeptic's Handbook of Parapsychology* edited by Paul Kurtz (Prometheus Books, New York, 1985), p.327.

144. John L. Randall, "Harry Price: The Case for the Defence", SPR *Journal*, Vol.64, No.860, July 2000, p.169.

145. "A Note on Borley Rectory" included in *A Skeptic's Handbook of Parapsychology* edited by Paul Kurtz (Prometheus Books, New York, 1985), p.327-328.

146. *Ibid*, p.328.

147. Quoted by Hall in *Search for Harry Price* (1978), p.6.

148. *Four Modern Ghosts* (1958), p.35.

149. Elected 30 March 1932.

150. *Four Modern Ghosts*, 1958, p.66 and *Search for Harry Price*, 1978, p. 201.

151. *Op. cit.* p.129.

152. *Op. cit.* p. 130.

153. *Op. cit.* p. 130.

154. *Op. cit.* p.182.

155. *Four Modern Ghosts* (1958), p.64.

156. *Four Modern Ghosts* (1958), p.9.

157. *Op. cit.* p.9.

158. *Op. cit.* p.59.

Chapter 10 – The Dingwall and Hall Investigation

159. *Four Modern Ghosts* (1958), p.54.

160. *Four Modern Ghosts* (1958), p.54.

161. *Ibid*, p.54.

162. *Ibid*, p.54 – both quotes.

163. *Ibid*, p.55.

164. *Ibid*, p.54.

165. *Four Modern Ghosts* (1958), p.54.

166. SPR *Journal*, Vol. 53, No. 799, February 1985, pp.40-41.

167. Vol.II, No.2, p.110.

168. *Ibid*, p.111. In his letter, Lambert incorrectly gives the date of his luncheon appointment with Price as the 10th of December.

169. *Ibid*, p.112.

170. *Price and His Spirit Child "Rosalie"* (1965), p.10

171. *Ibid*, pp.112-113.

172. *Four Modern Ghosts* (1958), p.55.

173. *Ibid*, p.57 – both quotes.

174. *Ibid*, p.55.

175. *Ibid*, p.58.

176. SPR *Journal*, Vol.39, No.697, September 1958, p.304.

177. *Ibid*, pp.304-306 – all quotes.

178. SPR *Journal*, Vol.39, No.698, December 1958, p.342.

179. "Postscript to Harry Price" included in *Mystery – An Anthology of the Mysterious in Fact and Fiction* (Hulton Press, London, 1952).

180. *Price and His Spirit Child "Rosalie"* (1965), p.57.

181. Brockley, today, is located in the Greater London Borough of Lewisham. Between 1889-1965 it was included in the old County of London. Before then it was part of the county of Kent.

182. *Four Modern Ghosts* (1958), p.61.

183. *Ibid*, p.62.

184. *Price and His Spirit Child "Rosalie"* (1965), p.52.

185. *Four Modern Ghosts* (1958), p.62.

186. *Four Modern Ghosts* (1958), p.60.

187. *Ibid*, p.62.

188. The authors do not state which house was examined and from the 1950-51 1:1250 OS map there are in fact three double-fronted corner houses with steps and bays which are potential candidates, nos. 51, 52 and 60. As they were following Price's description, no.51 would have been discounted as

it does not possess dormer windows. No.60 does have dormer windows in the roof but not 12 steps to the front door. This leaves no.52, on the corner of Geoffrey Road, now demolished and replaced with a block of flats (Geoffrey Court). David Cohen reported seeing what he took to be the house mentioned in *Four Modern Ghosts* during his visit to London in April 1962. As outline permission for the redevelopment of the site had only been granted by the London County Council the previous month (22 March), it seems highly likely that no.52 Wickham Road was still standing at the time of Cohen's visit, and this was the corner house examined by Eric Dingwall.

189. *Ibid*, p.62.

190. *Search for Truth* (1942), pp.47-48.

191. *Four Modern Ghosts* (1958), p.65.

192. *Ibid*, pp.66-67 – all quotes.

193. SPR *Journal*, Vol.39, No.697, September 1958, p.288.

194. *Ibid*, Vol.79, No.3438, Spring 1959, p.85.

Chapter 11 – The Ghost Hunter From Manchester

195. *Price and his Spirit Child "Rosalie"* (1965), p.79.

196. See Edwin F. Bowers, *The Phenomena of the Séance Room* (Rider & Co., London, 1936); Edward Cope Wood, *Death – The Gateway to Life* (Exposition Press, New York, 1958); Harry Edwards, *The Mediumship of Jack Webber* (Rider & Co., London, 1940); Harry Edwards, *The Mediumship of Arnold Clare* (Rider & Co., London, 1942); Alan Crossley, *The Story of Helen Duncan – Materialization Medium* (Arthur H. Stockwell Ltd., Ilfracombe, 1975); Robin Foy, *Witnessing the Impossible* (Torcal Publications, Diss, 2009); Victor Zammitt, *A Lawyer Presents the Case for the Afterlife*, 2006, 4th Edition – available as a pdf download from www.victorzammit.com – Retrieved on 29 September 2009 – Chapter 3 "My Sensational Materialization Experiences" covers Zammit's work with physical medium, David Thompson.

197. In a letter to Paul Tabori dated 17 August 1966 (Author's Collection), Cohen qualified this figure as being 'close to 2,000'.

198. *Price and his Spirit Child "Rosalie"* (1965), p.101.

199. In an undated letter in the present author's collection to a Miss Lawrence concerning a visit to a medium named Lees, Cohen states that two pages of *The International Psychic Gazette* for March 1933 'are given in this

magazine to my articles in the Press'. He makes the additional comment that this 'must have been the year I started serious investigations'.

200. All these cases date from the early 1960s. The allegedly haunted locations investigated were a private house, a clothing mill, two public houses, a hotel and a Conservative club. Cohen also gives brief details of a number of other cases examined by his Manchester Society, most of which came to his attention initially via newspaper publicity.

201. *Price and His Spirit Child "Rosalie"* (1965), p.101.

202. Throughout her book, Gregory mistakenly refers to David Cohen as 'John Cohen'.

203. *Price and His Spirit Child "Rosalie"* (1965), pp.84-85 – all quotes.

204. *Daily Express*, Friday 18 March 1960.

205. *Op. cit.* p. 5.

206. *Op. cit.* p. 101.

207. An edited account of this case was published in *Ghosts & Gallows* (The History Press, Stroud, 2012) by the present author.

208. *Memories of Murder: The Great Cases of a Finger-print Expert* (Grafton Books, London, 1988), p.139.

209. *The Ghost Hunters* (Robert Hale, London, 1985), pp. 15-16.

Chapter 12 – The Cohen Investigation

210. 11 November 1962 (Author's collection).

211. *Price and his Spirit Child "Rosalie"* (1965), p.17.

212. *Ibid*, p.46.

213. *Ibid*, pp. 46-47.

214. *Ibid*, p.46.

215. *Ibid*, p.50.

216. *Borley Postscript* (White House Publications, Haslemere, 2001), p.151. During the same meeting, Mrs Price referred to 'another man, long after Harry's death' whom she described as 'snooping about and asking the rector and other people questions'. Underwood assumed that this would have been Trevor Hall during the time of the SPR 'Borley Report', but it seems likely that she was referring, here, to David Cohen's visit six years before.

217. *Price and his Spirit Child "Rosalie"* (1965), p.52.

218. 19 November 1962 (Author's collection).

219. *Experiments in Psychics* (E.P. Dutton & Co., Inc., New York, 1939).

220. *Harry Price – The Psychic Detective* (2006), p.198.

221. *Photographing the Invisible* (Revised edition – L.N. Fowler, London, 1922).

222. Johnson was a member of The Society for the Study of Supernormal Pictures, an organisation established in 1918 to promote the scientific examination of alleged paranormal photographs. Its Presidency was first held by Abraham Wallace, and Henry Blackwell served as an inaugural Vice-President.

223. The Mary Evans Picture Library describes the image on its website (www.maryevans.com) as the '[a]lleged spirit photograph of "Rosalie" the little girl whose materialisation at a séance in Brockley, south London, was attested to by Harry Price' – Retrieved 3 March 2016.

224. *Price and his Spirit Child "Rosalie"* (1965), p.56.

225. *Ibid*, p.55.

226. *Ibid*, p.54.

227. See Peter Underwood's *The Ghost Hunters* (1985), pp.166-169.

228. "An Examination of the Dieppe Raid Case", SPR *Journal*, Vol.45, No.740, June 1969, pp.55-66. A subsequent project to carry out an investigation into the paranormal compositions of Rosemary Brown, the musical medium, was never realised. Hastings died from a stroke at his home in Llandre, Wales, on 15 August 1973.

229. SPR *Journal*, Vol.42, No.721, September 1964, p.371.

230. *Ibid*, p.372.

231. *The Spiritualists* (1962), p.*xiv*.

232. "Mr Hall and the S.P.R.", SPR *Journal*, Vol.43, No.724, June 1965, p.54.

233. *Tomorrow (Quarterly Review of Psychical Research)*, Vol.12, No.1, Winter 1964, pp.17-29.

234. SPR *Journal*, Vol.42, No.722, December 1964, p.421.

235. A facsimile reissue of *The Spiritualists* was published as *The Medium and the Scientist* by Prometheus Books of New York in 1984. No revisions or changes were made to this new edition, despite the fact that the Medhurst and Goldney paper had identified several mistakes and historical inaccuracies. A similar situation occurs on the 'Rosalie' case in Hall's *Search for Harry Price* (1978). A footnote (p.201) cites his earlier *Four Modern Ghosts* as having 'critically examined' Price's claims, but fails to mention that several of the joint authors' findings had by then been discredited.

236. *Price and his Spirit Child "Rosalie"* (1965), p.113.

237. *Ibid*, p.11.

Chapter 13 – Cruising the Streets – Medhurst and Barrington

238. *International Journal of Paraphysics*, Vol.6, No.3, 1972, p.110.

239. Despite holding the SPR Presidency between 1950-51, Soal's posthumous career in psychical research, like that of Harry Price, has been affected by accusations of fraud and malpractice. His famous experiments with the South African portrait photographer Basil Shackleton (*c*.1900-1978), despite the efforts of others, such as Renée Haynes and Richard Medhurst himself, have now been largely discredited. In the recently established SPR online Psi Encyclopedia, Donald West describes the case as 'the single most serious case of fraud to have occurred in the field of parapsychology' – Retrieved 10 September 2016 from www.psi-encyclopedia.spr.ac.uk. For concise accounts of the Soal controversy see also "The Establishment of Data Manipulation in the Soal-Shackleton Experiments" by Betty Markwick in *A Skeptic's Handbook of Parapsychology* edited by Paul Kurtz (Prometheus Books, New York, 1985), pp.287-311 and Renée Haynes, *The Society for Psychical Research 1882-1982: A History* (Macdonald & Co., London, 1982), pp.152-156.

240. *Beyond the Senses*, Souvenir Press, London, 1971, pp.211-212.

241. SPR *Journal*, Vol.42, No.722, December 1964, p.421.

242. The original carbon copy of this letter now appears to be lost as the Senate House Library, today, holds only a photocopy. This loss may have occurred in the mid-1970s when it was removed from the archive to enable graphology and psychometric tests to be carried out by the Ghost Club.

243. See *The Borley Rectory Companion* (2009), pp.209-210.

244. SPR *Journal*, Vol.43, No.726, December 1965, p.206.

245. *Ibid*, pp.206-207.

246. *Ibid*, p.207.

247. See *The Borley Rectory Companion* (2009), pp.50-52. De Lotbiniere subsequently spent the night of 13-14 December 1937 at Borley in the company of Henry Douglas-Home and a BBC colleague, John Snagge. The Borley ghosts refused to perform on this occasion and de Lotbiniere lost interest in the project. As a result, the projected second live haunted house broadcast never took place.

259

248. SPR *Journal*, Vol.43, No.726, December 1965, p.207.

249. *Ibid* (all quotes) pp.208-209.

250. SPR *Journal*, Vol.43, No.728, June 1966, pp.327-329.

Chapter 14 – 'Yours Sincerely, Rosalie'

251. *Beyond the Senses* (1971), p.149.

252. 17 August 1966 (Author's collection). Cohen is referring to the famous materialisations of the past including Florrie Cook's 'Katie King' and 'Marie', Marthe Béraud's 'Bien Boa', and Helen Duncan's 'Albert', all of whom were photographed wearing their personal 'spirit robes'. Similar portraits of 'Silver Belle', the spirit guide of Ethel Post-Parrish, and an un-named phantom by Béraud (as Eva C from the Schrenck-Notzing sessions), were included as illustrations in *Spirit Child*.

253. 11 May 1965 (Author's collection).

254. *Harry Price: The Biography of a Ghost-hunter* (1950), p.252.

255. *Beyond the Senses* (1971), p.167.

256. *Ibid*, p.163.

257. *Ibid*, p.164

258. *Ibid*, pp.167-168.

259. SPR *Journal*, Vol.46, No.749, September 1971, p.194.

260. Author's collection.

261. *Op. cit.* p.17.

Chapter 15 – Searching for Mrs Mortimer

262. *The Beaver Book of Horror* (Hamlyn, London, 1977) has a photograph and a small piece on the Borley case. *The Hamlyn Book of Ghosts in Fact and Fiction* (Hamlyn, London, 1978), fondly remembered by ghost hunters and other interested parties of a certain vintage, has a lavishly illustrated section on Borley. There are also chapters on other notable haunted sites including the Tower of London, the Petit Trianon and Berkeley Square, as well as accounts of the careers of investigators Elliot O'Donnell and Peter Underwood.

263. Issued as Vol.7 of "The Dennis Wheatley Library of the Occult" (Sphere Books, London, 1974), a collection of both fiction and non-fiction titles.

Other books in the series include Stoker's *Dracula*, *Moonchild* by Aleister Crowley, and William Hope-Hodgson's *Carnacki the Ghost-Finder*.

264. SPR *Journal*, Vol.43, No.726, December 1965, p. 208.

265. Founded by Findlay and novelist Shaw Desmond in December 1933, The International Institute for Psychical Research existed up until the outbreak of World War II when, like the Price's University of London Council, it was disbanded. Miss Beenham appears to have been released from Price's employment following the closure of Roland Gardens, rejoining her former employer once the move to Berkeley Street had been completed. At this time she worked part-time for both the IIPR and Price's ULCPI. As they were effectively rival organisations, Miss Beenham's presence in both is interesting, particularly given the fifth columnist activities that 'Mollie' Goldney admitted to much later in associating with Price following the Schneider fiasco in 1933.

266. SPR *Journal*, Vol.42, No.720, June 1964, pp.316-323.

267. *Op. cit.* p.118.

268. SPR *Journal*, Vol.43, No.726, December 1965, p. 208.

269. *Preliminary Studies of a Vaudeville Telepathist*, published as Bulletin III of the University of London Council for Psychical Investigation, London, 1937.

270. SPR *Journal*, Vol.66.1, No.866, January 2002, p.63.

271. The Ancestry.co.uk and Findmypast.co.uk websites were used for genealogical research, both for historical aspects of the 'Rosalie' case as well as our modern investigation. Historic Ordnance Survey maps were accessed using the Old-maps.co.uk website. Google Maps and Google Streetview were used to check present day roads and buildings.

272. Information retrieved from www.nhs.uk – 24 July 2016.

273. *The Times*, 1 June 1940.

274. Charlie Mortimer, *Dear Lupin – Letters to a Wayward Son* (Constable, London, 2012); Louise Mortimer, *Dear Lumpy ... Letters to a Disobedient Daughter* (Constable, London, 2013); Jane Torday, *Dearest Jane ... My Father's Life & Letters* (Constable, London, 2014).

Chapter 16 – 'Rosalie' –
Summing Up An Extraordinary Case

275. Letter from Kathleen Goldney to Robert Hastings, 4 December 1958, SPR Archive, Cambridge University Library.

276. "Time for action", an online editorial in *Psychic News* – Retrieved from www.psychicnews.org.uk – 3 October 2016.

277. *The Strange Case of Rudi Schneider* (1985), pp.329-330 including the quoted passage.

278. See E.J. Dingwall, "The Need for Responsibility in Parapsychology: My Sixty Years in Psychical Research", *A Skeptic's Handbook of Parapsychology*, Ed. Paul Kurtz (Prometheus Books, New York, 1985), pp.161-174.

BIBLIOGRAPHY AND
FURTHER READING

Adams, Paul, Brazil, Eddie & Underwood, Peter, *The Borley Rectory Companion* (The History Press, Stroud, 2009)

Archer, F.M., *The Soul of a Dog: Illustrated by True Stories* (The Churchman Publishing Co. Ltd., London, 1931)

Baker, Douglas, *The Phenomena of Materialisation* (Baker Publications, Essendon, 1981)

Cohen, David, *Price and His Spirit Child "Rosalie"* (Regency, Press, London, 1965)

Cornell, Tony, *Investigating the Paranormal* (Helix Press, New York, 2002)

Dingwall, Eric J., Goldney, Kathleen M. & Hall, Trevor H., *The Haunting of Borley Rectory* (Gerald Duckworth & Co. Ltd., London, 1956)

Dingwall, Eric J. & Hall, Trevor H., *Four Modern Ghosts* (Gerald Duckworth & Co. Ltd., London, 1958)

Edmunds, Simeon, *Spiritualism – A Critical Survey* (Aquarian Press, London, 1966)

Edwards, Harry, *The Mediumship of Jack Webber* (Rider & Co., London, 1940)

Fletcher, Tony, *Memories of Murder* (Weidenfeld & Nicholson Ltd, London, 1986)

Foy, Robin, *In Pursuit of Physical Mediumship* (Janus Publishing Co., London, 1996)

Foy, Robin, *Witnessing the Impossible* (Torcal Publications, Diss, 2008)

Gauld, Alan, *The Founders of Psychical Research* (Routledge & Kegan Paul, London, 1968)

Gregory, Anita, *The Strange Case of Rudi Schneider* (The Scarecrow Press, London, 1985)

Hall, Trevor H., *Search for Harry Price* (Gerald Duckworth & Co. Ltd., London, 1978)

Hall, Trevor H., *The Spiritualists – The Story of Florence Cook and William Crookes* (Gerald Duckworth & Co. Ltd., London, 1962)

Hartley, Robert, *Helen Duncan: The Mystery Show Trial* (H Pr [Publishing], London, 2007)

Harrison, Tom, *Life After Death – Living Proof* (Saturday Night Press, 2004)

Haynes, Renée, *The Society for Psychical Research 1882-1982: A History* (MacDonald & Co., London, 1982)

Jarman, Archie, *High Jinks on a Low Level* (Peter Wynford & Co., London, 1970)

Morris, Richard, *Harry Price – The Psychic Detective* (Sutton Publishing, London, 2006)

Myers, F.W.H., *Fragments of Inner Life: An Autobiographical Sketch* (Society for Psychical Research, London, 1961)

Playfair, Guy Lyon, *The Flying Cow* (Souvenir Press, London, 1975)

Podmore, Frank, *Modern Spiritualism: A History and a Criticism* (Methuen & Co., London, 1902)

Price, Harry, *Confessions of a Ghost-Hunter* (Putnam, London, 1936)

Price, Harry, *Fifty Years of Psychical Research* (Longmans, Green & Co. Ltd, London, 1939)

Price, Harry, *Leaves From a Psychist's Case-Book* (Victor Gollancz, London, 1933)

Price, Harry, *Search for Truth – My Life for Psychical Research* (Collins, London, 1942)

Randall, John L., *Parapsychology and the Nature of Life* (Souvenir Press, London, 1975)

Schrenck-Notzing, Baron von, *Phenomena of Materialisation* [English translation by E.E. Fournier d'Albe] (Kegan Paul, Trench, Trubner & Co. Ltd., London, 1923)

Seymour, Charles J., *These Things Happen – Evidences of contact with another world* (Odhams Press, London, 1957)

Shubik, Irene (Ed.), *The Mind Beyond* (Penguin Books, Harmondsworth, 1976)

Smith, Alson J., *Immortality: The Scientific Evidence* (Prentice-Hall, Inc., New York, 1954)

Solomon, Grant & Jane, *The Scole Experiment: Scientific Evidence for Life After Death* (Piatkus, London, 1999)

Tabori, Paul & Raphael, Phyllis, *Beyond the Senses: A Report on Psychical Research and Occult Phenomena in the Sixties* (Souvenir Press, London, 1971)

Tabori, Paul, *Harry Price – The Biography of a Ghost-hunter* (Athenæum Press, London, 1950)

Underwood, Peter, "Harry Price – Ghost Hunter", *Book and Magazine Collector*, No. 211, October 2001 (Diamond Publishing Group Ltd, Ealing)

Underwood, Peter, *Into the Occult* (George G. Harrap & Co. Ltd., London, 1972)

Underwood, Peter, *The Ghost Hunters: Who They Are and What They Do* (Robert Hale, London, 1985)

West, Donald J., *Psychical Research Today* (Penguin Books, Harmondsworth, 1962)

Wilson, Colin, *Poltergeist!: A Study of Destructive Haunting* (New English Library, London, 1981)

INDEX

'Rosalie' report of, 68-70
attempts to hold another sitting,
79-81, 99
reveals details of 'Rosalie', 81-83
views on 'Rosalie' case, 98, 100
death of, xvii, 63, 100, 229
posthumous reputation of, xvii,
103, 126-127
house in Pulborough, 4, 153, 206
Prince, Walter Franklin (researcher),
11
Psychic News, xviii, 81, 94, 126, 161,
162, 179, 182, 191, 250
*Psychic Practitioners (Regulation)
Bill*, 87, 94

R

Randall, John L. (researcher), 2, 9,
105, 193
Rasmussen, Anna (medium), 14
Revelations of a Spirit Medium, 8, 17,
42, 45
Rhine, J.B. (researcher), 21, 78, 89
Richards, Clarice, 60, 88, 123, 153-
154, 157-158, 163, 187
Richet, Charles (researcher), xiii, 6,
11-12, 26, 49, 132
Roll, Michael (researcher), 58, 96,
250
'Rosalie' case & circle,
first public awareness of, xvi
Price contacted by, 27-29
possible locations of, 33
history & members of, 35-37
presence of Airedale dog, 43-44,
55, 176, 236
layout of sitters, 47
end of séances, 99-100, 174
investigation by present author,
186-225

'Rosalie' letter',
sent to David Cohen, 173
allegations of, 173-174
full text of, 233-244
investigation by Ghost Club, 180
handwriting analysis of, 210-212
'Rosalie' photograph, 154-156
Royal Societies Club, 59-60, 78, 147,
202

S

St Donatts Road, New Cross, 3-4,
196
Salter, William (researcher), 63-64, 103
Schneider, Rudi (medium), 10, 14-16,
38, 41, 50, 63, 74, 119, 122, 133,
157, 179, 184, 228-229
Schneider, Willi (medium), 8-10, 17,
49, 133
Schrenck-Notzing, Baron Albert
(researcher), 6, 8-9, 11-12, 14, 37-
38, 155, 159, 260
Scole Experimental Group (SEG),
xii-xvi, 28, 38, 60, 130, 228, 248
Scole Experiment, The, xiii
Scole Report, The, xiii
Search for Harry Price, 2, 23, 247
Search for Truth, xix, 1, 4, 11, 33, 74,
97, 125, 191
Soal, Samuel (researcher), 69, 166,
188, 192
Society for Psychical Research,
investigations of, xiii, 6, 15
relationship with Harry Price,
xvii, 16, 63
Society for the Study of Supernormal
Pictures, 5, 258
Spiritual Scientist, xv
Strange Case of Rudi Schneider, The,
16, 133

Paperbacks also available from White Crow Books

Elsa Barker—*Letters from a Living Dead Man*
ISBN 978-1-907355-83-7

Elsa Barker—*War Letters from the Living Dead Man*
ISBN 978-1-907355-85-1

Elsa Barker—*Last Letters from the Living Dead Man*
ISBN 978-1-907355-87-5

Richard Maurice Bucke—
Cosmic Consciousness
ISBN 978-1-907355-10-3

Stafford Betty—
The Imprisoned Splendor
ISBN 978-1-907661-98-3

Stafford Betty—
Heaven and Hell Unveiled: Updates from the World of Spirit.
ISBN 978-1-910121-30-6

Ineke Koedam—
In the Light of Death: Experiences on the threshold between life and death
ISBN 978-1-910121-48-1

Arthur Conan Doyle with Simon Parke—
Conversations with Arthur Conan Doyle
ISBN 978-1-907355-80-6

Meister Eckhart with Simon Parke—
Conversations with Meister Eckhart
ISBN 978-1-907355-18-9

D. D. Home—*Incidents in my Life Part 1*
ISBN 978-1-907355-15-8

Mme. Dunglas Home; edited, with an Introduction, by Sir Arthur Conan Doyle—*D. D. Home: His Life and Mission*
ISBN 978-1-907355-16-5

Edward C. Randall—
Frontiers of the Afterlife
ISBN 978-1-907355-30-1

Rebecca Ruter Springer—
Intra Muros: My Dream of Heaven
ISBN 978-1-907355-11-0

Leo Tolstoy, edited by Simon Parke—*Forbidden Words*
ISBN 978-1-907355-00-4

Erlendur Haraldsson and Loftur Gissurarson—
Indridi Indridason: The Icelandic Physical Medium
ISBN 978-1-910121-50-4

Goerge E. Moss—
Earth's Cosmic Ascendancy: Spirit and Extraterrestrials Guide us through Times of Change
ISBN 978-1-910121-28-3

Steven T. Parsons and Callum E. Cooper—
Paracoustics: Sound & the Paranormal
ISBN 978-1-910121-32-0

L. C. Danby—
The Certainty of Eternity: The Story of Australia's Greatest Medium
ISBN 978-1-910121-34-4

Madelaine Lawrence —
The Death View Revolution: A Guide to Transpersonal Experiences Surrounding Death
ISBN 978-1-910121-37-5

Zofia Weaver—
Other Realities?: The enigma of Franek Kluski's mediumship
ISBN 978-1-910121-39-9

Roy L. Hill—
Psychology and the Near-Death Experience: Searching for God
ISBN 978-1-910121-42-9

Tricia. J. Robertson —
"Things You Can do When You're Dead!: True Accounts of After Death Communication"
ISBN 978-1-908733-60-3

Tricia. J. Robertson —
More Things you Can do When You're Dead: What Can You Truly Believe?
ISBN 978-1-910121-44-3

Jody Long—
God's Fingerprints: Impressions of Near-Death Experiences
ISBN 978-1-910121-05-4

Leo Tolstoy with Simon Parke—
Conversations with Tolstoy
ISBN 978-1-907355-25-7

Howard Williams with an Introduction by Leo Tolstoy—*The Ethics of Diet: An Anthology of Vegetarian Thought*
ISBN 978-1-907355-21-9

Vincent Van Gogh with Simon Parke—*Conversations with Van Gogh*
ISBN 978-1-907355-95-0

Wolfgang Amadeus Mozart with Simon Parke—*Conversations with Mozart*
ISBN 978-1-907661-38-9

Jesus of Nazareth with Simon Parke—*Conversations with Jesus of Nazareth*
ISBN 978-1-907661-41-9

Thomas à Kempis with Simon Parke—*The Imitation of Christ*
ISBN 978-1-907661-58-7

Julian of Norwich with Simon Parke—*Revelations of Divine Love*
ISBN 978-1-907661-88-4

Allan Kardec—*The Spirits Book*
ISBN 978-1-907355-98-1

Allan Kardec—*The Book on Mediums*
ISBN 978-1-907661-75-4

Emanuel Swedenborg—*Heaven and Hell*
ISBN 978-1-907661-55-6

P.D. Ouspensky—*Tertium Organum: The Third Canon of Thought*
ISBN 978-1-907661-47-1

Dwight Goddard—*A Buddhist Bible*
ISBN 978-1-907661-44-0

Michael Tymn—*The Afterlife Revealed*
ISBN 978-1-970661-90-7

Michael Tymn—*Transcending the Titanic: Beyond Death's Door*
ISBN 978-1-908733-02-3

Guy L. Playfair—*If This Be Magic*
ISBN 978-1-907661-84-6

Guy L. Playfair—*The Flying Cow*
ISBN 978-1-907661-94-5

Guy L. Playfair — *This House is Haunted: The True Story of the Enfield Poltergeist*
ISBN 978-1-907661-78-5

Carl Wickland, M.D.—*Thirty Years Among the Dead*
ISBN 978-1-907661-72-3

John E. Mack—*Passport to the Cosmos*
ISBN 978-1-907661-81-5

Peter & Elizabeth Fenwick—*The Truth in the Light*
ISBN 978-1-908733-08-5

Erlendur Haraldsson— *Modern Miracles*
ISBN 978-1-908733-25-2

Erlendur Haraldsson— *At the Hour of Death*
ISBN 978-1-908733-27-6

Erlendur Haraldsson—*The Departed Among the Living*
ISBN 978-1-908733-29-0

Brian Inglis—*Science and Parascience*
ISBN 978-1-908733-18-4

Brian Inglis—*Natural and Supernatural: A History of the Paranormal*
ISBN 978-1-908733-20-7

Ernest Holmes—*The Science of Mind*
ISBN 978-1-908733-10-8

Victor & Wendy Zammit —*A Lawyer Presents the Evidence For the Afterlife*
ISBN 978-1-908733-22-1

Casper S. Yost—*Patience Worth: A Psychic Mystery*
ISBN 978-1-908733-06-1

William Usborne Moore—*Glimpses of the Next State*
ISBN 978-1-907661-01-3

William Usborne Moore—*The Voices*
ISBN 978-1-908733-04-7

John W. White—*The Highest State of Consciousness*
ISBN 978-1-908733-31-3

Lord Dowding—*Many Mansions*
ISBN 978-1-910121-07-8

Paul Pearsall, Ph.D. — *Super Joy*
ISBN 978-1-908733-16-0

All titles available as eBooks, and selected titles available in Hardback and Audiobook formats from www.whitecrowbooks.com

www.ingramcontent.com/pod-product-compliance
Lightning Source LLC
Chambersburg PA
CBHW021501090426
42739CB00007B/416